The Irish Freedom Movement handbook
the
IRISH WAR

junius

The Irish War: the Irish Freedom
Movement handbook—3rd edition
1. Northern Ireland—Politics and
government—1969-
941.60824   DA990.U46
ISBN 0-948392-08-8

First edition, 1983
Second edition, 1985
Third edition—updated and extended, 1987

Typeset by Junius Publications Ltd (TU)
Printed by Russell Press Ltd (TU)
Copyright © Junius Publications, BCM JPLtd,
London WC1N 3XX

CONTENTS

WAR FACTS

Introduction

In February 1987 the *Daily Express* published the results of a poll which seemed to show that the majority of British people wanted to end the war in Ireland by pulling out the troops. About 22 per cent of the poll's sample supported an immediate withdrawal, and 39 per cent favoured withdrawal 'within a pre-set period'; only 34 per cent believed that the British Army should stay in Northern Ireland 'as long as the violence continues'. A third for staying, two thirds for getting out. The *Express* claimed that its poll would prompt 'shock' and 'dismay' on the part of British politicians. In fact, a closer look at the poll's findings revealed how successful British politicians and the British media have been in influencing public opinion with their view of Irish affairs.

The best example of British officialdom's propaganda successes on Ireland came when people were asked about the cause of 'the troubles'. While 45 per cent thought that the roots of the conflict lay in religion, no other explanation reached even 10 per cent support. Only six per cent believed that the presence of the British Army provoked the violence, and just two per cent blamed partition and the Border dividing Ireland.

The idea that the war in Ireland is some sort of hangover from a historical religious feud has always been popular with politicians and the press in Britain. It allows the authorities to throw up their hands in mock exasperation at the 'irrational' and 'tribal' Irish, and to pose as referees trying to keep the peace. What it denies is the fact that the cause of the conflict in Ireland lies with Britain.

From the Act of Union in 1801 to the partition of Ireland in 1921, British governments divided Ireland and denied the Irish people their right to self-determination. British governments built and sustain the sectarian state of Ulster, with its artificial majority of privileged Protestant Loyalists and its oppressed minority of Catholic nationalists. For 18 years, the British Army has upheld the status quo with a fierce war against those fighting for Irish unity and independence. Yet today, British politicians and the British media have succeeded in getting the mass of the population to put the war in Ireland down to religion—and not to the British occupation.

The low priority British people assign to the Irish issue is further proof of how the establishment view of Ireland has prevailed here. All the major British parties have an unwritten agreement that they will not use the Irish War as a 'political football'. They recognise that the threat from the nationalist community to British domination is too big for it to be the subject of narrow party politicking. The wall of silence which Labour, Tory and Alliance leaders have built around Ireland means that, according to the *Express* poll, more than 90 per cent of people in Britain spend less time worrying about a war being fought within the 'United Kingdom' than they do worrying about the EEC.

'This handbook is for people in Britain who want to end the war in Ireland,' we wrote on the first page of the first edition of *The Irish War*. Four years on, ending the Irish War is even more urgent. One of the reasons why the war has dragged on for so long is the absence of a powerful movement in Britain to stop it. Tens of thousands of people in Britain are sympathetic to Ireland's fight for freedom and suspicious of the propaganda that justifies Britain's continuing occupation. But as the *Express* poll revealed, ignorance and confusion about the Irish War hold back any movement against it. The British media has concealed the truth about events, obscured the issues. Above all, politicians—left, right and centre—have nurtured a consensus which backs up every act of repression in Ireland and marginalises dissent about the war at home.

The information and arguments that follow are for people who want to end the war and to win wide support for the cause of Irish freedom. We provide the answers to the questions that come up every time the war is discussed. Why does Britain stay in Ireland? Why don't they just pull the troops out? What about the Protestants? Why can't a political solution work? We examine both the Northern Ireland statelet and British strategy there to clear up these questions and many more. This third edition of *The Irish War* contains an assessment of the Anglo-Irish agreement, the major development since the second edition was published in 1985. We draw out the implications of the accord for all the participants in the Irish War.

This book contains a lot of data and analysis concerning Ireland, but its central focus is Britain. The real problem of the Irish War is the success of the British government in making its behaviour in Ireland acceptable to the vast majority of people at home. Thus we look closely at Britain's use of political initiatives and the legal process which exists to give its rule in Northern Ireland an image of respectability and fairness. We review the use of the law in Northern Ireland to cast as a criminal anybody who opposes British domination; but we focus more closely on the Prevention of Terrorism Act, a British legal device designed to confer legitimacy on the occupation of Ireland by criminalising its opponents in Britain.

This Irish Freedom Movement handbook is more than just a compendium of useful facts and figures. It is a guide to action. Hence we include an outline of the way forward for anti-imperialists in Britain in solidarity with the Irish liberation struggle. Our conclusion is that the only way to end the Irish War is by fighting in Britain for immediate withdrawal of British troops from Ireland. If it is your conclusion too, then join the Irish Freedom Movement—see page 303 for details.

1.Why Britain stays

The 'Irish question' has haunted British politics for generations. Today an answer to it seems no nearer than in the days when Ireland was a pawn in the struggle for the English throne 300 years ago, or when it was central to the British elections of the nineteenth century. Indeed it has become widely accepted that Britain has no political solutions to the Irish War. The results of a *Daily Express* opinion poll in 1987 revealed that most British people did not believe that their government's latest political initiative—the Anglo-Irish deal—offered any hope of an end to hostilities. Officialdom has steeled itself for more years of bloody conflict.

The British establishment and press go to great lengths to blame all the paralysis on those fighting against British rule. The papers denounce the IRA as 'gangsters', 'psychopaths', 'religious fanatics', or just 'murdering bastards'. Those who try to inquire beyond the headlines find little illumination. They are met by a united front of British politicians and academics who describe the Irish War as a series of irrational events, as a highly complicated maze with no simple exits. Ireland generates more public hatred and confusion in British political life than any other issue. Why?

The meaning of partition

Britain's ruling classes have always regarded Ireland as a colony with a difference. In the past, Ireland's proximity to England gave it a strategic importance greater than any other overseas possession. After the Protestant Reformation in the sixteenth century, successive monarchs feared that Catholic Ireland might ally with Spain or France—England's historic enemies. The Crown regarded control over Ireland as essential to the defence of the realm. But the Irish people refused to accept rule by the English as natural and fought to drive them out. Armed force was never enough to subdue Ireland. In the seventeenth and eighteenth centuries the government tried to shore things up by settling Scottish and English Protestants in the North-east. But the presence of the forebears of today's Loyalist community could not restrain the national aspirations of the Irish people.

After the United Irishmen's rebellion of 1798, Britain's rulers took the unprecedented step of integrating Ireland into their own state—through the Act of Union of 1801. Ireland remained under military occupation, yet in constitutional terms was no longer a colony, but part of the United Kingdom.

Neither military terror nor constitutional manoeuvres succeeded in solving the Irish problem. The people of Ireland wanted to run their own nation, not to be citizens of Britain. The Act of Union could redefine the borders of the British state, but it could not define the national movement out of existence. The attempt to subjugate Ireland through the Act of Union brought the struggle for Irish freedom into the heart of British politics.

Ireland could not be subdued by the mere stroke of a legislator's pen. Throughout the nineteenth century and beyond, national revolt simmered and periodically erupted. Britain's brutal suppression of the 1916 Easter Rising only strengthened the Irish people's determination to rid themselves of their oppressors. In 1918, in the last election ever held over the whole of Ireland, 80 per cent of the electorate voted for Sinn Fein and national independence. Within a year Ireland was engulfed in the Tan War between the republican movement and the British Army.

The British establishment could not afford to lose control over Ireland. Ireland's incorporation into the United Kingdom meant that independence was a non-starter: it would have undermined the legitimacy of the British state at home and right across the Empire too. Irish independence and the break-up of the United Kingdom

● Early Irish risings

1534: Rebellion led by the Earl of Kildare, King Henry VIII's Irish deputy. Kildare was defeated by Henry, who established a permanent English garrison in Ireland.

1565: Shane 'The O'Neill' revolted in Ulster. The Crown overthrew O'Neill and sought to divide his land among loyal settlers—another step towards colonisation proper.

1569-1579: Anglo-Irish Lord James Fitzmaurice rose in Munster in a 'Catholic crusade' against the English 'heretics'. Fitzmaurice was killed and 12 000 colonists were shipped on to his land by 1598, when renewed rebellion drove them off again.

1594-1603: The O'Neill and O'Donnell clans of Ulster fought a nine-year war against Queen Elizabeth I. After their defeat and the exile of their earls, the Crown moved to 'Anglicise' Ireland by planting Ulster with settlers. 'There will be no difference or distinction between us', said one Elizabethan statesman 'except the Irish Sea.'

1641-1653: A peasant rising began in Ulster with a revolt against 100 000 English and Scottish settlers. Oliver Cromwell invaded to put down the widespread rebellion. His forces slaughtered 2000 at Wexford and more at Drogheda:

'It hath pleased God to bless our endeavours at Drogheda....The enemy were about 3000-strong in the town....I do not think 30 of the whole number escaped with their lives.'

In 1652 the English imposed a policy of 'to Hell or Connaught'. The people of Ulster, Munster and Leinster were driven west into Connaught and County Clare. The penalty for not moving was death. Ireland's population had been halved since the rising began—616 000 dead, 40 000 fled to Europe, 100 000 transported as slaves.

1689: Catholic King James II fled to Ireland after being dethroned by William of Orange. James' Irish-backed army was defeated by William and the Loyalists at the bloody Battle of the Boyne in 1690. The Crown imposed a system of penal laws. Catholics could not practise their religion, vote, teach, own guns, or work for the state. Irish Catholics now owned only 14 per cent of their own land, compared to 59 per cent when Cromwell arrived.

● *Revolts against the Union*

1798: Inspired by the French and American revolutions, Wolfe Tone's Society of United Irishmen rose for national independence, but was mercilessly put down by Britain and its local allies. More than 50 000 Irish people were slaughtered as British troops wheeled mobile gallows across the Irish countryside. Sentenced to hang, Tone committed suicide in jail.

1803: Even after the massacre of the United Irishmen and the 1801 Act of Union, the nationalist movement fought on as Robert Emmet led 200 supporters in an attack on Dublin Castle. Emmet was hanged.

1848: Despite the horror of the Great Famine, which killed a million Irish people and drove two million more out of the country, the Young Ireland movement took up arms against Britain. But its revolt was shortlived and its leader, Smith O'Brien, was transported to Tasmania.

1867: The Irish Republican Brotherhood, or Fenian movement, rebelled in Ireland with support from Irishmen in Britain and America. Britain's use of informers helped it crush the rebellion. Three Irishmen—the 'Manchester Martyrs'—were hanged in Britain for killing a policeman in a Fenian jailbreak, despite a huge campaign for their release led by Karl Marx. In December a Fenian bomb exploded at London's Clerkenwell prison—the first republican bombing in Britain.

1916: On Easter Monday 1600 members of James Connolly's Irish Citizen Army and the Irish Volunteers staged a rising in Dublin. Their efforts were doomed to defeat by the betrayals of middle class Volunteers' leaders. But their heroic resistance held key Dublin buildings for a week against British artillery and forces which outnumbered them by 20 to one. The rebels published a 'Proclamation of the Republic' which still forms the programme of today's IRA. In all 450 soldiers and civilians were killed and 2600 wounded. Crown forces made 3500 arrests and deported 1850 to be interned in England. The leaders were executed, including Padraig Pearse, James Plunkett and James Connolly, so badly wounded that he had to be tied to a chair and shot sitting down.

would have been an admission to the world that the British machine of government was neither invulnerable nor inviolate. Before the outbreak of war in 1914, Liberal leader Herbert Asquith told the cabinet that 'interests in India, the industrial world and throughout the Empire might be broken up by catastrophe in Ireland' (quoted in P Jallard, *The Liberals and Ireland*). If this was true before the war, there was an even stronger case for holding on to Ireland in the period of labour unrest and colonial revolt that followed it. Unionist leader Edward Carson painted a frightening picture for the British government of the international consequences of defeat in Ireland:

'If you tell your Empire in India, in Egypt, and all over the world that you have not got the men, the money, the pluck, the inclination and the backing to restore order in a country within 20 miles of your own shore, you may as well begin to abandon the attempt to make British rule prevail throughout the Empire at all.' (Quoted in M Beloff, *Imperial Sunset*)

Liberal prime minister David Lloyd George agreed. Speaking of the independence demanded by the Irish, he observed:

'Supposing we gave it to them? It will lower the prestige and dignity of this country and reduce British authority to a low point in Ireland itself. It will give the impression that we have lost grip, that the Empire has no further force and will have an effect on India and throughout Europe.' (Quoted in T Jones, *Whitehall Diary*, Vol 3)

Divide and rule

Any attempt by British politicians to compromise with the demand for independence was fiercely resisted by the state. In March 1914, British Army officers stationed at the Curragh camp near Dublin mutinied in anticipation of being commanded to enforce a Home Rule Bill, even though that would have only conceded a limited measure of devolved government to Ireland. Soldiers, Loyalists and Conservatives united to thwart Liberal efforts to weaken the British connection with Ireland. The authorities in London did not suppress this military revolt against the sovereignty of parliament. Instead the government assured the leading Curragh officers that troops would 'not be called upon' to enforce home rule (quoted in G Dangerfield, *The Damnable Question*). The British ruling class was prepared to back a military coup at home rather than concede Irish independence.

The Tan War of 1919-21 presented the ruling class with a seemingly intractable problem. Britain could not win in Ireland, but neither could it risk defeat. At the height of the war for independence Lloyd George endorsed the only diplomatic initiative which could extricate Britain—partition. The plan divided Ireland into a 26-county area with a degree of autonomy and a six-county region which was fully integrated into Britain. From Westminster's point of view partition appeared to be the perfect formula. It met Irish demands for national freedom by granting token independence to an 'Irish Free State' in the South. And it recognised the wishes of the Loyalist community in the North-east to retain the Union with Britain.

In fact partition was no fair and equitable solution. It was the mechanism through which Britain could continue to dominate Ireland—and not just the North, but the whole island. Partition divided the Irish nationalist movement and split the working class. It was only accepted after a civil war between intransigent republicans and the British-backed regime in the South, and Loyalist pogroms against the nationalist communities in the North. The defeat of the anti-imperialist movement enormously strengthened Britain's hand against the Irish people. Having foisted the partition treaty on to Ireland through a combination of military coercion and diplomatic skulduggery, Lloyd George celebrated it as 'the greatest day in the history of the British Empire' (Dangerfield). He was not exaggerating. The partition of Ireland ended the Tan War and reinforced British rule over its oldest and most important colony.

The Irish revolutionary James Connolly had warned against the dangers of partition back in 1914:

'Such a scheme would destroy the labour movement by disrupting it. It would perpetuate in a form aggravated in evil the discords now prevalent, and help the home rule and Orange capitalists and clerics to keep out their rallying cries before the public as the political watchword of the day. In short it would make division more intense and confusion of ideas and parties more confounded.' (J Connolly, *Selected Writings*)

To this day Ireland has remained divided and confused.

For half a century partition worked reasonably well from the British point of view, and it certainly remains the key to British control over Ireland. Partition has given rise to all the myths that justify the British occupation of the North and all the spurious accounts of why Britain stays. The propaganda value of partition was that it appeared to be a democratic compromise. Nobody got all they wanted, but everybody appeared to get something. The nationalists did not win a 32-county republic, but they got a 26-

county state. This could be presented by British politicians, and their Irish stooges, as a major concession and as a big step towards full national freedom. The Loyalists did not succeed in preserving the formal union of the whole of Ireland with Britain. But they did ensure that the six counties in which they predominated were bound even more tightly within the United Kingdom.

The British authorities presented themselves as honest brokers, concerned only to bring peace and harmony to Ireland's fractious sectarian communities. The superficial democracy of partition disguised the reality that Ireland was being carved up by a foreign power as a means of consolidating its rule. The 26 counties of the 'Irish Free State' were no more free from British domination than were the six counties of 'Northern Ireland'. Let's look at the two regimes established by partition.

The unfree state

Partition has been particularly successful in the 26 counties of the South. The substitution of indirect for direct control by Britain has allowed the Dublin state to maintain all the appearances of an independent country. But the Irish capitalist class is too weak to exist as an independent force. Its survival depends on the continued division of the working class enforced by partition.

Successive Dublin governments have proclaimed their independence and have tried to maintain a discreet distance from Britain. In 1921 the Irish collaborators who set up the new 26-county regime called it the 'Irish Free State'. The new regime promoted the Irish language and Irish culture in an attempt to assert an independent identity. But the British cabinet discussions leading up to the acceptance of the partition treaty indicate that the 'free' in the 'Irish Free State' was a fiction.

London insisted that an oath of allegiance to the Crown be made the condition for the ratification of the partition treaty. It was an issue, as Lloyd George put it, 'upon which no British government can compromise' (quoted in C Younger, *Ireland's Civil War*). When the cabinet put its ultimatum to Free State negotiators Arthur Griffith and Michael Collins, an accompanying diplomatic note clarified the significance of the Crown:

'The Crown is the symbol of all that keeps the nations of the Empire together. It is the keystone of the arch in law as well as in sentiment.' (Quoted in F Pakenham, *Peace By Ordeal*)

By swearing their loyalty to the British King, the Free State collaborators made their land one of His Majesty's dominions within the Commonwealth. Thus did the Irish parliament become a slave to the sovereignty of the English Crown.

In 1949 the Dublin government cut all its institutional ties with Britain and declared the Irish Republic. This step caused little concern in Whitehall. Labour premier Clement Attlee dismissed the whole affair as a publicity stunt. He appreciated that the Dublin politicians were more concerned to raise the prestige of their 26-county domain than they were to push forward to a united Ireland. He told the cabinet that Dublin 'laid more store on formal independence than on the Union of Ireland' (Cabinet minutes, 12 January 1949). The Irish Republic could renounce the Commonwealth, remove the British governor general, join the United Nations and exchange ambassadors around the world. But Ireland as a whole remained under Britain's thumb. As Attlee put it, 'Eire was not to be regarded as a foreign country even though she ceased to be part of His Majesty's dominions.'

Recurrent controversy over defence relations between Dublin and London underlines Ireland's continuing subordination to its old imperial master. The terms of partition stipulated that Britain remained in control of the so-called 'Treaty Ports' at Lough Swilly, Cobh and Berehaven. In its early days, the Free State's military affairs were effectively run by Westminster. By the thirties, however, the British authorities acknowledged the popular pressure on the Dublin government to assert its independence from London. Hence they returned the Treaty Ports in 1938 and respected the Free State's formally neutral stand in the Second World War.

Since 1945 the Irish government has preserved a non-aligned posture in international affairs and has stood aloof from Nato. Its refusal to back Britain's war against Argentina in 1982 reinforced perceptions that Dublin can take an independent line on foreign policy. But in fact the Irish Republic's much-vaunted neutrality disguises the extent to which it has remained a vassal of the British Crown.

Britain has always got what it wanted from Dublin. Before the Second World War Eamon de Valera, the former republican leader who was Ireland's popular nationalist prime minister through most of the thirties and forties, backed a series of key British diplomatic initiatives towards Italy and Germany. Neutral in the war itself, the Free State allowed Britain to use its airspace and coastal waters with impunity. More than 50 000 Irishmen enlisted in the British services.

The de Valera government interned republicans and communists to calm Churchill's fears of a fifth column in Ireland. Although de Valera entered a bitter public dispute with Churchill over Ireland's neutrality, he still borrowed the British hangman to execute republicans during the war. In 1940 the British armed forces were alerted to invade Ireland, a move called off only because it was regarded as unnecessary.

Britain obtained all the support it wanted from Dublin without encountering the snags of an open invasion. As Churchill said in a broadcast at the end of the war, Britain never laid a violent hand on the Irish, 'though at times it would have been quite easy and quite natural' (*The Irish Press,* 17 May 1945).

Today Ireland stands outside Nato. But Nato has schemes to use the Shannon and the west coast for its submarines, and plans, too, for the military use of ports and airfields. The Mount Gabriel radar station on Ireland's south coast, which is tied into Nato's network, is jointly funded by London and Dublin. More than 4000 Nato aircraft overfly the Republic annually (*Sanity,* March 1985). There is even rumoured to be a plan to evacuate the Queen and the British prime minister to Donegal in the event of a nuclear strike in London.

In the past control over Ireland was integral to Britain's defence. During the First and Second World Wars Britain feared that Ireland might be occupied and used by the Germans. As long as the threat came from a naval armada or from warships and submarines, direct military occupation of the whole of Ireland was an indispensable strategic option for Britain. With today's long-range missiles, Britain's military needs are fully met by indirectly including the Twenty-six Counties under its nuclear umbrella. The most important sphere of Anglo-Irish military cooperation, however, has been in relation to the war in the North.

The extensive deployment of the Irish army in counter-insurgency operations in the Border areas shows up its role as an adjunct of the British forces. Throughout the current war the Dublin government has proved a most reliable ally of the British state. It has harassed, hunted down, imprisoned and extradited republicans without relent. The Republic's soldiers, like its police, courts, prisons and intelligence services, operate to all intents and purposes as an arm of British repression. Cross-Border joint security operations are standard practice.

Irish neutrality is a myth. It obscures what goes on behind the partition of Ireland—the fact that the whole country remains under British domination.

The fatal flaw

The success of partition in the South stands in stark contrast to its failure in the North. Despite its incorporation into the United Kingdom, Northern Ireland has remained a colonial outpost wracked by instability and conflict. The local parliament that Britain established at Stormont Castle in 1921 stood for Loyalist privilege and the crushing of the nationalist people. A cycle of repression and resistance, and more repression and resistance, finally erupted into open conflict in the late sixties.

Partition has made things even more difficult for Britain. The division of Ireland meant amalgamating the Six Counties with Britain. Ever since partition events within Northern Ireland have had immediate consequences for the British state at home. But the London establishment has never faltered in its determination to keep Ulster British. As early as 1916, when the details of partition were still moot, Lloyd George told Carson:

'We must make it clear that at the end of the provisional period Ulster does not, whether she wills it or not, merge with the rest of Ireland.' (Quoted in A Coughlan, *Fooled Again?*)

The response of the British authorities to the emergence of a popular campaign against partition throughout Ireland in the late forties illustrates the firmness of Britain's commitment to the Union. In 1948 Lord Rugby, the foreign office's representative in Dublin, warned Downing Street about the rising tide of republican sentiment in Ireland:

'My forecast is that unless a move is made now on our side to anticipate and disperse the forces and influences now gathering we shall have bloodshed in Ireland, a grave state of disorder in the North with world opinion once again only too ready to believe that England is misbehaving herself in Ireland.' (Cabinet minutes, 20 November 1948)

The declaration of a Republic in the South prompted an unusually explicit statement of Britain's position in a memo sent to Attlee by Norman Brook, secretary to the Labour cabinet:

'Now that Eire will shortly cease to owe any allegiance to the Crown it has become a matter of first-rate importance to this country that the North should continue to form part of His Majesty's dominions. So far as can be foreseen, it will never be to Great Britain's advantage that Northern Ireland should form part of a territory outside His Majesty's jurisdiction. Indeed, it seems unlikely that Great Britain would ever be able to agree with this even if the people of Northern Ireland desired it. There should, therefore, be no political difficulty, as circumstances now are, in giving a binding assurance that Northern Ireland shall never be excluded from the United Kingdom without her full and free consent.' (Cited in S Cronin, *Irish Nationalism*)

Brook's memo explodes the myth that Northern Ireland has been preserved by Britain to uphold the democratic wishes of its majority Protestant population. Brook made clear that Britain would never agree to Irish unity 'even if the people of Northern Ireland desired it'. Britain sustains Northern Ireland, not out of respect for Loyalist aspirations, but because of naked self-interest. The commitment of successive British governments to make no change in the constitutional position of Northern Ireland 'without the consent of the majority of its people' is simply a disguise for imperialist interests. While the leaders of the Labour government privately admitted their indifference to the will of the people of Northern Ireland, the Labour government's Northern Ireland Act of 1949 kept up the pretence:

'In no event will Northern Ireland or any part thereof cease to be part of His Majesty's dominions and of the United Kingdom without the consent of the parliament of Northern Ireland.'

Attlee commented that 'troops were present in Northern Ireland...to ensure that the will of the majority will not be overridden by pressures from outside the United Kingdom' (Cronin). In fact troops were present to ensure that the will of another majority—that of the Irish people in its entirety—was ignored.

There is no Loyalist veto

The myth that the Loyalist community has the whip-hand over British policy on Northern Ireland is widely accepted in Britain. During the Loyalist backlash which followed the signing of the November 1985 Anglo-Irish deal, many in the labour movement argued that the Unionists had a 'veto' on political initiatives in the North. This idea covers over the domination of Ireland by Britain. It means blaming the Loyalist community in the Six Counties, a community which is but an instrument of British policy. The British government uses its artificially created majority in the North to legitimise partition. Loyalist intransigence is only a product of the intransigence of the British state over Ireland. Throughout the current war, successive British governments have displayed a consistent commitment to the unity of Northern Ireland with Great Britain.

In 1969 Labour prime minister Harold Wilson said that sending in the troops was vital to keep the peace there. But he was quick to reiterate the position outlined by Attlee 20 years previously:

'Nothing which has happened in recent weeks in Northern Ireland derogates from the clear pledge made by successive United Kingdom governments that Northern Ireland should not cease to be a part of the United Kingdom without the consent of the people of Northern Ireland....The Border is not an issue.' (H Wilson, *The Labour Government 1964-70*)

The pledge made by Wilson in this famous 'Downing Street Declaration' was repeated by Labour home secretary James Callaghan, who declared that 'the Border will remain. That is as flat and as unequivocal as I can make it, and any policies that are pursued derive from that beginning.'

In 1971 Callaghan, who played a key role in formulating the Irish policy of the Wilson government before taking over as prime minister, recalled:

'We attached very great importance to reaffirming the pledge about Northern Ireland not ceasing to be part of the UK without the consent of the people of Northern Ireland. Indeed the home office would never present me with a draft speech or statement at that time without automatically including it by way of a preface.' (J Callaghan, *A House Divided*)

When Wilson suggested cutting subsidies to a Belfast firm, former Labour minister Richard Crossman recalled the cabinet discussion:

'It was pointed out that if we did this they would still get the subsidies from us because of the way Northern Irish finances relate to UK finances. At this point I said, "I am an ignoramus; may I be told what is the exact financial arrangement?" Nobody could say. Neither Jack Diamond nor the chancellor knew the formula according to which the Northern Ireland government gets its money. In all these years it has never been revealed to the politicians and I am longing to see whether now we shall get to the bottom of this very large, expensive secret.' (RHS Crossman, *The Diaries of a Cabinet Minister*)

In fact there is no secret. Whatever the whims of individual ministers or governments, the British state must rule in Ireland.

On countless occasions after the introduction of the Anglo-Irish accord, leading British politicians reaffirmed their undying commitment to the permanency of the Union. 'I am a Loyalist' declared Margaret Thatcher, reassuring angry Loyalists that the Union was safe with her. She told the house of commons that the Hillsborough agreement 'does not detract from British sovereignty in Northern Ireland....Decisions North of the Border will continue to be made by the United Kingdom government. This is a fundamental point. There can be no misunderstanding' (*Hansard,* 26 November 1985). Northern Ireland secretary Tom King went even further:

'We have signed an agreement in which the prime minister of Ireland, notwithstanding the fact that he faces and has to live with a constitution which has aspirations of sovereignty over Northern Ireland, has in fact accepted that for all practical purposes and into perpetuity, there will not be a united Ireland.' (Brussels speech, 3 December 1985)

King's statement enraged Dr Garret FitzGerald, the Taoiseach. But King was careful to apologise only for claiming that Dublin accepted the partition of Ireland. He did not apologise for his own view, shared by British politicians across the political spectrum, that Ireland will never be united. Anyway, in Anglo-Irish relations what Dublin thinks is of no consequence. The power-strings in Ireland are pulled by British Kings and Thatchers.

The British establishment cannot disengage itself from the Six Counties without undermining the credibility of state institutions essential to its rule at home. Let's look at this central issue of state power more closely.

Why Britain can't withdraw

To maintain its domination over Ireland the British establishment has been forced to extend its state apparatus into Ulster. The institutions which sustain the Six Counties are intertwined with those of the British state. To withdraw from Ireland now would be tantamount to dismantling part of the British state itself: a setback which would have profound repercussions for the whole of the state machine. No significant section of the British ruling class could ever countenance such a step as it would severely undermine its capacity to enforce its interests over society. What is at stake for the British establishment in Ireland is not merely its continued domination of another nation, but the maintenance of its own state apparatus. This is the revolutionary significance of the 'Irish question' for British workers. Defeat in Ireland would be a direct body blow to the British state, which would seriously weaken the ability of the capitalist class to defend its way of life.

The state is the central agency for preserving the rule of the capitalist class. In all capitalist countries it has played a central role in establishing and maintaining stable conditions for the accumulation of wealth in the hands of the few. The two key institutions of the state are an administrative bureaucracy and a repressive apparatus. Every capitalist state has a standing army and police force to guard its wealth from threats at home and abroad. To enforce its interests the capitalist class requires stable and coherent institutions of coercion. Anybody who questions the legitimacy of these institutions can expect to feel the full force of the state's repressive hand.

Coercion alone cannot guarantee stability. The strength of the state depends on the degree of popular support it enjoys. It is always preferable to rule by consent rather than through naked coercion. One reason why the capitalist class in Britain has had such an easy ride is the widespread support given to the state by ordinary people. Public support for the institutions of the British establishment has meant that the state apparatus is seldom put to the test. The very legitimacy enjoyed by these institutions is itself a source of power. That is why the British ruling class so jealously guards against any threat to the authority of the state. By putting to question the legitimacy of the state in one part of the 'United Kingdom', withdrawal from Ireland would undermine its authority throughout Britain. Britain cannot pull out of Ireland without seriously undermining its state institutions. With the question of state power at issue, withdrawal from Ireland is not an option for Britain's rulers.

Under the Union Jack

The rise of capitalism in Britain and the establishment of the British state took place through the incorporation of Wales, Scotland and later Ireland. Wales and Scotland were integrated into the wider entity of Great Britain at an early stage of capitalist development. Yet by the early nineteenth century and the emergence of full-scale industrial capitalism and of the working class, the authority of the British state among its domestic subjects was uncontested. In Ireland, however, things were different.

In the eighteenth century English rule over Ireland was precarious. The 1801 Act of Union subordinated Ireland to the British state within the United Kingdom, with the result that nationalist revolt

Ireland's Oath of Allegiance
to the British Crown,
1921

'I...do solemnly swear true faith and allegiance to the Constitution of the Irish Free State as by law established, and that I will be faithful to His Majesty King George V, his heirs and successors by law, in virtue of the common citizenship of Ireland with Great Britain and her adherence to and membership of the group of nations forming the British Commonwealth of Nations.' (Oath of Allegiance, as incorporated in the Irish Peace Treaty, 1921)

The British government insisted on the Oath as essential to the partition treaty. Lloyd George enthused: 'The terms of the Oath to be taken by members of the parliament of the Irish Free State are remarkable and are better in many respects than the terms of the Oath of Allegiance ordinarily required in Great Britain.'

dominated British politics throughout the nineteenth century. While the British state presided over the most rapid phase of development and industrial innovation in its history, it now encompassed another nation in which most people neither respected nor accepted its authority.

The Act of Union ensured that the Irish question remained central to British politics. It meant that the tensions and conflicts that formerly existed between two countries now had to be contained within one 'United Kingdom'. The dangers posed by continuing turmoil in Ireland were more serious than those presented by Britain's other conflicts in Europe, Africa or Asia. Ireland was part of the United Kingdom, fully represented in parliament at Westminster. In addition, large-scale Irish emigration to Britain in the mid-nineteenth century brought the Irish question into every British city, underlining its potential threat to the established order. Ireland was a domestic rather than an international issue. It meant Empire—and the revolts of 'the natives' that always accompanied Empire—right here at home. It was thus a more serious menace to the British ruling class.

In 1882 Frederick Engels noted that the British establishment could not entertain defeat or a withdrawal from its oldest colony. It 'would grant the Irish open-handedly everything they asked for—only not complete independence' which was 'not at all desirable' to the establishment (*Marx and Engels on Ireland*). In the next 40 years the struggle for Irish independence brought constant upsets to political life in Britain.

Ireland's disruptive effect on the British state reached its peak in the stormy period leading up to the First World War. In these years the struggles of the Irish people converged with those launched by campaigners for universal suffrage, and with those taken up by workers fighting for better wages and conditions. All these struggles were prepared to challenge the state authorities on the streets. The result was a grave crisis for the British establishment and one which it survived only by keeping an iron grip over Ireland. In his 1918 manifesto, Lloyd George pointed out that to a large degree so long as the Irish question remained unsettled, there could be 'no political peace either in the United Kingdom or in the Empire'. True before partition, this statement is a hundred times truer today.

Today the Six Counties is fully integrated into the United Kingdom. The invasion of British troops in 1969 and the imposition of direct rule in 1972 removed the last vestiges of autonomy from Britain. Even though borders were specially designed to install a

Loyalist majority, Northern Ireland still contains a 500 000-strong 'disloyal' minority. The nationalist people make up a third of the population of Northern Ireland and they do not respect the British state. Yet they are locked within its boundaries and for the last 15 years have been under its direct military and political domination. The conflict which results from this—between the republican movement on the one hand and the Army and paramilitary police on the other—is thus a direct threat to the British state. Unionist and Tory politicians have long proclaimed that the counties of North-eastern Ulster are as British as Yorkshire, Derbyshire or Kent. This is Britain's way of asserting its authority in Ireland; but it also means that unrest in Ireland is dangerously close to home.

The enemy within

Events during the 1984-85 miners' strike underlined the potential danger of the Irish War for the British ruling class. Violent clashes on picket lines began to expose the myths which uphold popular consent for state rule. Many striking miners saw that the police were the hired thugs of the coal board bosses and the Tory government. Many learned that the courts imposed a rule of law that prevented effective picketing, imprisoned scores of strikers and bankrupted the National Union of Mineworkers. Not a few discovered that 'British democracy' was a smokescreen for fulfilling the dictates of the capitalist class.

In the summer of 1984 observers of all kinds were struck by the similarity between the rioting in British coalfields and that in the ghettos of West Belfast and Derry. At the time a significant number of miners and other workers sympathetic to their struggle refused to accept the authority of the state and proved willing to fight its institutions. The parallel between the petrol bombs and barricades in South Yorkshire and those in Northern Ireland filled the British ruling class with terror.

Because the nationalist people in Northern Ireland refuse to consent to the rule of law or to respect the legitimacy of the state, the British establishment has been obliged to impose its rule in Ireland by force. This has led to more conflict and instability. It is a state of affairs which the bosses are very reluctant to introduce at home. The breakdown of respect for capitalist law and order in the miners' strike underlines the importance for the British ruling class of keeping the lid on the situation in Northern Ireland and preserving the image of the British state as a source of authority.

The public response to the IRA bomb attack on the Tory leadership during the Conservative Party conference in October 1984 revealed a change in the climate of British opinion. The bomb killed five top Tories and injured many more, including senior minister Norman Tebbit. In the wake of previous IRA bombings in Britain, popular resonance for anti-Irish hysteria had been widespread. But after six months of the miners' strike reactions were different. Working class people expressed little sympathy for the Tories. 'Pity they missed' was a phrase on many lips and jokes about Norman Tebbit found a ready audience.

Thatcher's speech to the Tory conference emphasised the concern of the ruling class at the growing disrespect for the state and its institutions:

'The battle to uphold the rule of law calls for the resolve and commitment of the British people. Our institutions of justice, the courts, and the police, require the unswerving support of every law-abiding citizen.' (Quoted in M Hume, *After the Brighton Bomb,* Junius)

Thatcher cast striking miners and IRA bombers as twin threats to British democracy. 'Britain', she continued, 'faces now what is probably the most telling crisis of our time—the battle between the extremists and the rest.'

Thatcher understands that, once people begin to rubbish the British state, it is revealed for what it is—a body of armed men protecting the ruling class. The Irish liberation struggle is a threat to the British capitalist class because it displays a constant defiance of all British institutions. It is all the more menacing since it comes from within the United Kingdom. The state cannot be divided into its British and 'Ulster' sections. One British state must represent the interests and power of an entire capitalist class. A defeat for the state in one part of its territory, whether Belfast or Birmingham, would do irreparable damage to the whole apparatus. It would jeopardise existing power relations throughout the United Kingdom.

The Irish struggle stands as an example to workers, or black people, or women, or any section of society which finds itself in conflict with the repressive forces of the state at home. The Irish people have already demonstrated their ability to shake the authority and confidence of the capitalist class. By exposing the state as an instrument of ruling class coercion, the war in Ireland opens up the possibility of building wider resistance to the rule of British capital.

As Thatcher well knows, the six counties of Northern Ireland contain a threat to Britain that is much more explosive than the gelignite that blew up the Grand Hotel in Brighton. The only way to contain this threat is to confine it within Northern Ireland, maintain the existing constitutional arrangements and repress the nationalist community. This is the policy that has been pursued with ruthless consistency by successive Labour and Tory governments for the past 18 years. While it is a logic fully grasped by the ruling class, it is one which has escaped the British left.

The opposition underestimates

One of the great failures of the British left is its underestimation of the importance of Ireland. This follows directly from its misconceptions about the capitalist state. British socialists have long viewed the state as a neutral or mediating force in society, rather than as the agency of capitalist rule. Indeed they have often seen the state as an instrument that could be used to chip away at or even completely transcend the domination of capital. They have underestimated how crucial the integrity of the United Kingdom of Great Britain and Northern Ireland is to the stability of British capitalism, and have failed to recognise the mortal threat the Irish liberation struggle poses to the British state. As a result, British socialists tend to fall back on impressionistic theories to explain why Britain stays in Ireland.

Radical commentators often draw superficial parallels between Ireland and other colonies. 'Britain withdrew from Cyprus and Kenya, so why can't it withdraw from Ireland?' the argument runs. In fact such parallels only draw attention to Ireland's peculiar position. Britain was reluctant to lose its colonies overseas, but there, at least, its basic survival was not at stake. The British state pulled out of Asia and Africa, but remained intact. With Ireland, by contrast, matters are different. The fact that Ireland could only be contained by incorporating it within the British state means that the British ruling class is in the direct line of fire of the Irish liberation movement.

Other colonial struggles help to illustrate the peculiarity of the Irish War. Algeria's links with France went some way towards the closeness of Anglo-Irish relations. Thus the war of liberation in Algeria led to the collapse of France's Fourth Republic, a military coup by Charles de Gaulle, the mutiny of a section of the armed forces, and widespread violence on the streets of Paris and elsewhere. Likewise the defeat of the Portuguese in Angola and Mozambique in 1974 led to the overthrow of dictatorship in Lisbon and an era of class conflict which even today finds capitalist rule in Portugal fragile and unsteady.

Two views of Ulster

The public view

'In no event will Northern Ireland or any part thereof cease to be part of His Majesty's dominions and of the United Kingdom without the consent of the parliament of Northern Ireland.'(Labour's Northern Ireland Act, 1949)

The private view

'It will never be to Great Britain's advantage that Northern Ireland should form part of a territory outside His Majesty's jurisdiction. Indeed, it seems unlikely that Great Britain would ever be able to agree with this even if the people of Northern Ireland desired it.' (Cabinet secretary's memo to Labour prime minister Attlee, 1949)

Northern and southern Africa have, therefore, profoundly upset the rule of the bourgeoisie in two of Western Europe's Latin countries. Yet neither France nor Portugal had nearly as much at stake in their colonies as Britain has in Ireland. Nor were their predicaments complicated by the deep recession that reduces Britain's room to manoeuvre in Ireland today. Ireland is a colony *in Europe*. It is a colony *inside the United Kingdom,* and the 'UK' economy is *in crisis.* These are the simple facts which Mrs Thatcher's opponents so often choose to ignore.

Where they stand

The British ruling class knows that it stands or falls in Ireland. Its intransigence on Irish affairs contrasts with its flexibility towards opposition at home. Compromises with the trade unions are always possible. But when it comes to the integrity of the state itself, concessions are out and negotiations can only have a perfunctory character. The British ruling class has never flinched from the measures necessary to safeguard its rule in Ireland. The editor of *The Times* summed up the establishment's view in 1979:

'The differences so stubbornly insisted upon in Ulster concern the most fundamental of all political issues: allegiance, national identity, the legitimacy of the state....These are issues which are usually disposed of only when one side prevails decisively over the other.'

Every British government has grasped the importance of prevailing decisively over Ireland. In 1921 Winston Churchill expressed unease at a cabinet cover-up of atrocities committed by the infamous Black and Tan constabulary. Yet he admitted he was 'ready to go on with the policy of coercion so long as they challenge us in our vital interests' (T Jones, *Whitehall Diary*). Over the past 18 years, the immense economic, political and military costs of the Irish War have often frustrated British politicians. But they have never been deterred from spending and doing whatever is necessary to keep the lid on Northern Ireland. In 1974, Labour prime minister Harold Wilson complained bitterly that British parents had 'seen their sons vilified and spat upon and murdered' in the Six Counties. Meanwhile British taxpayers' money had been 'poured out, almost without regard to cost' to support the state where the spitting and murdering was being done. But Wilson did not allow his emotional outbursts to interfere with the job of securing the Six Counties.

When, in August 1969, Wilson sent in the troops to Northern

Ireland, he did so despite ministry of defence predictions that this would lead to an 'unstoppable escalation' in the number of troops required to contain the situation (*Sunday Times* Insight Team, Ulster). The likely cost of full-scale invasion and prolonged occupation never occurred to Wilson. His 'Downing Street Declaration' emphasised that Britain was in Ireland to stay, whatever hardships were to come. 'The Border', declared Wilson, 'is not an issue.' In a real sense the financial costs of the Irish War are irrelevant to the establishment. With capitalist stability in Britain dependent on its domination over Ireland, more is at stake than figures on a Treasury balance sheet.

Since 1969 numerous establishment politicians have openly admitted that withdrawal from Ireland would have disastrous consequences for Britain. This remarkable consensus can only be compared with those which surrounded Britain's entry into this century's two world wars. Politicians have differed only in their speculations on the grave consequences withdrawal might entail for the British ruling class. Enoch Powell, once a leading member of the British Conservative Party and a former Ulster Unionist MP, has spoken out clearly for his class:

'Ulster is Britain's test of its own will to be a nation. A nation that will not defend its frontiers or recognise the rights of its own people is well on the way to being no nation.' (*Guardian*, 15 February 1980)

Powell's emphasis on the threat that Ireland now poses to the very fabric of the state is the key point.

Parliamentary united front

On the few occasions it is discussed at all, Labour and Tory do criticise each other's policies on Ireland. But both have held firm to the basic premise that Ireland is above party politics. Partition is generally seen as a reasonable arrangement designed to guarantee the democratic aspirations of the Protestant majority in the Six Counties. Britain's presence is accepted as legitimate and its troops are depicted, not as aggressors, but as keepers of the peace. As a result the status of the Six Counties is placed above debate. All corners of the house of commons agree with Margaret Thatcher's statement on the eve of the 1979 general election—that Northern Ireland must never be 'a political football'.

What has now been achieved is what establishment politicians in the years leading up to partition had always hoped for: consensus on Ireland. Lloyd George, for example, agreed with leading Unionists that Ireland should not force itself on to the centre of the political stage. In his 'Criccieth memorandum' of 1910, he made it clear that Ireland was an issue that should not excite party controversy. In the period leading up to home rule, Ireland moved from being a most contentious issue to a taboo subject. In 1913 Lloyd George told Lord Birkenhead that the differences between the parties—especially on home rule—were 'very artificial' (quoted in RJ Scally, *The Origins of the Lloyd George Coalition*). Ulster Unionist leader Lord Carson lobbied privately to have Britain's control of Ireland struck off the agenda at Westminster.

To this day Ireland remains outside party politics, and a bipartisan policy between the Labour and Tory parties holds the floor. They have little to debate because both are loyal servants of the British state. When the state faces a major threat, political debate is either suspended or directed towards discussion of how the interests of the state can best be preserved. Bipartisanship is the natural, reflex response of the parliamentary parties to what is evidently a mortal danger to the British ruling class.

Not even the mass internment of republican suspects in 1971 could force the Labour Party to break from bipartisanship. Indeed Wilson and Callaghan went out of their way to give this repressive measure their approval. *The Times* congratulated the Labour leaders on their patriotism:

'Mr Wilson and Mr Callaghan have ensured that the essentials of bipartisanship on Northern Ireland remain unchanged. That is a service to the nation....At moments when national responsibility is squarely upon them...Mr Wilson has never acted in such a way as to damage the political fabric of the nation, and the same is true of Mr Callaghan....Ireland is an issue on which, conceivably, the political stability of the nation could again be put at risk, as it was in the nineteenth century when, besides nearly bringing parliamentary life to the brink of collapse, it was a deeply destructive force threatening the coherence of British society.' (26 September 1971)

Labour cabinet minister Richard Crossman recalled with pride how, in 1969, leading Tory opponents such as Edward Heath and Reginald Maudling were unable to fault home secretary Callaghan's colonial policing policy in Ireland:

'It is the most messy kind of civil war one has ever seen. Nevertheless, from the point of view of the government it has its advantages. The Tories are with us on this. Maudling has been strongly supporting us and Ted Heath will find it very difficult to disagree with anything Jim does.' (RHS Crossman, *The Diaries of a Cabinet Minister*)

In 1981 the Labour Party conference adopted a policy of 'eventual Irish reunification' which was hailed by the left as a break with bipartisanship. But the new policy was little more than an attempt to present an electoral alternative to the Tories—it had the same reactionary content, but was just repackaged in form. Labour remained committed to military rule from Westminster for the foreseeable future. In practice nothing was to change.

After its defeat in the 1983 general election, Labour retreated into full-blooded support for the British occupation. On a trip to Derry in December 1984, Labour's new leader, Neil Kinnock, went on record as backing the use of 'every force' against republicans. This was just days after an SAS shoot-to-kill gang in Derry shot to pieces two IRA men, using five pistols, three submachine guns and two assault rifles. Even the jury that presided over the inquest into the killings in December 1986 concluded that the SAS unit 'should have tried to arrest' Danny Doherty and Willie Fleming 'in order to save their lives'. But saving the lives of those fighting for Irish freedom was the last thing on Kinnock's mind when he said where he stood in the Irish War in Derry in 1984.

Labour and Tory, Liberal and Social Democrat: all understand that the war in Ireland is an immediate and mortal threat to the British ruling class. Opening the parliamentary discussion on the Anglo-Irish agreement in November 1985, Thatcher herself observed: 'Whatever the differences that may emerge in our debate...we shall all be united in our determination to end the violence and to bring to justice those who are guilty.' Closing the debate for the Labour Party, deputy Northern Ireland spokesman Stuart Bell agreed: 'We want a massive majority for the agreement, not because it's bipartisan, but because it's right for the people of Northern Ireland, the United Kingdom and the ultimate aspirations of the Labour Party' (*Hansard*, 26, 27 November). This was the man who, in a debate following the IRA bombing of Newry RUC barracks eight months earlier, made clear that Her Majesty's loyal opposition would condemn the armed struggle in Ireland 'today, tomorrow and always' (*Hansard*, 4 March 1985).

2. The longest war

In 1985 a briefing by two top advisers to the Tory Party admitted that 'the essential challenge of the IRA' in Ireland could be met only 'by victory or surrender' (Sir Patrick Macrory and TE Utley, *Britain's Undefended Frontier: A Policy for Ulster*). They were right. Britain's is a foreign army of occupation—and is seen as such by the nationalist community. Therefore the central objective of the liberation movement is the physical expulsion of the troops. This is well-recognised by Britain's most expert military men. When the BBC asked former Army commander in Northern Ireland Sir Harry Tuzo whether he saw any prospect of IRA men being handed over by the nationalist population, he dismissed the idea as 'going completely against the national character and against all the trends of history' (*The Listener,* 17 June 1971).

The alien character of the British interlopers was well summed up by *Daily Telegraph* defence correspondent Clare Hollingworth:

'The units are growing more experienced in anti-insurgency and doubtless too, their intelligence is better; but it is difficult to understand why the British Army which penetrated the Malaysian communist rebel organisation has been unable to plant successful agents in an organisation whose members share the same round eyes, pale skins and cultural background.' (14 November 1977)

This isolation of the British Army from the nationalist population is particularly striking in the Border areas of South Armagh. All supplies and personnel are airlifted in and soldiers rarely venture out of camouflaged bunkers below ground. When they do, it is with the back-up of considerable firepower. South Armagh is where no British soldier can ever feel safe.

The British ruling class cannot afford to admit that it is fighting a colonial war within the United Kingdom. Most of the time it cannot admit that it is fighting a war at all, for that would raise questions about the basis of British authority in the Six Counties and elsewhere. Thus the British establishment has tried to present the war as either a local conflict between two tribes of religious bigots or as a simple problem of law and order.

Sometimes the ruling class goes to absurd lengths to pretend that the war does not exist. In 1974 SAS commando sergeant Barry Davies, who had been on active service in Northern Ireland, received an MBE for 'services to community relations'. But whether they call it religious strife, criminal behaviour, or 'community relations', our rulers know they are fighting a war in Ireland. Politicians may promise new initiatives, but they never lose sight of the central military objective. As Wilson put it to parliament in 1971: 'No political solution can come about, or be put into effect, until what is called the military solution is effective—until the security problem is solved and seen to be solved' (*Hansard,* 25 November 1971). Characteristically, Powell has been even blunter. He argues that the role of the British Army is 'to act as what it is: a killing machine, at the moment when the authority of the state judges that order can no longer be maintained or restored by any other means'. Powell is all in favour of 'controlled and selective killings'(quoted in D Hamill, *Pig in the Middle: The Army in Northern Ireland 1969-1984*).

Since troops first invaded the Six Counties, British strategy has been modified and refined. During the first phase of the war, from 1969 to 1972, the British plan was to prop up Stormont and use the Army to quell nationalist revolt. When the war erupted almost out of control, this plan had to be abandoned. Since the collapse of Stormont in March 1972, Westminster has sought to make direct rule more acceptable through a series of schemes designed to give Catholic politicians a limited stake in the system.

Until 1981 the British authorities combined a ruthless military drive against the IRA with a package of reforms designed to restore the appearance of 'normality' to the streets of the Six Counties. This phase of the war came to an end when a mass campaign in support of the H-Block hunger-strikers proved beyond doubt that the situation was far from normal. After the 1981 hunger-strikes, the British state reverted to its earlier emphasis on counter-insurgency solutions—of which the most infamous was the shoot-to-kill policy. This assassination campaign claimed more than 20 nationalist lives in the two years following Sinn Fein's October 1982 assembly election success. In more recent years Britain has combined selective coercion with a sophisticated political attempt—the Anglo-Irish deal—to undermine the republican movement.

In this chapter we look at British strategy and republican resistance from the beginnings of the Irish War in the civil rights campaigns of the sixties, through to the repression behind the Anglo-Irish agreement today.

War efforts

The Irish War is the longest period in history of open armed conflict between Ireland and Britain. By the beginning of 1987 it had claimed more than 2500 lives. Common prejudice has it that the IRA started the violence. But nationalist resistance actually began in a peaceful civil rights movement in the sixties.

Throughout 1968 and 1969 the nationalist ghettos were seething with anger. Organised through the Northern Ireland Civil Rights Association, protests were met with violent repression. Demonstrations demanding basic democratic rights were either banned by Stormont or set upon by Loyalist mobs. The sectarian Royal Ulster Constabulary, and its much-hated paramilitary reserve, the 'B' Specials, unleashed a campaign of terror against the campaign for civil rights. But indiscriminate repression only provoked more nationalist resistance. The violence came to a head after the traditional Loyalist Apprentice Boys march on 12 August in Derry. Rioting following the march led to the siege of the Bogside, Derry's nationalist ghetto. The RUC and 'B' Specials attacked the nationalist community in force. Armoured cars with machine guns rolled through the streets and for the first time CS gas was used by police in British uniforms.

More than 200 people were wounded in the first day of the battle, but Bogside would not surrender. The RUC was forced to retreat and

barricades were erected. 'Free Derry' was declared a 'no-go' area for
the forces of repression. Rioting spread to other towns and cities and
the Six Counties edged towards a total collapse of law and order. On
14 August 1969, Wilson's Labour government ordered British troops
into action in Northern Ireland. The longest war had begun.

The British establishment had no choice but to invade Northern
Ireland and put down the civil rights movement. The demands for
'one man, one vote, one man, one house' might seem to have posed
little danger to British interests. But in the context of Northern
Ireland they were political dynamite. Britain had built the repressive
Loyalist regime on a bedrock of religious sectarianism. Catholic
demands for civil rights struck at the foundations of the Northern
Ireland state. The Labour government could not grant such demands
without signalling the collapse of British rule in Belfast.

As far as British interests were concerned the troops arrived not a
minute too soon. The local security forces had proved incapable of
keeping 'the Queen's peace' and enforcing British law and order.
Indeed, their techniques of repression only served to rouse
international feeling against Stormont. Millions of television viewers
across the world saw British uniformed police wading into unarmed
and peaceful demonstrations with clubs and batons, CS gas and
water cannons—violence on a scale unfamiliar in Western Europe.
Something had to be done to improve Britain's image and to re-
establish social stability. The unashamed, random brutality of the
RUC had to be replaced by a more discreet, and more systematic,
deployment of British terror.

Once the troops were on the streets, Britain's first priority was to
salvage Stormont. Westminster politicians knew that some of the
more vicious excesses of the RUC and 'B' Specials were counter-
productive: they only provoked nationalist anger. They believed that
a few well-publicised reforms could sort out the problems and allow
order to be restored. In October 1969, the Wilson government
accepted recommendations on policing from the Hunt Commission—
set up to investigate the earlier disturbances in Derry. Hunt proposed
that the RUC be reorganised and the infamous 'B' Specials
disbanded. The Specials were to be replaced by a full and part-time
paramilitary force under the control of the British Army. This force
later became known as the Ulster Defence Regiment.

The Hunt reforms were entirely cosmetic. There was never any
question of establishing a non-sectarian 'peace-keeping' force. The
aim was to demonstrate to public opinion in Britain and beyond that
Westminster was even-handed. In reality the 8000 'B' Specials were

 War firsts

● **First shooting, 26 June 1966:** Gusty Spence's Loyalist Ulster Volunteer Force guns down four young Catholics in Belfast. Eighteen-year old Peter Ward is shot dead.

● **First bombing, March 1969:** Ulster Volunteer Force bombs electricity pylons and pipelines in the hope that the IRA will be blamed.

● **First civilian fatality, July 1969:** Samuel Devenney, 43-year old Catholic, dies in Derry after being savagely beaten by the Royal Ulster Constabulary three months earlier.

● **First policeman killed, 10 October 1969:** Constable Victor Arbuckle is shot dead by Belfast Loyalists rioting against disbanding of the 'B' Specials.

● **First armed resistance by IRA, 27 June 1970:** A handful of Belfast Provisional IRA men defend St Matthew's church against Loyalist mobs in an all-night gun battle in the Catholic enclave of Short Strand.

● **First Catholics killed by Army, July 1970:** Five Catholic civilians shot dead and a dozen wounded as 3000 British troops rampage through Belfast's Falls Road for two days.

● **First soldier killed by IRA, 6 February 1971:** Robert Curtis, 20-year old gunner in the British Army, is shot dead by the Provisionals—18 months after the British invasion.

replaced by the same number of British troops, and the new UDR turned out to be little more than a better-armed and more professional version of the 'B' Specials. Half the UDR's first recruits were former 'B' Specials, and all former Specials had been sent forms inviting them to join the UDR.

The reorganisation of the security forces backfired on both Stormont and Westminster. The repression continued: the reforms failed to appease the nationalist community. Increasing numbers of Catholics realised that their only protection against sectarian pogroms lay in military organisation. The new proposals also antagonised the Loyalist community. Many Protestants took the changes at face value and resented the abolition of their traditional militia, the 'B' Specials. The announcement of the Hunt Commission's proposals led to rioting in the Loyalist Shankill Road in Belfast. Instead of bringing stability, the first year of British military rule only heightened sectarian tensions. The Loyalist establishment sought to defend its privileges by threatening pogroms. This was met by the resistance of the nationalist community. The result was the emergence of the modern republican movement.

The Army was in the front line of the drive to re-establish order. The iron fist of the British state, it quickly lost its 'non-sectarian' image as it turned to smash nationalist resistance. It was clear that from then on Molotov cocktails, rather than tea, would be the only refreshment the Irish handed out to the occupying Army. After a series of riots on the nationalist Ballymurphy estate in Belfast in 1970, Army commander-in-chief Lieutenant-General Freeland declared war on nationalist rioters. In April he warned that the Army would shoot petrol bombers on sight. Home secretary Callaghan backed him up, telling parliament: 'Some honourable gentlemen may not like the choice of language, but the way to avoid it is very simple. Do not go out with a petrol bomb' (*Hansard,* 7 April 1970). Freeland boasted that his select marksmen were equipped with the latest night-sight rifles: 'I will not elaborate on this,' said Freeland, 'but you do not want to get in the way of one' (*The Times,* 4 April 1970). This was no empty threat: within three months British troops had shot dead three civilians. By November, soldiers were instructed not to wait to see what was being thrown at them, but to shoot first (*Guardian,* 9 November 1970).

The moment that the basic conflict between Irish nationalists and British imperialism came to the fore at Ballymurphy, there could be no easy end to the Irish War. 'Some problems you can't solve, you have to live with,' Callaghan told a Labour Party meeting after the riot. 'This', he continued, 'is one I think we have got to live with' (*Irish News*, 21 April 1970).

The British authorities turned to try to crush the nationalist community because they realised that the movement for civil rights had become a movement for Irish unity. The manifest failure of the campaign to reform Stormont forced Catholic people to the realisation that nothing less than a united Ireland could meet their needs. British troops found themselves face to face with a movement of national liberation. Even worse, this was no longer just a political campaign of protests and demonstrations. By the summer of 1970 a revitalised IRA had emerged as the defensive arm of the nationalist community. The IRA showed that it was back in June 1970 when its Belfast Brigade successfully resisted a sectarian invasion of the Short Strand, an isolated Catholic ghetto.

In July 1970 the Army launched the first of many operations designed to crush the national liberation movement. The Army sealed off the nationalist Falls Road area of Belfast and saturated it with troops. It imposed a curfew and soldiers went on a house-to-house rampage. To show that everything was back to normal, the Army drove leading Loyalist politicians around the area to inspect the newly captured terrain. As a result of this and many smaller operations of a similar kind, the battle-lines soon became clearly drawn, with the British Army on one side and the IRA on the other. The British state acknowledged this in January 1971 when the Army entered negotiations with the IRA and a temporary truce was arranged. For the IRA the breakdown of this truce meant a formal declaration of war. On 6 February 1971, the IRA shot dead its first British soldier. The longest war was now out in the open.

The year 1971 marked a watershed. Thousands of British troops poured into Northern Ireland, so that by December the Army of occupation was 15 000-strong. This enormous military invasion indicated that there was no going back to Stormont. To prove it the IRA launched a bombing campaign designed to stretch the Army to the limit. The bombings gathered momentum from month to month. In April there were 37 major explosions, in May the number rose to 47, in June it was 50 and in July it reached 91. The movement of nationalist resistance grew from strength to strength. The killing of two youths in Derry in July provoked three days of nationalist rioting. Although the British Army opened up with tear gas, truncheons, rubber and real bullets, it could not break the nationalists. On the contrary, nationalist youths flocked to join the IRA.

Instead of curbing resistance, Army repression only unified the nationalist community around the IRA. Even the middle class Catholic Social Democratic and Labour Party, founded in 1970 to reconcile the nationalist community to a reformed British rule, could not remain immune from the groundswell of nationalist fervour. Yielding to public pressure, the SDLP's representatives withdrew from Stormont in July. The last links between Stormont and the nationalist population were thus broken.

The nationalist revolt created panic in establishment circles. A small-scale security operation had turned into a full-blown war. After two years on the ground, the British Army was even less in control of the situation than when it went into action in August 1969.

Reasserting British authority required drastic action. On 24 July 1971 the Army announced that it was going on to the offensive. In a series of dawn raids on 9 August, the British seized hundreds of republican suspects and interned them without charge or trial in special concentration camps. Internment was a public admission that Britain was fighting a colonial war against a people who did not recognise that their land was a part of Britain. With a wave of the hands *The Times* dismissed liberal objections that internment would antagonise the nationalist population, noting that 'the populace could hardly be more antagonistic than it was' (10 August 1971).

Towards direct rule

Internment was a failure. Leading republicans evaded the Army net, and the nationalist community could not be cowed into submission. The majority of the 342 detainees were civil rights campaigners, old republicans or people who just happened to live in Catholic ghettos. The RUC's intelligence proved to be inaccurate and out of date. In Armagh, British troops arrived to arrest a man who had died four years earlier. The only positive result of the massive security operation was that it allowed the British Army to gather useful information on its opponents and to reorganise its intelligence services. An Army spokesman later justified the raids on the grounds that 'it took seven years in Malaya to build up the equivalent intelligence we have gained in a few months' (*Observer,* 30 January 1972).

Internment was also a political disaster. The raids, house searches, harassment and intimidation of the nationalist community helped destroy what little illusions remained in British democracy. Internment gave the green light for Loyalist pogroms. Within 24 hours 13 people had been shot dead. Catholic families were forced to abandon their homes. Then came the reports of the indignities and torture suffered by internees in Long Kesh, Hollywood barracks and in the prison ship *Maidstone.* The systematic beatings and new experiments in sensory deprivation techniques became public knowledge. Internment generated an unprecedented level of solidarity in the nationalist areas and there was a dramatic rise in support for the republican movement.

In the months following internment the Six Counties was plunged into warfare on a scale not experienced since 1921. Nationalists put up barricades in virtually every Catholic quarter. In the 'no-go' areas of Belfast and Derry the IRA operated as a virtual provisional government. A group of Belfast women launched a rent and rate strike which took off throughout the Six Counties. By the end of the year more than 23 000 families were refusing to pay their bills to the state. The war itself acquired a new ferocity: 30 soldiers and 11 members of the local security forces were killed within four months of internment. The IRA's extensive bombing campaign showed that its military powers were on the increase.

The upward spiral of violence in the aftermath of internment had a profound impact on the British ruling class. The more far-sighted British politicians now realised that Northern Ireland could no longer be ruled in the old way. Two years of mounting chaos convinced them that the very existence of a separate Six Counties state would continue to provoke nationalist resistance. In December 1971, Tory home secretary Reginald Maudling shocked some observers by admitting that the republican movement would 'not be defeated, not completely eliminated', but would rather have their violence reduced to 'an acceptable level'. Maudling acknowledged that British control meant more repression. Accordingly on 30 January 1972 the government ordered the Army to open fire on an unarmed march against internment in Derry. The slaughter of 14 Catholics on Bloody Sunday was a clear indication of what was intended by the Army's new policy of 'maximum repression'.

Bloody Sunday led directly to the fall of Stormont. The outraged reaction throughout Ireland and abroad put the British state on the defensive. Tens of thousands marched in protest against the massacre in Dublin (where the British embassy was burnt down), Belfast and Derry itself, as well as in London and other capital cities around the world. Inside Northern Ireland Bloody Sunday precipitated even greater polarisation and conflict. The republican movement went on the offensive and Loyalist politicians mobilised their paramilitary units to defend the British way of life. The Stormont regime could not stand the strain: on 24 March 1972 it was dissolved and direct rule from Westminster was instituted.

From August 1969 to March 1972 the war developed from sporadic riots into a conflict of arms, bombs and the high-technology weapons of modern counter-insurgency. During this period Britain's role as the oppressor of Ireland became more and more obvious, culminating in direct rule—the clearest expression yet of British domination. The first three years of open conflict showed that what was at stake was not some obscure religious feud, but a war between oppressor and oppressed. A decade later, the voice of the British ruling class reiterated the major lesson of the period:

'If one rules out British withdrawal from Ulster, as we do, the only conceivable alternative that has been put forward is the maintenance of direct rule more or less *sine die.* The trouble with direct rule is that it offers no hope for the future. Its main achievement was once described by a previous secretary of state as leading to an "acceptable level of violence"....Direct rule is thus in many ways a euphemism for military rule.' (*Financial Times,* 25 October 1982)

The destruction of Stormont was a major blow against British imperialism. It meant that British rule could only be enforced through military occupation. Stormont, the body that for 50 years had tried to give imperialist oppression a democratic veneer, could no longer play any part in disguising it.

Living with direct rule

Direct rule brought all aspects of social, economic and political life in the Six Counties under the control of Westminster. It was the only way Britain could keep a firm grip on the deteriorating situation. But direct rule itself could not solve the underlying problems. The liberation struggle still raged and, to make matters worse for Britain, Loyalist gangs also extended their activities to seek revenge for the loss of Stormont. In March 1972 a successful one-day Loyalist strike, backed by the Ulster Defence Association, added to the climate of instability.

Squeezed from both sides, British strategists seemed to have run out of plans. Until the middle of 1974 the authorities floundered, at one moment seeking a negotiated compromise, at another trying to set up a revamped version of Stormont and again going all-out for coercion. In the summer of 1972 the British government was in such a weak position that it was prepared to hold talks with the IRA. On 7 July home secretary William Whitelaw met a delegation from the republican movement in London. The talks proved inconclusive. On 9 July the British Army broke the ceasefire which had accompanied the secret negotiations. In reply, the republican movement announced to the press that its leaders had been discussing with the British government. Embarrassed by these revelations, the Tory regime launched a new offensive to demonstrate that it was still in control in Northern Ireland.

On 24 July Whitelaw announced in the house of commons that his first priority was to destroy the IRA. A week later 'Operation Motorman' set out to do just that. Motorman was the largest military initiative up to that stage of the war. Its objective was to destroy the 'no-go' areas from which most attacks were launched. It involved 21 000 British troops—the highest concentration ever in the Six Counties. Hundreds of armoured vehicles, landrovers and scout cars lined up in ranks which were 12-deep in places. At 4am, led by specially converted 60-ton Centurion tanks, Motorman smashed through the barricades. In Belfast the IRA withdrew in the face of overwhelming odds and there was little fighting. In Derry there was considerable resistance and the Army shot two people dead. When it was all over, the ghettos of West Belfast and Derry were like one vast concentration camp. Schools and community centres were turned into local bases and observation posts. Perimeter fences and security gates were scanned by closed-circuit television. Squads of soldiers patrolled every backyard, every tiny front garden.

Between 1972 and 1974 the British state followed up the success of Motorman. The number of houses searched quadrupled from 17 262 to 74 919 between 1971 and 1974 (*Belfast Bulletin,* Spring 1982). In 1973 plastic bullets replaced rubber bullets in the armoury of the security forces.

In an attempt to restore its rather tarnished 'fair-play' image, the British state began to pull back the Army from front-line combat. The aim was to dissociate the Army from the more gruesome atrocities necessary to enforce the British way of life on the uncooperative Irish. Yet in practice, Army officers maintained informal relationships with Loyalist murder gangs. Indeed, what emerged were new, covert security units which combined the Special Air Service with local Loyalist forces. Operating under the name of the Military Reconnaissance Force, these units unleashed a reign of terror in 1972.

IRA VOLUNTEER CHARLES ENGLISH

● *Why my son joined the IRA*

Michael English lives in the Bogside district of Derry. Above the fireplace in his front room, set in a carved frame, is a picture of his eldest son. The inscription is simply 'Gary English. Aged 19 years. Murdered by British troops, Easter Sunday 1981'. On the back wall is a picture of his second dead son, dressed in the military uniform and mask of the IRA and carrying a machine gun, underneath which is printed the legend 'Volunteer Charles English'. Charles English was killed when a rocket-launcher went off prematurely as his IRA unit attacked the RUC in August 1985.

Michael English's eldest son Gary was 19 when, in 1981, Irish republican prisoners went on hunger-strike for their right to be recognised as prisoners of war. Gary was not involved in the republican movement: 'but he knew where his sympathies lay'. Like thousands of Irish people in Derry, he joined the annual Easter Sunday march to remember those who had died fighting for Irish freedom. After the march Gary went off to play football. It was to be his last game.

'There was trouble between some of the local boys and the British Army near the ballpark,' Michael remembers. 'Gary and the people playing football heard the crowd running and the firing of plastic bullets. So they stopped playing and went to see what was happening. They had just arrived when two Army landrovers came tearing down the hill, a gradient of about one in six, at about 60 miles an hour. They just ploughed through a crowd that wasn't rioting, and killed two boys. One of them was my Gary. They drove in line behind him, they lined their vehicle up deliberately to strike him down. As he lay on the ground the Army vehicle reversed over him, and at that point in time my son's life was squeezed away.'

The soldiers who murdered Gary walked out of court with a caution. The judge told them to watch their 'careless driving'.

Charles English was just 18 when the Army killed his brother. He had seen enough of 'British justice' in Ireland. He joined the IRA. His father tried to persuade him that there was a peaceful way to fight back. But as he now admits, he lost the argument. 'I felt it was important to show that if a person was persistent enough justice could be obtained. I've learnt that was a mistake on my part. Justice can't be obtained in Northern Ireland because it does not suit the British establishment. Charles decided the only justice they seemed to understand is the justice of an armed struggle. He, like many more young men, followed a path they believed in, and it's a path I wouldn't now contradict.'

So what kind of man was Charles English? A 'terrorist'? 'It's a word used by the British propagandists,' says his father. 'There was a time not so long ago in relation to the Irish struggle when people like my Charles were called "rebels". But "rebel" meant they had something to rebel against, and the British would like you to believe that young people here have nothing to rebel against, that they are terrorists for the sake of being terrorists. But I knew my Charles, knew him as a person. He loved life, he thought it was precious. But still he had principles which he thought were worth fighting for. And he died for them as well.

'He wasn't afraid of death, because he'd grown up with death: Bloody Sunday in 1972 he was nine years old; 1981 when his brother Gary was murdered, he took the message over the phone that his brother was dead; 1983 the best friend that he had in the world, Richard Quigley, was killed in an operation against the British Army of occupation. So death was all around him. I know from the people who took him from the place where he was injured to hospital that he said "I'm not afraid to die, but I don't want to die alone like my brother, stay with me." And he died in their arms.

'That's the calibre of person the British Army and government have to overcome if they want to keep the British ruling Ireland. And there's no way they're going to do it, because they are fighting people with convictions. The British Army get paid, 90 per cent of them do it for the wages. People like my Charles do it through conviction, they do it from the heart. And there's no way you can beat a man like that.'

Charles English's funeral hit the headlines around the world. Noraid spokesman Martin Galvin broke a ban on entering Northern Ireland and carried Charles English's coffin with leading republican Martin McGuinness. It was a gesture of defiance against the British Army and the RUC, who had tried to abuse and intimidate the English family the night Charles died.

Charles English's coffin was carried every step of the three miles from his home to the cemetery by friends, family and supporters. 'Even his mother, his sisters and his girlfriend carried him,' says Michael, 'that was a highly emotional thing, and it wasn't given any publicity in the British press. Because I don't care how hard you are, to see them six girls carrying that coffin, it just tugged at the heart. And the last thing the British propagandists wanted was for anybody to feel any kind of sympathy for the family of a "dead terrorist".'

(From an interview in *the next step*, 18 October 1985)

The assassinations continued into 1973 and, by the middle of the year, rumours began to filter through to the media that Army operations were directed specifically at killing IRA leaders in a 'top 30' death list (*The Times,* 17 May 1973). Six unarmed IRA men were murdered in February and another in May. The *Guardian* reported that two criminals, the Littlejohn brothers, had been hired to assassinate prominent IRA members, including its chief of staff (9 August). In March 1974 the establishment publicly admitted what everyone had suspected all along. *The Times* reported that SAS units were operating in the Six Counties. This was the first time that such operations had been launched within the 'United Kingdom'. The report noted that 'the political implications of bringing the SAS into Northern Ireland are enormous' and proudly boasted of the ability of the SAS 'to kill swiftly and silently behind enemy lines' (19 March 1974).

Undercover intelligence work increased dramatically during this period. The scale of the operations was made public in August 1974, when the *Observer* reported that every soldier in the Six Counties was being trained in routine intelligence work. Up to 20 per cent of any battalion could be involved in full-time intelligence work at any one time (11 August 1974).

Whitelaw's policy of dirty tricks and maximum brutality achieved a number of successes but failed to restore order. The British government realised that it could not rely on repression alone. That would expose too starkly its oppressive role in Northern Ireland. To give British rule a semblance of legitimacy, Whitelaw began to search for alternative forms of control. The Tories granted a number of minor concessions to encourage the collaboration of middle class Catholics and the SDLP. Whitelaw even dropped hints about ending internment.

In March 1973 the government announced plans for a new 'power-sharing' assembly and executive. The idea was to create a middle ground of moderate opinion which could help extricate Britain from direct involvement. The Sunningdale conference of December 1973 added to the proposed assembly a 'Council of Ireland', a talking shop with representatives from both North and South, as a further concession to the SDLP. The assembly met, the executive was chosen. By mid-1973 the quest for the middle ground seemed on the point of yielding results.

In fact the assembly never had a chance. It was unrepresentative of both the nationalist and Loyalist communities. Indeed the rhetoric which launched the assembly only frightened Loyalists, whose sole

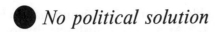 ## No political solution

1972:	Stormont collapses and direct rule from Westminster is imposed.
1973:	Tories set up 'power-sharing' assembly and executive, including major Unionist parties and the Social Democratic and Labour Party. Sunningdale conference brings the Southern government into the deal.
1974:	Loyalist Ulster Workers' Council strike, backed by British Army, brings down 'power-sharing' institutions.
1975:	Labour's constitutional convention elected, then immediately stalemated by Unionist demands for a return to Stormont and for no concessions to the nationalists.
1976:	Convention recalled to discuss power-sharing. Talks between Unionists and SDLP break down within 60 minutes. Convention collapses.
1980:	Tory Northern Ireland secretary Humphrey Atkins' devolution conference opens, closes, reopens, recloses and packs up as Unionists take 'no surrender' stance.
1982:	James Prior sets up 'rolling devolution' assembly for gradual transfer of local powers to Belfast. Immediately rolls into trouble as Sinn Fein wins five seats and SDLP is forced to join the nationalist boycott of the assembly. In June 1986 Northern Ireland secretary Tom King dissolves the assembly which had ceased to function after the Anglo-Irish deal.
1985:	Tory prime minister Margaret Thatcher and Irish Taoiseach Dr Garret FitzGerald sign the Anglo-Irish agreement. It holds firm despite vociferous and violent opposition from Ulster Loyalists.

concern was to cling on to their privileges. The last thing they wanted was any 'power-sharing' with Catholics. The leadership of the Loyalist community united to destroy the assembly. In May Loyalist paramilitaries organised the successful Ulster Workers' Council strike, which paralysed the Six Counties within days and dealt a death blow to the assembly. The middle ground disappeared.

The defeat of the 'power-sharing' assembly set a precedent for future political initiatives. From the constitutional convention of 1975 to the Tory 'rolling devolution' scheme of 1982, events have shown that the prospects for a new Stormont, however reformed, are very dim. The conflict of interest between British imperialism and the nationalist community cannot be resolved through assemblies or constitutions. The Loyalist dimension further complicates matters. Even the most modest reforms—such as the mere suggestion that Irish flags and street names be made legal under the Anglo-Irish agreement—threaten to provoke a Loyalist backlash and thus exacerbate 'the troubles'.

When the new Labour government assumed office in 1974 the war had reached a new stalemate. The republican movement was strong enough to inflict embarrassing blows against British imperialism but it lacked the means to defeat the Army. The British security forces were sufficiently organised and equipped to prevent a complete collapse of the Northern Ireland state, but were not in a position to turn the tables on the IRA. It was left to the new Labour administration to come up with one of the most sophisticated strategies ever devised to destroy the movement for Irish liberation.

Ulsterisation

From 1974 to 1979 the Labour government engineered a policy of containment designed to isolate and crush the IRA. Northern Ireland minister Merlyn Rees, and his successor Roy Mason, were committed to the policy of maximum repression. But they also wanted a policy which would give British imperialism moral authority and pin the blame for 'the troubles' on the IRA. Their chosen path was Ulsterisation—the replacement of British troops by 'Ulster' policemen. Ulsterisation aimed to localise the conflict and extricate British troops from direct public combat.

Hand in hand with Ulsterisation went normalisation and criminalisation. In Britain it is not normal to have soldiers on the streets. Police however, are normal. Wars of liberation are not normal either, but crime and punishment are accepted features of the British way of life. Hence the British propaganda machine played up the police and played down the Army ('normalisation'), as well as presenting the Irish War as merely a conflict between vicious petty criminals and an impartial police ('criminalisation'). Ulsterising, normalising and criminalising the forces of revolt in Ireland was the Labour government's way of turning the collective national fight for freedom there into a matter of individual, local larceny and violence for material gain.

On 4 April 1974 Rees explained the new strategy to the house of commons. He began by stating that the 'overriding consideration must always be that of security'. That was, he went on, a political question:

'The cornerstone of security should be a progressive increase in the role of the civilian law enforcement agencies in Northern Ireland....Sufficient numbers of the Army will remain in Northern Ireland to assist in maintaining law and order. But the government believed that in the long term it must be the community itself and normal police activities, not military operations alone, which will finally defeat the terrorist.'

● *Internment*

● 342 nationalists interned without trial on 9 August 1971.

● Fourteen internees subjected to the 'five techniques' of British torture: hooded, made to stand flush against walls for hours, denied sleep, given little food and water irregularly, subjected to constant 'white noise'. Many are mentally and emotionally scarred for life.

● Other hooded internees thrown backwards out of helicopters hovering a few feet above ground after being told they were flying high over Belfast.

● Over next four years more than 2500 are interned in Long Kesh concentration camp, where they are kept in unheated huts surrounded by floodlights and barbed wire.

● In 1975 home secretary Merlyn Rees admits that £300 000 had been paid to 473 internees in compensation for false arrest and beatings.

Rees' emphasis on a return to a 'normal' police activities meant that
every step possible would be taken to make the streets of Northern
Ireland appear as placid as those of his Leeds constituency. Rees
went as far as to legalise Sinn Fein. He countered criticism from
Loyalist politicians by arguing that it was a gamble well worth
taking. Anything that could help defuse military resistance was
worth a try.

The government abolished internment in 1975 as part of its
continuing campaign to restore normality. Internment was no longer
needed, because the policy of criminalisation was now in place. The
withdrawal of special-category status from Irish prisoners of war in
1976 meant that they would be treated as ordinary criminals. A crude
but efficient system of judicial terror, consisting of no-jury courts
and convictions obtained on the basis of confessions extracted
through torture, provided the framework for criminalising the
resistance movement. The number of prisoners soon far
outnumbered those detained under internment. In 1975 the RUC
held and tortured 320 people; in 1976 the figure more than doubled
to 708 and by the first quarter of 1977 it was 904. The number of
prisoners increased from 1644 in 1973 to 3450 by mid-1977 (*Northern
Ireland Digest of Statistics,* September 1977; *The Times,* 26 July
1977). The system of judicial violence provided the security forces
with a considerable amount of hard intelligence and eventually
forced the IRA to reorganise its operational units.

Criminalisation was accompanied by a determined effort to
project the Six Counties as slowly returning to normal. Every few
weeks Roy Mason announced that the IRA was on the run. He
launched plans to rebuild the economy, schemes for housing and
other community projects. Even the RUC received a face-lift. The
sectarian boot-boys began to operate youth clubs and organise 'Blue
Lamp discos'. RUC community workers 'continually emphasise', an
RUC officer explained, 'that they are policemen first and community
relations officers second, and the Community Relations Branch is
just another specialised unit which a modern police force requires if it
is to serve the community properly by reducing or preventing crime
and helping to produce responsible citizens' (*Ulster Commentary,*
May 1975).

Criminalisation and normalisation are familiar counter-insurgency techniques. Whether or not they work depends on the extent to
which the unruly colony is really getting back to normal.

Local security forces

During the seventies the total size of the Loyalist security forces increased from 10 955 to 19 287. The Labour government clearly intended that the RUC and the UDR should move into the front line of the war. But these units could not replace the Army by force of numbers alone. They had to be trained and equipped to carry out these responsibilities. In September 1973, Englishman Kenneth Newman was made deputy chief constable of the RUC. Over the next three years he established the framework for Ulsterisation. The RUC's intelligence operations were improved and its weapons were updated. Newman streamlined and reorganised the RUC's operational procedures.

But it was not just sophisticated technology that improved the RUC's effectiveness. The arbitrary powers granted by the Emergency Provisions Act of 1973 and the Prevention of Terrorism Act of 1974 allowed the RUC to oversee a system of detention, torture and conviction in no-jury courts. Newman's reorganisation meant building a truly systematic instrument of terror.

In July 1976 the Labour government announced plans for restoring the 'primacy of the police'. In practice the RUC's extended role meant that it would concentrate on collating criminal intelligence. A second aspect of the RUC's higher profile was its development of selective hard policing. On the basis of RUC intelligence, chosen targets were picked up, beaten into submission and shunted down the 'conveyor belt' to prison. The treatment meted out to prisoners in Castlereagh interrogation centre is well-documented. In 1976 some 875 complaints of assault were made against the RUC, double the figure for 1975. To aid this side of its work, the Six Counties Special Patrol Group was reorganised in 1977, to give each police district its own special assault squad. The new Divisional Mobile Support Units were highly trained and mobile.

Brutal attacks on selected individuals went together with a softer approach towards the nationalist community as a whole. The number of house raids fell dramatically from 34 039 in 1976 to 4106 in 1980 (*Belfast Bulletin,* Spring 1982). House searches were replaced by the 'screening of civilians' allowed under the RUC's extensive powers of stop and search. This double-edged policing was given the seal of British approval in January 1977 when formal responsibility for security in the Six Counties was handed over to the RUC.

The increased public exposure of the RUC did not mean that

Ulsterisation was really being implemented. The Army remained in strength. The only difference was that now most of the repression was carried out behind the scenes—through Loyalist paramilitaries, covert Army units and detentions. In 1976 the SAS unleashed a reign of terror in Armagh designed to destroy the IRA command structure. One SAS officer boasted of the success of the assassination squads in dealing with the top 10 local IRA leaders: 'We got four of them; the other six were chased down South' (T Geraghty, *Who Dares Wins*). From late 1977 to late 1978 selective murders were stepped up. The most infamous was the summary execution of a three-man IRA unit on 21 June 1978. An undercover team of SAS and RUC assassins surrounded Jim Mulvenna, Jackie Mealey and Dennis Brown. They pumped more than 200 rounds into their victims, also wounding passers-by—one fatally.

In a speech reasserting his determination to 'capture' and 'nail' the leaders of the IRA, Mason proudly announced that the size of the SAS and other covert units would be increased. He declared that henceforth those 'conspiring' to murder would receive life imprisonment (instead of 10 years) and 10 years (rather than five) for membership of the IRA (*Financial Times,* 9 June 1977). Soon Mason's normalisation policies were getting results. The prison system became one of Northern Ireland's few growth industries. In 1972, before Newman's arrival, there were 555 prison officers in the Six Counties. By 1978 that number rose to 2339 (*Belfast Bulletin,* Spring 1982). Private firms supplying security guards—often financed by the state—also mushroomed in the same period.

Mason's strategy had further consequences. With hundreds of volunteers either dead or behind bars, the IRA was forced to tighten up its structure and reorganise its service units into a cell-type organisation. Mason rejoiced over the decline of IRA military initiatives and often told the press that the IRA was on the run. He was soon forced to eat his words.

The reorganisation of the IRA and the emergence of the Irish National Liberation Army led to the renewal of the bombing campaign in November 1978. This was followed up by a series of engagements in 1979, the most spectacular of which were the assassination of leading Tory Airey Neave, and then of Lord Mountbatten on the same day as the bombing of 18 British soldiers at Warrenpoint. However, in general, the stalemate on the military plane which preceded 'Ulsterisation' continued. Nothing lasting had been achieved in the drive to destroy the IRA. A secret British Army document captured by the IRA in 1979 appreciated the resilience of British imperialism's No 1 enemy:

Joe Boatman

SPOT THE TERRORIST?

'The Provisionals' campaign of violence is likely to continue while the British remain in Northern Ireland. We see little prospect of political development of a kind which could seriously undermine the Provisionals' position.' (Quoted in *An Phoblacht/Republican News*, 10 May 1979)

The Army document only confirmed what was already general knowledge in Northern Ireland. In 1980 more than 31 000 security personnel were tied down in the Six Counties and normalisation was as far away as ever.

The struggle against criminalisation

In addition to its military aspects, Ulsterisation had an important ideological component. It was designed to isolate the IRA and legitimise British rule in Ireland. Its aim was to stress the criminal character of the IRA and to portray British troops as upright defenders of justice and democracy. The strategy had little prospect of convincing members of the nationalist community that their friends and relations were criminals. But Mason hoped that this version of the war would influence international opinion, and especially opinion in Britain.

The central importance of criminalisation to British strategy made nationalist resistance inevitable. The withdrawal of special-category status provided the focus for one of the most dramatic campaigns of the Irish War. In January 1976 the republican movement stated that Irish prisoners of war would not accept the change in their status because it denied the legitimacy of the national liberation struggle. Two months later the Belfast Brigade of the IRA announced that those manning Britain's war prisons in the Six Counties would now be regarded as legitimate targets (*An Phoblacht/Republican News*, 20 March 1976).

Prisoners themselves joined the struggle. On 14 September 1976, Kieran Nugent became the first republican to be denied special-category status. His refusal to wear a prison uniform launched the blanket protest campaign. By spring 1978 there were nearly 300 men 'on the blanket'. The protest in the H-Blocks was joined by women political prisoners in Armagh jail. The protest against the withdrawal of special status received widespread support in the nationalist community. The Relatives Action Committee organised protest marches in 1978 and 1979. Inside the prisons conditions deteriorated and the conflict between the republican prisoners and the authorities became more and more intense. On 10 October 1980

YET ANOTHER BRITISH ARMY RAID IN DERRY

the prisoners in the H-Blocks announced their intention of launching a hunger-strike to restore political status:

'We demand, as of right, political recognition and that we be accorded the status of political prisoners. We claim the right as captured combatants in the continuing struggle for national liberation and self-determination. We refute most strongly the term "criminal" with which the British have attempted to label us and our struggle.' (*Irish Times,* 11 October 1980)

The first wave of hunger-strikes was called off after 33 days before any prisoners had died. When promised concessions failed to materialise the prisoners launched the second wave of hunger-strikes on 1 March 1981. This lasted until 3 October and led to the death of 10 hunger-strikers. The hunger-strikers—and the popular response they received—destroyed criminalisation once and for all.

The hunger-strikers could not achieve their objective of winning political status. But their heroism inspired tens of thousands throughout the world. In Ireland—North and South—a new generation of youth joined the struggle for political status and Irish freedom. When Bobby Sands, the IRA hunger-strikers' leader and the first to die, was elected to Westminster on 9 April 1981 in Fermanagh-South Tyrone, criminalisation was dead. In one area of Northern Ireland—outside Belfast, Derry and South Armagh —30 492 people went out and voted to make one simple point to the British parliament: in their eyes Bobby Sands was no criminal. On 11 June, voters in the Twenty-six Counties elected two blanket men—Paddy Agnew and Kieran Doherty—to the Dail in Dublin in the general election. After the death of Bobby Sands, his election agent Owen Carron was elected in August for the same seat, on a ticket of support for the prisoners' demands for political status. The prisoners' electoral victories, together with the massive demonstrations of public sympathy throughout the Six Counties, showed the world the continued commitment of the nationalist community to the struggle for national liberation. Only in Britain could the lie that republican prisoners were criminals receive any degree of popular approval.

Despite all the resources, sophisticated technology and repression behind it, Mason's strategy failed on both military and ideological levels. By the end of the hunger-strikes the British state was back to square one. It had not broken the stalemate, and could only hope that the 'acceptable level of violence' would not be too high. Before we move on to look at the present situation, let's look more closely at

● Ten who died for political status

Bobby Sands MP, (IRA) died 5 May 1981 after 66 days without food
Francis Hughes, (IRA) died 12 May after 59 days
Raymond McCreesh, (IRA) died 21 May after 61 days
Patsy O'Hara, (INLA) died 21 May after 61 days
Joe McDonnell, (IRA) died 8 July after 61 days
Martin Hurson, (IRA) died 13 July after 46 days
Kevin Lynch, (INLA) died 1 August after 71 days
Kieran Doherty, (IRA) died 2 August after 73 days
Thomas McElwee, (IRA) died 8 August after 65 days
Mickey Devine, (INLA) died 20 August after 66 days

what an 'acceptable level of violence' means for the people on the receiving end of it.

The other war

An incident in February 1987, when an Ulster Defence Association gang raided the UDR barracks at Coleraine and took 170 rifles and guns, revealed how close links are between the official security forces and the Loyalist paramilitaries. Two serving officers of the UDR, both of whom admitted membership of the UDA, were later charged with complicity in the arms raid.

The Loyalist murder gangs are an auxiliary arm of British terror in Ireland. The Ulster Defence Association, the Ulster Volunteer Force, the Red Hand Commandos, the Ulster Freedom Fighters, the Protestant Action Force and other front organisations have been torturing and murdering Catholics since the mid-sixties. Sometimes the paramilitaries have gone too far and the British government has been obliged to denounce them. But in general the Loyalist gangs have played a valuable role for the authorities.

The British media, and even the British left, often label the republican movement and the Loyalist paramilitaries as equally 'sectarian'. The real alignment of forces in the Irish War exposes the superficiality of this view. The republican movement may be supported by Catholics, but its supporters blame, not Protestants, but the British state for the oppression and poverty they experience in Northern Ireland. The republican movement directs its attacks on British soldiers, policemen and prison officers. For republicans, the armed representatives of the British state are legitimate targets.

There have been isolated cases of sectarian assassinations of Protestants by Catholics. The killing of 10 Protestant workers at Bessbrook in County Armagh in 1976 and, in 1983, of three worshippers at a Protestant chapel at Darkley, also in Armagh, are widely publicised examples. But such incidents are rare, and always a response to Protestant attacks on Catholics. Five Catholics were killed in South Armagh on the day before the Bessbrook incident. The Darkley shooting was carried out by the 'Catholic Reaction Force' in retaliation for a two-year campaign of anti-Catholic terror by the Protestant Action Force, a group with close links to the Ulster Defence Regiment.

The republican movement has always rejected the policy of sectarian attacks. Loyalist paramilitaries, however, exist solely to organise random terror against Catholics. In their anger over unemployment, bad housing and poverty, Loyalists cannot turn

ALEX MASKEY, SINN FEIN COUNCILLOR AND ELECTION AGENT FOR GERRY ADAMS, SURVIVED AN ASSASSINATION ATTEMPT DURING THE 1987 GENERAL ELECTION

● *Sectarian slaughter since the Anglo-Irish deal*

In the first year after the Anglo-Irish agreement, Loyalist sectarian-assassins murdered 14 Catholics. On 14 September IRA volunteers executed a Protestant—John Bingham, 'military commander' of the Loyalist paramilitary Ulster Volunteer Force, because he organised the murder of at least five Catholics in North Belfast. The IRA statement on Bingham's death confirmed its opposition to sectarianism: 'At no time will we involve ourselves in the execution of ordinary Protestants but at all times we reserve the right to take armed action against those who attempt to terrorise or intimidate our people into accepting British/Unionist rule.'

14 January 1986:	The sectarian murder of Catholic Leo Scullion in Ligoniel, North Belfast, begins a spate of Loyalist killings which continues throughout the year.
31 January 1986:	Martin Quinn shot in his bed in the nationalist enclave of Bawnmore in North Belfast.
13 March 1986:	John O'Neill, from Ballysillan, North Belfast, becomes the third victim of Loyalist murder gangs in as many months.
7 May 1986:	North Belfast woman Margaret Caulfield, a Protestant, shot dead in her bed in Ballysillan by Loyalists because she was married to a Catholic; her husband Gerry is seriously wounded.
10 July 1986:	Brian Leonard, a Tyrone man working on a building site on the Loyalist Shankill Road in Belfast, shot in the head by Loyalist gunmen; dies two days later.
14 July 1986:	North Belfast man Colm McCallan, standing at his front door in Ligoniel, is dragged away by a roaming Loyalist gang and shot three times in the head.
19 July 1986:	North Belfast man Martin Duffy lured to his death by a bogus call to his taxi firm. He is shot three times and dies shortly afterwards.
26 August 1986:	The Ulster Freedom Fighters (a front for the UDA) claimed responsibility for the murder of West Belfast taxi driver Paddy McAllister who was shot dead in his home in St James's.
16 September 1986:	Father of four Raymond Mooney is murdered by Loyalist gunmen as he left a church committee meeting.
17 September 1986:	Joseph Webb from Saintfield is gunned down near Belfast city centre; two other Catholics in a shoe shop near the Shankill Road, together with another man from Newtownards, are all shot at, but escape unharmed.
16 October 1986:	76-year old Catholic woman Kathleen Mullan and her son Terry are slaughtered in their farmhouse by the UDA/UFF at Ballynahinch, County Down.
6 December 1986:	Loyalist sectarian killers claim their thirteenth victim of the year, beating Catholic Paul Bradley to death in a bar, in Lisburn, County Antrim.
20 December 1986:	Liam McShane killed when Loyalists bomb the pub he was using in Maghera, County Derry.

against the British state. The Loyalists rely on Britain to sustain their privileged access to jobs and housing. It is precisely because the advantages of the Loyalists over the Catholics are marginal that, in a situation of mounting economic ruin, they become so important. In these circumstances Protestant anger is turned, not against Britain, but against those who threaten British rule. Thus while Catholics hate the British state, Loyalists simply hate all Catholics. The paramilitaries are the extreme expression of the sectarian outlook which permeates Loyalism.

Loyalist paramilitaries have killed nearly 700 Catholics. The ferocious brutality with which these murders have been carried out is the hallmark of Loyalist sectarianism. The victims, usually randomly selected, are often tortured before being killed. Bodies have been found covered with innumerable scars, or with eyes gouged out. The object here is to terrorise the Catholic population as a whole.

The paramilitaries also harass and intimidate the nationalist community in non-lethal, but still devastating ways. In the early years of the war, they forced thousands of Catholics to move out of mixed residential areas. Between 30 000 and 60 000 people were estimated to have moved home in Greater Belfast alone in this period, and 80 per cent of them were Catholics (*The Times,* 4 August 1973). In the wake of the Anglo-Irish deal, Loyalist intimidation of Catholics left more than a dozen dead and hundreds homeless. In January 1987 the Northern Ireland housing executive revealed that, during 1986, cases of intimidation accounted for 1102 requests for rehousing, the highest recorded figure since the early seventies.

The reaction of the British security forces to Loyalist violence is different from their treatment of republicans. Many known Loyalist murderers are allowed to walk the streets safely. Lenny Murphy, the leader of the notorious 'Shankill Butchers', who carved 19 Catholics to death between November 1975 and March 1977, was never charged with any of these murders. His leading role was well-known, but it was left to the IRA to dispose of him in 1982.

The links between the British state and the paramilitaries go much further than turning a blind eye to murder. There is a tradition of dual membership of British forces and Loyalist murder gangs. The original Ulster Volunteer Force became a regiment in the British Army during the First World War. Today many members of the UDR and RUC are active in the UDA and UVF.

Out of uniform, UDR men have played a prominent role in the Loyalist paramilitary groups. Between 1973 and 1979, at least 35 serving or recently resigned members of the regiment were convicted

of offences ranging from membership of the illegal Ulster Volunteer
Force through armed robbery to sectarian murder. Hundreds more
committed outrages with impunity. Off-duty UDR members have
featured in some of the most grisly sectarian attacks during the 17
years since the UDR was formed.

Edward McIlwaine got 15 years in jail for his part in the Shankill
Butchers' murder campaign. In 1975 three Catholic members of the
Miami Showband were killed and two more were maimed when the
UVF bombed their bus and machine-gunned them. The bus had
been stopped by a UDR sergeant and corporal in uniform. Two
members of the regiment blew themselves up in the explosion.
Another two were later convicted of the murders. In January 1985
UDR private Geoffrey Edwards was convicted of killing Sinn Fein
activist Peter Corrigan in 1982. Edwards had used the regiment's
intelligence system to pick out his victim. A part-time UDR officer
told a British Sunday paper that Edwards was considered a hero for
killing Corrigan. Edwards had carried out 'an act of war, a matter of
pride' for the regiment.

In April 1985 a UDR member was arrested for the off-duty murder
of Catholic civilian Martin Love. The arrest of a regular British
soldier for the same murder showed Britain's complicity in the
Loyalist regiment's campaign of sectarian slaughter. Love was a 24-
year old unemployed Catholic from Enniskillen, County Fermanagh.
He had no republican connections, and his family supported the
moderate, pro-British Alliance Party. On Easter Sunday, on his way
home from a holiday drink at a local hotel, he was shot in the back
and the neck by Loyalist Ulster Freedom Fighters. Three days after
he died, Robert Kenny, a private in the UDR, was charged with his
murder. Kenny's arrest came within a week of the UDR's fifteenth
anniversary as an integral part of the British Army. Throughout
those 15 years and since, members of the UDR have doubled up as
gunmen for the Loyalist paramilitary organisations.

Members of the security forces who double up as Loyalist
paramilitaries can count on the sympathy of the Crown courts and of
the Crown itself. In 1980 a Northern Ireland judge sentenced to life
imprisonment two RUC men convicted of murdering a Catholic
shopkeeper. Their accomplices got off with suspended sentences.
The judge sympathised with the killers, telling them that their crime
was 'inexcusable' but 'understandable' (quoted in J Holland, *Too
Long a Sacrifice*). In November and December 1983, a dozen UDR
members from County Armagh were arrested in connection with
attacks carried out by the Protestant Action Force. Eight were

subsequently charged with the sectarian murder of Adrian Carroll, a Catholic, and five were convicted. Within days Thatcher made a special visit to the Armagh barracks where the murderers were based to express her full support for the UDR. Two months later the Duke of Edinburgh followed her to the barracks to put a royal seal of approval on the work being carried out by the armed forces in South Armagh. In 1985 Tory Northern Ireland secretary Douglas Hurd leapt to the UDR's defence, after its involvement in shoot-to-kill attacks, sectarian murders and kidnappings brought renewed calls for the regiment to be disbanded.

The close cooperation between security forces and the paramilitaries is sometimes strained by conflicts over how much violence to use against nationalists. Unlike the paramilitaries, the British state has to contend with international public opinion and maintain its 'peace-keeping' facade. Often when it appears that Britain is going 'soft' on the 'taigs', the Loyalist murder gangs go on the rampage. This strategy was explained in the UVF's journal in 1974:

'There is no essential moral difference between official government action and unofficial Loyalist action in the struggle against terrorism and subversion....In the event of political weakness on the part of the government leading to ineffective security measures, the UVF upholds the right to take such effective measures as it may, from time to time, consider necessary for the defeat of terrorism, aggression and insurrection.' (*Combat,* No 33, 1974)

The results of this division of labour between the British Army and the Loyalist paramilitaries are clear from a glance at the sectarian body count.

The two years in which the Loyalist murder squads were busiest were 1975 (150 murders) and 1976 (175 murders). These were the years in which Britain negotiated long ceasefires with the IRA. The repression which followed with the policy of Ulsterisation satisfied the UVF and the UDA, and they withdrew into the background. But the guns of the paramilitaries are still greased and they remain at the ready. Even the mere hint of Britain implementing meaningless 'reforms', such as those promised under the Anglo-Irish deal, is enough to let loose the Loyalist killers on innocent Catholics. Sectarian murders shot up in the months after the deal was signed.

● Victims of shoot-to-kill and sectarian slaughter

'The Royal Ulster Constabulary shot my brother Roddy, the Ulster Defence Regiment killed my brother Adrian. Now they're threatening me.'

Sinn Fein councillor Tommy Carroll, from the nationalist Mullacreevie estate outside Armagh, told *the next step* how they did it.

Inla volunteers Roddy Carroll and Seamus Grew were shot dead by an RUC assassination squad in December 1982, in an operation which was later investigated by Manchester policeman John Stalker before his removal from the shoot-to-kill inquiry.

'Roddy was 22 when the RUC murdered him and Seamie. The day they were shot was the day when my grandfather was buried and they were down at the funeral in Magherafelt. When they got back here the house was surrounded by UDR men. Roddy and Seamus sat in the house until they left, then took my sister down to Monaghan. They didn't know it, but the police followed them over the Border, into the Free State, then back up to Armagh.

'The police chased them into this estate and pulled up in front of them. An RUC man—Robinson—got out and walked over to the boys' car. He shot Roddy first. Obviously Roddy was shot in the back of his head because his face was all black and blue and disfigured. The bullets had gone into the back of his head and lodged at the front of his face.

'Seamie Grew must have got out of the car: his body was found on the ground. One of his fingers was shot off, so he must have had his hands up or something. There was no intention of arresting them. And there was no question of the boys trying to drive away from the police, because they weren't on the run, they were living openly. So the intention was just to kill them there and then.'

THE RUC TOLD TOMMY CARROLL: 'IT'S YOUR TURN NEXT'

There has been no inquest into Roddy Carroll's killing. In 1984 RUC constable Robinson was found not guilty of murdering Grew, although he admitted in court that there had been a high-level cover-up of the truth about the shooting. 'Clearance must have come from higher up that the trial would be rigged,' Tommy Carroll says. 'You just can't be a member of a police force and go out to shoot people and *hope* to get away with it. You must know beforehand that it's OK. The British authorities were behind the whole thing.'

It was a cold afternoon in November 1983. Twenty four-year old Adrian Carroll was walking home from his new job, painting railings for Armagh council. He had been married just four months. He was a Catholic, but lived in the Protestant part of the city because he had no interest in the war. As he turned up the entry to where he lived, a man disguised in cap and glasses followed. Carroll was partially deaf and could not hear his pursuer. The man behind pulled a gun and shot Carroll in the back of the head. He had become the latest victim of the Protestant Action Force, a gang of sectarian Loyalist killers operating in the Armagh area.

As the Protestant Action Force murderer tried to escape, an Ulster Defence Regiment patrol pulled up and arrested him. But, as Adrian Carroll's brother Tommy told us, it was no ordinary arrest: 'The UDR men came on the scene, pretended to arrest this man and took him away. But they didn't take him into custody. Instead they gave him his uniform to change back into. It was a UDR uniform. He was one of their patrol. They then went up to the police barracks and the police sent the same UDR men out to look for the terrorists who were after shooting Adrian.'

Since Roddy's death, the RUC has told Tommy that it's his turn next. 'I was walking up the estate and the police drew up. They shouted "Your day's coming Carroll." We should know what that means by now.'

(From an interview in *the next step,* 19 July 1985)

From shoot-to-kill to summits

The Anglo-Irish deal agreed between London and Dublin in 1985 was intended to be the political complement to criminalisation. By declaring that Dublin would have a new consultative role in matters affecting Northern Ireland, and by promising to reform some of the more extreme aspects of repression and discrimination in Ulster, Britain hoped to restore credibility to the constitutional nationalism of the SDLP and confirm the isolation of the republican movement as unreasonable extremists. Once this was achieved, the British would be well-placed to launch an all-out crackdown on the IRA and Sinn Fein.

The impetus for the agreement was the political and military polarisation that followed the hunger-strikes. The strikes brought an upsurge of anti-British feeling and IRA and Inla activity. The British security forces went on the offensive to restore the balance of power in a manner reminiscent of the open repression of the early years of the war. The lesson of the popular support for the hunger-strikers was grasped by all significant sections of the establishment. Top Tory adviser and *Daily Telegraph* columnist TE Utley urged Thatcher to pursue 'the policy of treating Ulster as a normal part of the Kingdom'—in other words, to hold fast to direct rule (*Daily Telegraph,* 18 February 1983). For Utley direct rule meant only one thing—military rule:

'Every device which the British government has used as a substitute for internment has attracted as much hostility as internment itself. This applies conspicuously to the use of supergrasses and the deployment of the SAS.' (*Daily Telegraph,* 8 December 1983)

Utley's case was clear: if every British stratagem is equally unwelcome to the nationalists, then Britain should forget about public relations and go for the device that best guaranteed continued physical control. In a pamphlet tribute to Ross McWhirter, the co-author of the *Guinness Book of Records,* who was killed by the IRA in 1975 for offering informers vast sums of money, Utley argued even more pointedly for ignoring nationalist opinion and concentrating on security: 'A dead martyr is rather less dangerous than a live terrorist' (TE Utley, *Terrorism and Violence*).

British imperialists took the point. Northern Ireland secretary Hurd accepted no limit to British violence. In 1984 he declared that the government's aim was 'no longer to contain terrorism, or to achieve an acceptable level of terrorist violence, but to eradicate it'.

MARTIN McGUINNESS HANDS THE TRICOLOUR, GLOVES AND BERET TO PATRICK KELLY'S WIDOW, MAY 1987

 The shoot-to-kill campaign

11 November 1982: IRA volunteers Gervais McKerr, Eugene Toman, Sean Burns shot 109 times at an RUC 'road-block' near Lurgan, County Armagh.

24 November 1982: Michael Tighe (17) shot dead by the RUC while innocently inspecting ancient rifles at a farmhouse near Lurgan.

12 December 1982: Inla members Roddy Carroll, Seamus Grew ambushed and shot to pieces by RUC at Mullacreevie estate, outside Armagh.

18 December 1982: Patrick Elliot (19) shot dead by British Army during the robbery of a chip shop in Andersonstown, West Belfast.

19 January 1983: Francis McColgan gunned down by RUC during the robbery of a petrol station, Lisburn Road, Belfast.

2 February 1983: Inla volunteer Eugene 'Niall' McMonagle is dragged from a flat in Shantallow, Derry, shot by an Army undercover squad and left lying in a pool of blood.

27 July 1983: Anthony O'Hare killed by RUC while running away from a post office robbery in Lurgan.

30 July 1983: Martin Malone (18) shot dead at point-blank range while arguing with a UDR patrol harassing Catholic youth in Armagh.

August 1983:	Inla volunteers Brendan Covery and Gerard Mallen killed by RUC in a shoot-out at Dungannon, County Tyrone.
9 August 1983:	Thomas Reilly shot in the back by an Army patrol while collecting dole in Whiterock, Belfast.
28 November 1983:	Bridget Foster (80) killed by RUC fire at a post office in Pomeroy, County Tyrone.
4 December 1983:	IRA volunteers Brian Campbell and Colm McGirr killed in SAS ambush near Coalisland, County Tyrone.
30 January 1984:	Mark Marron shot dead by British troops while joy-riding in West Belfast.
21 February 1984:	IRA volunteers Declan Martin and Henry Hogan killed by SAS in a gun battle at Dunloy, County Antrim, as they lay wounded on the ground.
13 July 1984:	IRA volunteer William Price shot by SAS in a stake-out in Ardboe, County Tyrone. He is left lying where he died for 10 hours.
12 August 1984:	John Downes killed by RUC during mass attack on West Belfast anti-internment rally.
2 December 1984:	IRA volunteer Tony McBride shot dead by SAS in gun battle near Kesh, County Fermanagh.
6 December 1984:	IRA volunteers Danny Doherty and William Fleming shot 30 times each by SAS in grounds of Gransha psychiatric hospital, Derry.
17 December 1984:	IRA volunteer Sean McIlvenna gunned down by RUC in County Armagh.
15 January 1985:	Paul Kelly (17) shot dead by UDR while joy-riding in West Belfast.
7 February 1985:	Gerry Logue (19) killed by RUC while joy-riding in West Belfast.
23 February 1985:	IRA volunteers Charles Breslin, Mickey Devine and Davy Devine (15) executed by SAS after surrendering in Strabane.
18 February 1986:	Francis Bradley murdered by SAS squad. On his twenty first birthday, Bradley went to see a friend about a car-part in Newbridge, County Derry. The SAS broke his leg, smashed his jaw and shot him through the neck.
22 February 1986:	IRA volunteer Tony Gough shot by British Army in Shantallow, County Derry.
26 April 1986:	IRA volunteer Seamus McElwaine killed by SAS in Rosslea, County Fermanagh.
13 September 1986:	Unarmed IRA volunteer James McKernan shot in the back at close range by a British Army patrol in Andersonstown, West Belfast.
8 May 1987:	IRA volunteers Declan Arthurs, Seamus Donnelly, Tony Gormley, Eugene Kelly, Patrick Kelly, Jim Lynagh, Patrick McKearney and Gerard O'Callaghan shot to pieces in an SAS ambush at Loughgall, County Armagh.

From 1982 to 1985 shoot-to-kill took the place of power-sharing and devolution as the central theme of British strategy in Ireland.

The terror unleashed against Irish nationalists in the period after the hunger-strikes had all the trappings of the classic colonialism of the early seventies. But the shoot-to-kill offensive and the supergrass policy, which ran from late 1982 to early 1985, were quite distinct from the internment/Bloody Sunday strategy of the period in which nationalist hostility to British rule was at a high point. Civilians were certainly shot after the hunger-strikes, and the supergrasses certainly named some innocents. But the thrust of Britain's new security offensive was to target known republicans. The British state had learnt the lessons of the earlier period. It wanted to intimidate its opponents and dampen the rising spirits of the nationalist community. But its concern to contain the conflict and improve the image of British rule dictated a greater selectivity with regard to its victims.

Over the whole of the Irish War, the Crown forces have killed almost equal numbers of nationalist civilians and republican activists. But during the two-year period of their sustained shoot-to-kill campaign, the British shot two IRA or Inla volunteers for every civilian. They used an improved intelligence system to ambush republicans on active service.

Selective assassination

Shooting to kill is nothing new in itself. Imperialist armies fighting wars against popular liberation movements never shoot to do anything else. But the Crown forces' assault was more systematic and more explicit than before. In the period from 1982 to 1985 shoot-to-kill became a British institution. The appointment of a former SAS commander to run the British war effort confirmed the government's emphasis on execution tactics. The Army and the RUC were restructured: ordinary members of the security forces were separated from the shoot-to-kill specialists—the RUC's Divisional Mobile Support Units and the Army's SAS.

The shoot-to-kill experts rarely wear uniforms. They hit known republicans from well-concealed ambushes, giving their victims no warning or chance of surrender. But despite their clandestine operations, they make no secret of what they are about. The security forces no longer even bother to pretend that they are involved in anything other than selective assassination. Members of Divisional Mobile Support Units have boasted in court that their training is based on 'speed, firepower and aggression'. Professional contract killers have a method of execution called 'cowboying' where the victim is literally blown apart as a warning to others. British shoot-to-kill squads now operate on the same principle, using unorthodox weapons like pump-action shotguns alongside their machine pistols.

In February 1983 plain-clothed soldiers shot dead Inla volunteer Niall McMonagle at his Derry flat and left him lying in a pool of blood. In February 1984 IRA volunteers Declan Martin and Henry Hogan were wounded in an SAS ambush in Country Antrim and executed as they lay helpless in a field. In February 1985 the SAS executed IRA activists Charlie Breslin, and brothers Michael and David Devine in Strabane. They fired 117 rounds without warning and then shot each volunteer in the head. The inquest into the shootings in early 1987 was told that the IRA men did not discharge their weapons, nor were they challenged. Dr Thomas Marshall, the state pathologist for Northern Ireland, said the trunk wounds inflicted on Michael Devine, who was hit at least 28 times, almost defeated interpretation. Many of the injuries had been sustained as Devine lay on the ground. Marshall said that never in his examination of gunshot fatalities had he seen such extensive injuries. The message was clear: all republicans are legitimate targets to be shot on sight.

The shoot-to-kill policy was only one aspect of the build-up of repression. Britain's treatment of its targets has become even more brutal. It is now common practice to leave dead volunteers where they have fallen for hours on end as a warning to those who might follow them. Republican funeral parades have been viciously attacked by riot police. The British clampdown reached a highpoint with an RUC raid on a Belfast anti-internment rally in August 1984. On 'Belfast's Bloody Sunday', the RUC shot and killed 22-year old nationalist John Downes and injured 20 others.

The British government boasted of its successful murder campaign. After IRA volunteers Brian Campbell and Colm McGirr met a hail of British bullets at the end of 1983, Northern Ireland secretary James Prior proudly remarked that 'from time to time' the SAS 'have an opportunity of showing us what they can do' (*The Times,* 6 December 1983). The shoot-to-kill policy was strongly supported by Loyalist politicians. Ian Paisley welcomed the shootings of republicans in Armagh and said that he would 'like to see these actions repeated across the province'. After Belfast's Bloody Sunday, Paisley's Democratic Unionist Party praised the RUC's 'positive action' and hoped that it would 'not be the last time

'BELFAST'S BLOODY SUNDAY', AUGUST 1984, RUC KILL 22-YEAR OLD NATIONALIST JOHN DOWNES AND INJURE 20 OTHERS

republican law-breakers are dealt with in such a positive manner'. In September 1984, replacing Prior in office, former diplomat and part-time novelist Douglas Hurd assured Unionist leaders that his arrival in Belfast meant 'a change in personalities, not policies'. This proved as fair about Hurd as it did about Tom King, who took over Hurd's job a year later.

Alongside the shooting spree came the supergrasses—paid informers used to give perjured evidence against republican suspects. Just 25 supergrasses were responsible for the detention of 600 people up to 1984 (see Chapter 5). But the supergrass system never had the same sweeping character as internment in the early seventies. The vast majority of detainees were known to have republican connections. The long list of retractions and acquittals based on the complete incompetence of the supergrasses led to the final collapse of the showtrial system by 1987. But it had been one of the most successful stratagems pursued by Britain in the Irish War. It took entire active service units off the streets overnight, and kept them in jail awaiting trial for up to three and even five years at a time. And it encouraged a mood of suspicion and demoralisation within the republican communities.

The Irish dimension

The overt repression of the early eighties made events in Northern Ireland more explosive than at any other time since 1974. One victim of the increased polarisation was the moderate Social Democratic and Labour Party, traditionally Britain's only friend inside the nationalist community. The growing hatred of nationalists for Britain forced the SDLP on to the defensive. Under grassroots pressure, the SDLP was forced to boycott the Ulster assembly in 1982. As more Irish people lost all faith in any British solution for Ireland, there was a republican revival at the polls. In the 1983 general election Sinn Fein won 100 000 votes on a platform of explicit support for the armed struggle of the IRA. Sinn Fein president Gerry Adams was elected to the house of commons, and promptly refused to go there on principle.

This was all thoroughly embarrassing for the British authorities. The SDLP, their agent within the nationalist community, was losing support to a movement which Westminster had spent the previous 13 years condemning as a small armed gang. British ministers, Irish bishops and even Loyalist politicians called on nationalists to vote SDLP and renounce republican terrorism. Official Unionist leader James Molyneaux summed up the fears of the establishment:

'The demise of constitutional nationalism, with all its imperfections, and the emergence of Sinn Fein as representative of mainstream minority opinion, would surely signal the beginning of the ultimate nightmare for all the people of Northern Ireland.' (*Irish Times,* 21 April 1984)

The nightmare behind the crisis of the SDLP was the growing alienation of the nationalist community, and the rise in support for Sinn Fein and the armed struggle against British rule. London desperately needed a new initiative to restore some belief in British benevolence, isolate the republican movement, boost the SDLP, and put the containment strategy back on course. Dublin could help here.

The Tories turned to the South for a deal that could mop up the mess the shoot-to-kill squads and the supergrasses had left behind. The illusion of reform could undermine the surge in republican support. Thatcher did not pursue her Anglo-Irish option with any enthusiasm. During the period when she was supposed to be perusing the proposals in the moderate nationalists' New Ireland Forum report, she was actually trying to persuade her civil servants to draw up plans for a repartition of Ulster! Rightly, from their point of view, officials refused to entertain such a non-starter. Instead, Thatcher was forced to the conclusion that there was nowhere else to go but South if she was to salvage any sort of settlement.

The 'Irish dimension' in the war has been an important totem for the SDLP since its formation in 1970. Protesting that the Dublin government should have a say in the affairs of Northern nationalists had been the staple SDLP alternative both to the republican struggle for Irish unity and to explicit support for the status quo in Northern Ireland. Support for an Irish dimension fitted perfectly the party's idea that the demands of both nationalists and Unionists could be satisfied in a new Ireland—what SDLP leader John Hume called, in 1978, 'the third way'. 'The third option open to the British government', announced Hume, 'is to declare that its objective in Ireland is the bringing together of both Irish traditions in reconciliation and agreement.'

But there is no third way in Ireland. Nationalists and Unionists cannot be reconciled, because each believes that a different state should exercise sovereignty over the Six Counties. Yet after the hunger-strikes the British government was prepared to recognise that paying lip-service to an Irish dimension might serve a useful purpose in fracturing republicanism. The result was the Anglo-Irish agreement.

There has been a good deal of confusion about the agreement's purpose. Loyalist opposition has helped convince some war-weary nationalists that there must be something in the accord for them. Meanwhile Dublin has helped keep the illusion of reform alive, allowing the SDLP to regain some lost ground. But the British politicians who debated the agreement in the house of commons after it was signed had no illusions about its central purpose—to sweep aside the IRA. Tom King, for the Tories, told the house that the agreement would 'help to isolate the men of violence' and 'help us to pursue more vigorously the attack against terrorism'. David Alton, for the Liberals, argued that 'this agreement is the bulwark against Sinn Fein.' Roy Mason, for the Labour Party, was most explicit:

'Running throughout the ministerial meetings in the last few years has been the urge to stifle the rise of Sinn Fein. That is why so much republican interference in Northern Ireland's affairs has been agreed—to pacify the green, to take politicking away from Sinn Fein and to let the minority community see that their interests are being progressed by the South and the SDLP in the North. This is designed to blunt the edge of Provisional Sinn Fein campaigning....We cannot effectively ban Sinn Fein, but we can isolate it. That is the objective of this political exercise.' (*Hansard,* 26 November 1985)

To give maximum scope for selling the deal to nationalists, North and South, the British war machine went into second gear for some time after the accord was signed. British politicians played the diplomat and let Loyalist murder gangs get on with the job of hounding the nationalist community while the SAS kept a low profile. Now that it seems to have scored some successes in bolstering the SDLP and undermining the republican movement, Britain hopes to deliver defeated Loyalists and revived moderate nationalists into a new devolved assembly, and the way will be clear for a new round of anti-republican repression.

In fact such repression never went away. Less than two months after Thatcher shook hands with FitzGerald after sealing their anti-IRA pact, security forces arrested 18 leading Sinn Fein members in what Sinn Fein councillor Jim McAllister called 'the first bitter fruits of the London-Dublin accord'. The RUC told Derry Sinn Fein chair Gerry O'Hara after his arrest that they expected to get 'internment both sides of the Border, so it could be very effective' and that they looked forward to a 10-mile 'hot pursuit' zone on the other side of the Border 'so they could go South and not have to tell the garda'

THATCHER'S DEAL WITH FITZGERALD CANNOT DO AWAY WITH REPRESSION OR RESISTANCE

(quoted in *the next step*, 11 April 1986). To put a stop to Sinn Fein's electoral successes, King announced plans to introduce an anti-violence oath for candidates in future local polls. Worse, the SAS death squads struck again, shooting 20-year old civilian Francis Bradley in Toomebridge in February 1986. By May 1987 shoot-to-kill was back with a vengeance: SAS assassins shot dead eight IRA volunteers outside the RUC station at Loughgall, County Armagh.

Thatcher's accord has as little prospect of ending the Irish War as every other British initiative. Like Labour's criminalisation policy, it contains the seeds of future conflict. The Tories cannot deliver on their promises of fundamental reform. The clearer this becomes, the more likely it is that nationalists will once again turn their backs on the idea of a British solution. In the meantime the promise of more repression against republicans can only harden the outlook of that section of the nationalist community which wants nothing to do with any London initiative. The IRA is thus guaranteed the recruits it requires to fight on for Irish freedom.

As the war moves into its eighteenth year the national liberation movement continues to defy imperialist oppression. While Sinn Fein can win the votes of nearly 100 000 people, the IRA is capable of audacious strokes: the mass escape of 38 republicans from Long Kesh in September 1983, the bombing of top Tories at Brighton's Grand Hotel a year later, the 1985 mortar attack on a Newry police fortress which killed nine RUC officers in the biggest single debacle the constabulary has ever suffered. In July 1986, IRA volunteers dressed in butchers' aprons penetrated a tight security cordon around Newry, attacked an armour-plated RUC car in the market square in broad daylight, and killed all three occupants. In April 1987 the IRA scored a major propaganda success when volunteers blew up Lord Justice Gibson, the man who congratulated RUC marksmen for bringing three republicans to 'the final court of justice', as he drove through Armagh with his wife Lady Cecily after a holiday in England. After 18 years the truth remains that there is no British solution to the Irish War. All that the British government can do is try to contain the resistance and do its best to stop the war overflowing into Britain and the South.

The republican movement will not go away. Repression breeds resistance and as long as Ireland remains divided, the struggle will continue. Despite the ravages brought by the seemingly interminable conflict, nationalists have not lost the will to fight. They have no choice but to resist British oppression. The republican movement has stood up against the most sophisticated counter-insurgency force in the world. In August 1986 King called the IRA 'a small bunch of thugs and terrorists who are increasingly isolated'. But as *The Times* editorial remarked of his claim to be beating the IRA, 'It is safe to assume that he has entered the world of wishful thinking.'

The republican movement cannot be beaten. But as long as the national liberation struggle remains restricted to Northern Ireland, the military stalemate will last. The success of the national liberation movement depends on winning mass support in the South and in Britain. For nearly 18 years the nationalist community in the Six Counties has fought more or less alone. These years of sacrifice must not be in vain. Workers in Britain have a special responsibility to do everything in their power to hasten the defeat of the military machine of their own ruling class. Extending the struggle beyond the Borders of the Six Counties is vital for the victory of the Irish people.

LOYALIST BIGOTS BURN THE IRISH TRICOLOUR

3. The sectarian state

In June 1985 George Seawright, a Loyalist councillor from Belfast, was appointed to sit on the local fire authority. In any normal circumstances such an innocuous move would merit no comment. But Belfast city council is not normal and George Seawright is not a man to be trusted with fire. In May 1984 he dismissed Catholic parents who objected to the British national anthem being sung in state-funded Irish schools as 'Fenian scum' and said they should be 'incinerated':

'Taxpayers' money would be better spent on an incinerator and burning the lot of them. The priests should be thrown in and burnt as well.' (*Guardian,* 1 June 1984)

Seawright's remarks caused uproar, a court case, his expulsion from Ian Paisley's Democratic Unionist Party and a short spell in prison. But they did not unduly disturb the British authorities. The department of education calmly announced that Seawright had said nothing that could lead to his removal from Belfast's education board.

The sectarian prejudices so forcefully articulated by bigots like Seawright are an integral part of Britain's oppression of the Irish people. Seawright's 'don't educate Catholics, burn them' speeches may be too explicit for many in the British establishment. But his basic message—that the security of the British state depends on the repression of the nationalist community—is the principle on which Northern Ireland was founded. Because Northern Ireland's link with Britain is artificial, it requires extraordinary measures for its maintenance. The sectarian discrimination and oppression that have prevailed in the Six Counties are essential to Britain's continuing domination there. Now and again the Loyalists and the British authorities fall out—as over the Anglo-Irish deal; but this amounts only to bickering about the best arrangements through which Britain should rule Northern Ireland. Both sides agree that the Union Jack should continue to fly over Belfast and Derry, and both are united in their determination to preserve the sectarian state.

A Protestant state for a Protestant people

The creation and survival of the Six Counties have both required the denial of the democratic aspirations of the Irish people. In February 1920, when the Government of Ireland Act set out the plan for partition, 40 000 British troops were engaged in a bitter struggle with the liberation movement. The war for Irish freedom still raged in the South when the parliament at Stormont opened its doors on 7 June 1921. Stormont was imposed on Ireland by force of arms. Its only supporters were Britain's Loyalist allies, who had acted for more than 150 years as the agents of British colonial rule over the whole of Ireland. When control over the whole country could no longer be retained in the old way, the Loyalists had to settle for territory over which they could guarantee their reign.

In March 1920 the Ulster Unionist Council abandoned its demand for a nine-counties state encompassing the whole of the historical province of Ulster. The Council accepted Lloyd George's reasoning that a smaller Ulster with a substantial Protestant majority (66 per cent) was far preferable to trying to cling on to the whole province with only a slender majority (56 per cent). Once these calculations were complete and the region accordingly carved up, the Loyalists turned their attention to the problem of how to guarantee the predominance of Protestant interest under the new regime.

In 1920 the Six Counties had a population of 820 000 Protestants and 430 000 Catholics. But superiority in numbers did not mean calm. The Catholic minority was strongly imbued with Irish nationalism and was therefore, almost by definition, disloyal. Though out-numbered two to one, the nationalists had substantial majorities in two of the six counties, Fermanagh and Tyrone, and in Derry, the largest city after Belfast. From the outset, the overriding objective of the Stormont regime was to contain and control the nationalist community.

Before the institutions of Loyalist rule could be fully established, the Six Counties had to be brought under control. Local elections in June 1920 confirmed the necessity for coercion—republicans won 25 out of 80 local council seats, including Derry. Loyalist politicians promptly dispensed with their democratic facade. Ulster Volunteer Force members fired into the nationalist Bogside from Derry's city walls. In Belfast, where Catholics were in a minority of 93 000, families were driven from their homes and 14 000 workers were forcibly ejected from their jobs in the shipyards and factories.

Britain's offensive against the nationalist community and the republican movement took the form of a sectarian pogrom. A division of labour between Westminster and Stormont allowed Loyalist mobs and paramilitaries to go on the rampage against the nationalist population, leading to indiscriminate killing and the burning of Catholic houses. This division of labour persists to this day—the Loyalists do the dirty work, with discreet British backing, while Westminster politicians talk loftily about democracy and political initiatives. This also provides the British establishment with a valuable propaganda weapon: the conflict can be presented as sectarian strife between rival communities.

To give Stormont a degree of legitimacy, Westminster had to put the Loyalist gangs into uniform. The idea of a Protestant police force was first suggested by war minister Winston Churchill in 1920, when the British authorities were still waging a war to keep the whole of Ireland under Crown control. The fight for Irish freedom had been concentrated in the south and west of the island, where the British authorities were at full stretch trying to contain the IRA. When the struggle spread to the north, Churchill suggested that Lloyd George's government look to loyal Protestants to police their areas. 'What would happen', he ventured, 'if the Protestants in the Six Counties were given weapons and...charged with maintaining law and order and policing the country?' (cited in M Farrell, *Arming the Protestants*). Churchill's brainwave soon became British strategy. An illegal Loyalist paramilitary force reformed after the First World War to defend the Union by terrorising Catholics, the UVF was stuffed into make-shift uniforms and renamed the Ulster Special Constabulary. It carried on attacking Catholics, but with the British government's blessing. After Ireland was partitioned and the province of Northern Ireland established in 1921, the USC evolved into the Royal Ulster Constabulary.

The RUC's job was to keep the sectarian state intact by repressing nationalists. Its rules on who were decent citizens and who were criminals differed from the state's normal standards. For the RUC, a person's innocence or guilt hung on whether they saluted the Union Jack or the Irish tricolour. Those who opposed British rule were automatically outside the law in Ulster, as Unionist leaders told the British authorities in discussing the new force's operational and recruitment policies: 'No rebel who wishes to set up a republic can be regarded merely as a "political opponent", but must be repressed.' They insisted that 'appointments to the constabulary should all be those who are prepared to accept this new form of government.' There could be no question of asking Ulster constables 'to act as mediators between those holding loyal views and those desirous of establishing a republic' (Farrell, *ibid*).

By the summer of 1922 the total number of security forces in the Six Counties had grown to include 16 Army battalions and about 20 000 in the UVF, backed by an undisclosed number of RUC men and the Specials. These were divided into four forces. The 5500 'A' Specials were full-time, uniformed and paid. The 19 000 'B' Specials were part-time but fully armed. The 'C' Specials were a reserve force for use in emergencies: they had few of the formal trappings of a police force, and amounted to little more than a front for arming the Loyalist working class. The new 'C1' Specials were a 7500-strong territorial army. Almost 20 per cent of the male Protestant population of Northern Ireland was in a branch of the Specials (Farrell, *Northern Ireland: The Orange State*). The machine eventually succeeded in breaking down the resistance of the nationalist population. By the end of 1922 'peace' was established and the Stormont regime got down to the business of consolidating its power.

A sham democracy

Nationalists are not supposed to get elected to the local citadels of Loyalist rule in Northern Ireland. When 59 Sinn Fein councillors

RUC BATON-CHARGE AT THE BEGINNING OF THE BATTLE OF THE BOGSIDE, 12 AUGUST 1969

did, in the district council elections in May 1985, the two Unionist
parties signed a pact after the polls whose purpose was, in the words
of DUP leader Ian Paisley, 'to make the lives of Sinn Fein councillors
as unbearable as possible'. In Craigavon Unionist councillors
transferred council business to committees from which nationalist
councillors were excluded. In Magherafelt, Loyalist leaders cracked
a chair over the head of councillor John Davey. In Omagh, Unionists
offered to cut the throat of Sinn Fein council leader Seamus Kerr,
whom they described as 'a Fenian papist bastard'. Ian Paisley's
daughter Rhonda made her council debut in Belfast by blowing a toy
trumpet whenever Sinn Fein councillors spoke. The reaction from
the Unionist camp to Sinn Fein's success at the polls revealed British
democracy in the occupied territories of Northern Ireland for the
charade it is.

Sectarianism is built into the Six Counties state. Its sectarian
character is not the product of fundamentalist religious ideology on
the part of Orange extremists, but a means of ensuring British
domination. Sectarianism operates through a system of comprehensive and systematic social discrimination. Without it the Six
Counties could not survive. Since partition, British imperialists have
turned a blind eye to it. They understand that British rule in Belfast
depends upon sectarianism, as Sir Robert Maxwell explained to the
Westminster cabinet in 1924:

'The accusation against the government of Northern Ireland of religious
discrimination is somewhat difficult to deal with. In one sense it is of
course obvious that Northern Ireland is and must be a Protestant "state",
otherwise it would not have come into being, and would certainly not
continue to exist.' (Cabinet minutes, 22 April 1924)

Today the British establishment still tries to justify its toleration of
Stormont's sectarian system. As Tory MP Julian Amery told
parliament during the debate on the Anglo-Irish deal, 'Stormont
did many good things. It preserved law and order in the province.'
But Stormont's law and order meant anti-Catholic measures of
horrific severity and the systematic denial of the rights of
the nationalists.

Discrimination in favour of Protestants of all social classes plays a
vital role for Northern Ireland's British creators. It welds together all
sections of the Loyalist community and keeps the nationalist areas in
a constant state of subjugation. It also forces the tightly knit Loyalist
bloc into a permanent alliance with Britain. The Loyalists are aware
that the source of their privileges is the Six Counties state created and

sustained by Westminster. This is why controlling the state machine—even at local government level—has been so important for the Loyalist establishment. Fixing elections has been a key political activity for Loyalists ever since partition.

One of the features of the Six Counties which has done so much to reinforce the notion that it is just another part of the UK is that people in it do at regular intervals go to the ballot box. What is more, they do so at the same time as people in Britain, sending 17 MPs to Westminster and electing local councillors on the same day as voters in Hackney or Sheffield. It is not widely appreciated in Britain that elections in Northern Ireland have more in common with the sort of bogus polls that take place in countries like El Salvador than anything that goes on in Western Europe.

Intimidation of Catholic electors, harassment of election campaigners, polling frauds—especially the impersonation of voters who have died or emigrated—are all longstanding characteristics of electoral contests in the Six Counties. It is said that in Northern Ireland resurrection is not regarded as a miracle, since the graveyards are all empty on polling day. Catholics who are too active at election time risk going to the grave. Sinn Fein election agent Peter Corrigan was murdered by the Loyalist Protestant Action Force during the October 1982 assembly elections.

The fact that violence at the polls has in general been less in evidence in Northern Ireland than in third world countries is mainly due to a sophisticated system of ballot-rigging which renders open violence superfluous. After partition, Westminster and Stormont constituency boundaries were drawn to ensure the return of a Loyalist majority. It was a fairly straightforward task to rig the large constituencies, but it was more difficult to stitch up local government elections. Yet control over local councils was the key to jobs and housing, as well as health, education and other services.

Stormont was determined never to allow nationalists to repeat their success in the 1920 local election, in which they won, as we have seen, 25 out of 80 councils. In 1921 the Loyalist parliament passed a law which dissolved all councils that refused to swear allegiance to Stormont and the British Crown, replacing them with government commissioners. In July 1922 proportional representation in local elections—originally introduced by Britain to reduce the Sinn Fein vote in the South—was abolished. This measure not only cut nationalist representation, but wiped out smaller parties and independent candidates.

In 1923 the British government appointed a judicial commission to fix new electoral boundaries. By the method commonly known as 'gerrymandering', wards were redrawn so that areas with a nationalist majority would nevertheless return mostly Loyalist councillors. This was done by concentrating nationalist votes in a few large wards returning a smaller number of seats. Given that the majorities thus achieved were subject to changes as a result of even small population shifts, gerrymandering had to become a continuous process. In slightly different forms, it has continued under direct rule. Until quite recently, the right to vote in local elections was restricted to ratepayers and their wives, excluding people who owned no private rateable property. In addition, a further restriction in 1923 confined the right to vote to individuals owning land worth £5 or more. According to one of the measure's supporters, the object was 'to disenfranchise a very large number of irresponsible people'.

It is not only Loyalist bigots who have fiddled the votes. In 1945 the British Labour government introduced universal suffrage and abolished the business vote for local elections in Britain; but Northern Ireland was exempt from this reform. Instead, Stormont introduced its own Representation of the People Act in 1946. This removed lodgers from the electoral roll and introduced the business vote for Stormont elections too. The aim was openly stated by Stormont chief whip Major LE Curran:

> 'The best way to prevent the overthrow of the government by people who had no stake in the country and had not the welfare of the people of Ulster at heart was to disenfranchise them.' (Cited in Farrell, *Northern Ireland*)

The result of all these measures was to make one Protestant vote equivalent to 2.5 Catholic votes. Local councils in areas with a nationalist majority were more often than not run by Loyalist politicians.

The effect of these fraudulent practices are shown in the table below. It provides the results from a number of district and county councils from the 1966 local elections.

	ELECTORS		COUNCILLORS	
	Adult Catholic	Adult Protestant	Nationalist	Loyalist
Armagh UDC	3139	2798	8	12
Dungannon UDC	1845	2041	7	14
Dungannon RDC	7329	7476	6	13
Fermanagh Co Cl	15884	15222	17	33
Derry Co Borough	18432	11340	8	12
Newry UDC	5843	1364	12	6
Omagh RDC	2605	1949	9	12

UDC=Urban District Council, RDC=Rural District Council
(The Cameron Commission, 1969)

The extent of electoral manipulations is particularly striking in the example of Derry's ward system.

	POPULATION		SEATS
	Catholic	Protestant	
North Ward	2530	3946	8 Unionist
Waterside	1852	3697	4 Unionist
South Ward	10047	1138	8 Nationalist

(The Cameron Commission)

The exclusion of Catholics from political institutions was the cornerstone of the system of social discrimination. It provided a framework for extending calculated injustice into the allocation of housing, social services and local government employment.

What discrimination means

Discrimination against Catholics in all spheres of social life is what holds the Loyalist state together. Until the late sixties, it was virtually government policy to discriminate against Catholics in giving out jobs, housing and services. The agents of discrimination were Protestant employers, Stormont and local government. After British troops intervened in 1969 a few things changed. Westminster removed housing and education from council control, and introduced proportional representation in local elections in the hope of encouraging middle class Catholics to participate in the institutions of the Six Counties state. These changes had no noticeable effect on Catholic housing and employment conditions. If anything discrimination got worse during the seventies. Since 1972 the British state itself has assumed a direct role in distributing resources and in preserving the sectarian character of the Six Counties. The British government's own reports confirm that sectarian discrimination continues today. Catholics are three times as likely to be unemployed as Protestants. In 1986 statistics showed only 16 Catholics among 116 officers on the government's own employment training schemes. It is the same story for Catholics right across the job market.

In the Six Counties jobs, homes and services are handed out as perks for Protestants. The Official Unionist Party has often freely admitted its commitment to sectarian discrimination. Basil Brooke, later Stormont prime minister and Lord Brookeborough, made his position clear in 1933:

'There were a great number of Protestants and Orangemen who employed Roman Catholics. He felt he could speak freely on this subject as he had not a Roman Catholic about his own place....He would appeal to Loyalists, therefore, wherever possible, to employ good Protestant lads and lassies.' (Cited in Campaign for Social Justice in Northern Ireland, *Plain Truth,* Dungannon 1972)

Democratic Unionist councillor Charles Poots has asserted the same principle more recently and more forcefully still:

'If I was in control of this country it would not be in the same state as it is in now. I would cut off all supplies, including water and electricity, to Catholic areas. And I would stop Catholics from getting social security. It is the only way of dealing with enemies of the state.' (Cited in *Belfast Bulletin,* No 9)

George Seawright's 'burn the Catholics' campaign is in the best traditions of Unionism.

Sectarian discrimination crushes the nationalist community. It dictates where Catholics can live and work, who they can marry, even where it is safe to walk at night. Statistics on emigration reflect the plight of the nationalists. Between 1937 and 1961, 90 000 Catholics and 69 000 Protestants left Northern Ireland. For Catholics this meant an emigration rate of 21 per cent; for Protestants, a rate of only eight per cent.

Homes fit for rebels

In housing segregation and discrimination are pervasive. The civil rights movement of the sixties started out as a campaign against the housing policies of one particular council—Dungannon. Here the population was 50.3 per cent Catholic, but the council was Loyalist-controlled. For 34 years not one new Catholic family had been allocated a permanent home, though Protestants had received more than 200. There were more than 300 families, almost all Catholic, on the waiting list, and some of them had been waiting for up to 12 years. When Catholic tenants were moved into prefabricated bungalows during a slum clearance operation, the council announced that the bungalows themselves were to be destroyed to make way for further house-building. It was later revealed that no such plans existed. Many old Catholic homes were claimed by slum clearance—without replacement.

In 1966 Derry Corporation, to contain the growth of the local nationalist community, decided not to build any more homes at all. By 1969 there were more than 1500 families on the waiting list and more than 1000 homes occupied by more than one family. The housing of seven or eight families in single-family dwellings was commonplace.

Segregation in housing has always been government policy. The social geography of Belfast and Derry has been sharply defined through sectarian housing and planning policies. Since 1969 the British state has reinforced segregation through innumerable check-points, Army forts and ghetto barriers. These encircle the Catholic population. In June 1984 the Northern Ireland Housing Executive—the body Britain set up in response to charges of sectarian housing distribution—completed a £250 000 wall around the nationalist areas of North Belfast. In nationalist districts of Derry, districts like Bogside and Brandywell, old streets have been

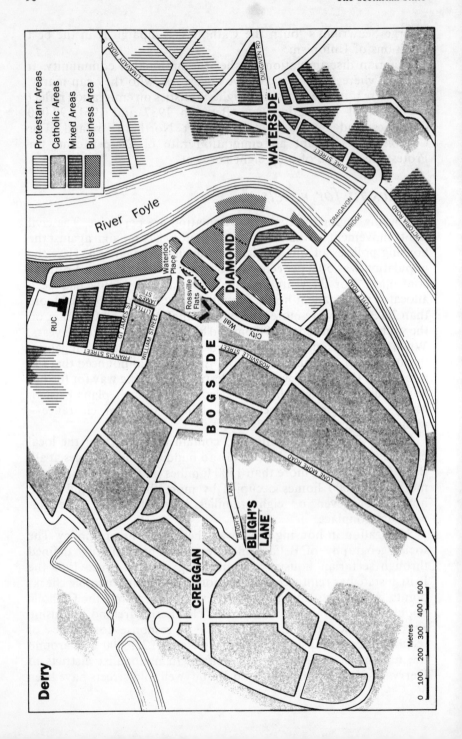

Derry

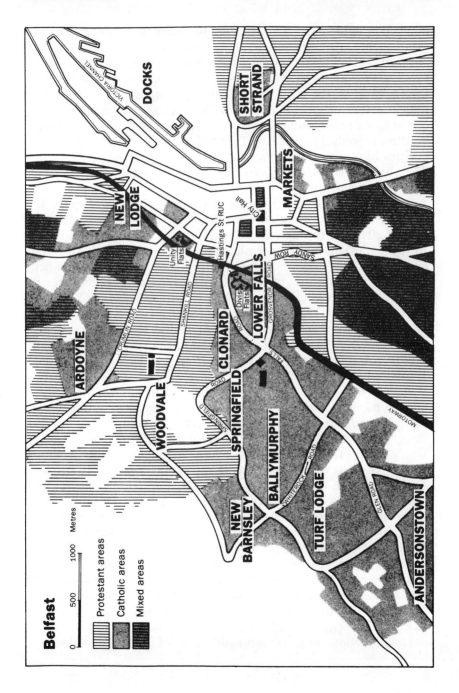

blocked off and new estates designed to ensure that they are not easy escape-routes for the IRA or for young rioters. The British authorities dress up these constructions as 'cul-de-sacs'; but, as locals explain, they are merely slums designed to suit the British security forces. In 1986 the authorities started pulling down the Rossville flats, not to satisfy the demands of Derry people for decent homes, but to give British gunmen easier access and an open line of fire into a hardline republican area. Apart from their military uses, segregation policies have played an important role in intensifying sectarianism. They help cohere the Loyalist community and fuel its traditional fear, hatred and bigotry.

Sectarianism has also influenced regional planning. One of the ways in which Stormont ensured that 'the Protestant people' were looked after was through the selection of areas for new investment. In the sixties, during the premiership of Terence O'Neill, Stormont encouraged industrial and infrastructural developments to compensate for the decline of engineering, shipbuilding and textile industries. Under the Matthew Plan, incorporated in 1965 into the Wilson Plan, the Protestant towns of Antrim, Ballymena, Lurgan and Portadown (renamed Craigavon) were designated as development areas. New investment was concentrated in the area in a 30-mile radius around Belfast in which 75 per cent of all Ireland's Protestants live.

As for new investment, Derry, the second largest city, with a natural harbour and other advantages, was neglected. Siting of new factories and plant on the eastern side of the Six Counties was a tactic designed to ensure that whatever employment could be generated would serve Loyalists who had lost their jobs in the declining industries. West of the River Bann, the country was left to rot. The Great Northern railway was axed, leaving Fermanagh, Tyrone and practically all of County Derry with no rail link.

Stormont's planners systematically discriminated against Derry, with its Catholic majority, in favour of Protestant-dominated Coleraine. A small town on the northern coastline with scarcely any industry or higher education, Coleraine was promoted as a Loyalist citadel remote from the heartlands of Antrim and Down. Industry was encouraged to set up in Coleraine and in 1965 it was chosen as the site of Northern Ireland's second university, after Queen's in Belfast. This selection was made despite the fact that Derry was the natural location, with its own institutions of higher education.

Jobs for the boys

Loyalist leader Ian Paisley blames Catholics' low standard of living on the size of their families. But the real blame lies with the British state, which helps bigots like Paisley keep Catholics at the back of the jobs queue. Even officially doctored surveys cannot disguise the scale of modern discrimination in favour of Protestants against Catholics. A report published in July 1985 by the research unit of the department of finance and personnel services showed that Catholics generally have fewer qualifications and worse jobs than Protestants. An incident a year earlier drew out the consequences of discrimination in the sphere of education. In July 1984 rumours spread that a Belfast firm was to open a factory in the west of the city, to provide jobs for Catholics. Loyalist spokesmen reacted angrily. Democratic Unionist Party deputy Peter Robinson insisted that the new jobs should go to Protestants:

'The fact is that there is a section of the community who are better equipped to do this skilled work and that happens to be the Protestant community.'

Robinson was right. Britain has allowed Loyalists to maintain a monopoly on skills and trades in industry and services. As a result, no matter where factories are built, Catholics need barely bother to apply for the few precious jobs on offer. Discrimination in employment is the most deeply rooted source of division in the North of Ireland, stretching back, beyond partition, to the formation of the Irish working class.

Industrialisation in the nineteenth century went hand in hand with the development of a divided labour market, in which Protestant workers emerged as a privileged layer. Protestant workers fought for the preservation and extension of their control over hiring and firing in industry, often against employers who sought to avail themselves of cheap Catholic labour. In Belfast, the centre of the developing shipbuilding and engineering industries, Protestants used various devices to assert their exclusive access to the best jobs. Vicious sectarian pogroms and forcible expulsions drove many Catholics out of the factories and yards, and often out of the city altogether. Craft-based Protestant workers' associations, with control over apprentice schemes, ensured that those Catholics who remained were kept out of the better-paid and prestigious posts (see A Clarkson and P Murphy, 'The Loyalist Working Class', *Revolutionary Communist Papers,* No 7).

In the late nineteenth and early twentieth century Catholic workers were regarded as a threat to Protestant wages and jobs. Protestant workers were devoted to the consolidation of privilege through mutual agreement with the state and the employers. Their privileged access to the labour market lay at the root of the Protestant all-class alliance. Protestant workers' concern to preserve the link with Britain and to prevent any moves towards home rule reflected a deep commitment to maintaining their privileged position in the job market. Britain was the source of the investment on which Protestant employment depended.

Political integration with Britain guaranteed the permanent smothering of nationalist ideals. Partition and the establishment of the Six Counties state made things even worse. Before we look at how the recession has ravaged the Northern Ireland economy and reinforced the inferior position of Irish nationalists, let's look in more detail at the state of the Union between Britain and the Loyalists.

There is no Loyalist veto

In a rare opinion poll on Northern Ireland published in the *Daily Express* in February 1987, 70 per cent of people put Democratic Unionist Party leader Ian Paisley at the top of the hate list of Irish politicians, above even Gerry Adams of Sinn Fein. The *Daily Express* picture of Paisley as the most evil man in the Six Counties corresponds to the widespread view that the Loyalists are the people who call the shots in the Six Counties. The idea that an intransigent Protestant community exercises an effective veto over Northern Ireland affairs contradicts the real role of the Loyalists as the agents of British imperialism in the North.

The Loyalists rely on the link with Britain to perpetuate their advantaged access to jobs, houses and power over their Protestant neighbours. This means Westminster has always been able to rely on them as dogged defenders of British rule in Northern Ireland. But it has also made Unionists sensitive to any move that threatens to shift the sectarian status quo, however slightly.

The lifeline that keeps Loyalists attached to their British paymasters is a slender and shaky one. The Union between Great Britain and Northern Ireland is entirely artificial. There is no natural or national justification for it. It can only be maintained through an extraordinary system of state controls—repressive laws that are the envy of South African statesmen and the presence of 30 000 troops and paramilitary police. The artificial Union is inherently unstable. The Loyalist community has a historical fear that any change to the existing set-up might jeopardise its pre-eminent position. Even moves to deprive Protestants of their petty privileges are liable to provoke a backlash. Catholic workers still have to put up with Loyalist bands and bunting being paraded through Northern factories during the summer marching season. Complaints have led to walk-outs and attacks on nationalists. The paraphernalia of Loyalist triumphalism plays the same role in cohering the Protestant community as petty apartheid does for South African whites. Anything that alters the established power relations in Ulster—like the Anglo-Irish agreement—has Unionists pressing the panic button.

The Loyalists have always tried to avoid pressure for reform by keeping political power in the province in their own pockets. They achieved this for 50 years, ruling Northern Ireland as they liked from their private parliament at Stormont, and subjecting Catholics to brutal treatment. Loyalists have also tried to isolate their state from outside pressures by excluding Northern Ireland from the process of political debate in Britain. As the Unionists' hero Lord Carson put it before partition, 'Ulster wants above all things to be removed from the area of party politics in the imperial parliament.' Carson's successors have never had cause to repeat his pleas. All parties have cooperated in making sure that Ulster is never used as a political football.

Conflicts between the Crown and the Loyalists occur because Britain takes a more long-term view of oppression in Ireland than the narrow-minded bigots of Ulster. The Loyalists are concerned with the issue immediately at hand—keeping the nationalists down. They want more military repression and they want to show their superiority by marching through Catholic streets with Union flags flying. British governments share the Unionists' concern to crush the republican struggle for Irish freedom and keep Irish nationalists under the heel. But Westminster has wider concerns too. It has to convince people in Britain that Northern Ireland is a fairly normal place. It has to keep international opinion on its side. And, increasingly, it has to stop the instability in the North from spilling over into the Southern Republic. So while joining the Loyalists to wage war on nationalists, it has to promote an image of British fair play and impartiality, by banning the odd inflammatory Orange march and having talks about 'peace' with Dublin governments.

These disagreements are only over how British rule is packaged in its Northern Ireland colony. They do not interfere with the essential unity of the Loyalists and the British authorities against supporters of Irish freedom. British governments can play around with the fringe features of Protestant power, by stopping them flying the flag or keeping Loyalist leaders out of their negotiations with Dublin. But the British authorities cannot undermine the essence of the Protestant ascendancy in Ireland without cutting their own throats.

Over the past decade, and during the strife over the Anglo-Irish accord in particular, the British ruling class has forced the Loyalists to recognise that they are the monkeys, and not the organ-grinder, in Ulster. Margaret Thatcher faced them down over the Anglo-Irish deal and showed that, while Britain relies on the Loyalists' support, it also has wider political concerns which they will not be allowed to upset. The Loyalists have been forced to concede that Britain really does rule the Ulster roost.

Since the present stage of the Irish War erupted in 1969, British governments have launched political initiatives to put a democratic veneer on their colonial regime in Ireland. And they have tried to tone down the more embarrassing excesses of Protestant privilege. None of these changes have challenged the basis of British power or Loyalist privilege. But they have panicked Protestant leaders by altering political arrangements in the North, and prompted some Loyalists to take on the authorities in an attempt to turn back the tide. Every episode of Protestant resistance reveals that, without the backing of influential sections of the British establishment, the Loyalists don't have a hope of getting their own way.

● **Abolition of the 'B' Specials, 1969**
In 1969, the Labour government decided to reorganise the RUC and disband the 'B' Specials to improve Britain's image abroad and help restore order on Irish streets. These reforms were entirely cosmetic. There was never any question of establishing a non-sectarian 'peace-keeping' force. Yet these empty gestures outraged the Loyalists and led to two nights of ferocious rioting on the Protestant Shankill Road. Angry Belfast Loyalists killed the first RUC man to die in the war.

● **Abolition of Stormont, 1972**
The British have always had the final say on how the Protestant state is governed. Thus in 1920, Britain gave the Loyalists a Six Counties parliament at Stormont when they didn't want it. And in 1972, Britain took it away from them again when they wanted it more than anything—and introduced direct rule from Westminster. The Loyalists saw the loss of Stormont as a betrayal of the

A NEW GENERATION OF ULSTER LOYALISTS VOICE THEIR OPPOSITION TO THE ANGLO-IRISH DEAL

Protestant way of life: the Unionist Party broke off formal links with the Conservatives in protest.

● **Labour's constitutional convention, 1976**

In 1976 the Labour government's constitutional convention, which had been scuppered by the Loyalists a year earlier, was recalled to discuss power-sharing. The idea was to create a middle ground of moderate opinion and remove Britain from direct involvement. But even these token measures unleashed a storm of protest from Loyalists. They formed a United Unionist Action Council and launched a shortlived strike on 3 May 1977, a strike which collapsed when Northern Ireland secretary Mason promised more repression against nationalists.

● **Anglo-Irish agreement, 1985**

Loyalist protests began even before Thatcher signed the Anglo-Irish deal, during the marching season in 1985. Loyalist leaders accused Westminster of being 'held to ransom by the Dublin government' and threatening the Union. In November Loyalist demonstrators attacked Tom King. Unionist MPs resigned their seats and fought by-elections on an anti-accord ticket. In March 1986 a 24-hour strike by Loyalists did more to expose the divisions in the Protestant camp than it did to frighten the authorities. The Loyalist campaign dragged on through 1986 and into 1987 losing conviction the longer it went on.

Not one of these campaigns by Ulster Loyalists had a chance of success because they did not get the backing of the British establishment. But on two occasions in the past, when Westminster considered making serious concessions to the Irish, the people with the real power in British society stepped in to support the Loyalists.

In 1912-14 Loyalists campaigning against the Liberal government's home rule policy had the support of influential sections of the Conservative Party for taking up arms, because the government's political initiative would have undermined the Union. In March 1914, British Army officers stationed at the Curragh camp near Dublin mutinied to show the strength of their opposition to home rule. The British Army, Ulster Loyalists and the Conservative Party joined forces to fight off any Liberal measure that might have undermined the Union. The British authorities turned a blind eye to the rebellion because they had some sympathy with its objectives and told their troops that home rule was not an option.

Similarly in 1974, the British establishment sided with the Loyalists against the Labour government's power-sharing plans. When Loyalist politicians and paramilitaries united behind the Ulster Workers' Council strike, the British Army refused to move against them. An Army officer involved at the time boasted about how troops backed the Ulster Defence Association against the government: 'The Army chose quite deliberately to give the UDA tacit support....For the first time the Army decided that it was right and that it knew best and the politicians had better toe the line.' The BBC gave the Loyalist strike very sympathetic coverage because its backers in the establishment were behind the Protestant protests.

The Loyalists have only had any leverage over British policy in Ireland when they have been backed by powerful British forces. A closer look at the failed campaign against the Anglo-Irish deal reveals a lot about the real relationship between Britain and its local allies in Northern Ireland.

Many people in Britain were struck by the sight of Loyalists marching with Union Jacks to declare their undying allegiance to the Union and then turning to hit Loyalist policemen over the head with their banner poles. Many people asked: 'How can the Loyalists be loyal if they fight the government?' But this misses the point. The Loyalists are loyal to the British state machine which perpetuates their privileged position in Northern Ireland. For them the state is symbolised by the sovereign. But this loyalty to the British state does not mean they always bow to the commands of whichever British party happens to hold a majority in the house of commons. If the Loyalists decide that the government is going against the interests of the Union, they will oppose it. Unionist newspaper adverts warned RUC members that the Anglo-Irish deal 'radically alters the role of the RUC officers who are employed and who took an oath to "truly serve" our sovereign'—and not, the message implies, to serve Thatcher.

Loyalists can campaign ferociously against British government initiatives which they fear might alter the Ulster status quo. But, as the campaign against the accord exposed, they cannot sustain an armed struggle against the state that sponsors their existence. In a revealing interview a year before the deal with Dublin, Ulster Defence Association leader Andy Tyrie drew on the experience of the failed 1977 Loyalist strike to admit the limits of Loyalist resistance:

'The British government stopped taking the Loyalists seriously after 1977 because they saw them divided. What they learnt from 1977 was that

people here are more concerned with their jobs, their British status and
their respectable image because they're British. The government studied
this and found that the most it can expect from Loyalists is to march about
and protest. But if it means taking on the British establishment in a civil
war situation, that is totally different.' (*Fortnight*)

The point of conflict between the Loyalists and Britain is too
narrow for anything like civil war to develop.

Behind all the hot air the Unionists' protests against Thatcher's
pact with Dublin were pretty tame. The Loyalists' dependence on
the link with Britain means there are limits to how far their protests
can go. The contradiction of fighting the forces of the Crown under
the Union Jack quickly began to work itself out, fragmenting the
Unionist alliance against the accord. Frustration at Britain's refusal
to dump the Anglo-Irish deal sent Loyalist hardliners on to the
streets. But it concentrated the minds of the more level-headed
Loyalist leaders who began to talk of the need to reach an
accommodation with Westminster. Official Unionist Party general
secretary Frank Millar made it clear that the only alternative to
accepting the accord was to break the Union: 'Failure to make an
honourable peace with London would drive us inevitably to a
radical reassessment of our relationship with the Irish Republic.'
This meant there was no alternative for the Loyalists but to submit.

The history of conflicts between Ulster Loyalists and the British
state gives the lie to the idea that the Loyalists have a veto over events
in Northern Ireland. Loyalism is a product of Britain's oppression
of Ireland, and it depends on British support for its survival. The
people with the veto over political change in Ireland are the
unelected Army generals and establishment politicians who pull the
power levers in British society. The Loyalists are merely the agents
of British rule in Ireland. What ensures the continuation of
sectarianism and oppression is not just Unionist shouts of 'No
surrender', but the determination of the British authorities to keep
Northern Ireland under Crown control. The British state is the
central force for violence on Irish soil.

Discrimination in the recession

Since the emergence of the civil rights movement in the late sixties
and the subsequent explosion of nationalist protest into a full-scale
war, Britain has been forced to modify some of the worst excesses of
sectarian discrimination. However, despite a few changes (not least,
the massive increase in public sector employment), the basic

sectarian structure of the labour market has remained unaltered.

The campaign of bombing commercial targets which the IRA launched across the 'province' in late 1986 and early 1987 was intended to make the point that, contrary to British government claims, Northern Ireland Ltd was not a 'normal' part of UK PLC. The Northern Ireland economy has been hit by the war, and hit even harder by the recession. The British establishment is now paying out more than £4.75 billion to keep the Irish War going and the Ulster economy afloat.

Traditional heavy industries have collapsed and newer industries have failed to flourish. In early 1987 Noel Stewart, Coopers & Lybrand's senior partner in Belfast, declared that Northern Ireland could no longer be considered a manufacturing economy. More than 62 000 jobs have been lost since 1975, together with a third of the province's manufacturing industry. Between 1981 and 1985 the decline became precipitate. The worst-hit sectors were man-made fibres (down 52.7 per cent), motor vehicles and parts (down 50.1 per cent) and mechanical engineering (down 33.5 per cent). Manufacturing now accounts for only 21 per cent of Northern Ireland's remaining jobs, compared with 32 per cent in 1975. In that year manufacturing accounted for a quarter of Northern Ireland's gross product; by 1987 it had fallen to only a fifth, smaller than in any other region of the 'United Kingdom'—including the traditional service economies of the South-east and South-west.

The collapse of the Six Counties economy has compounded the problems facing British imperialism in Ireland. The loss of skilled engineering and shipbuilding jobs directly hit Protestant workers. To maintain stability, jobs had to be found for them. The Wilson regime embarked on a massive programme of state intervention, consisting of subsidies for industry, incentives for investors and the widening of public sector employment. The aim was to achieve 'parity with the UK' in unemployment levels. Between 1974 and 1980, public sector employment rose by 23 per cent. More than 55 per cent of the growth in male public sector employment was due to expansion in the police and in the prison service.

State subsidies prevented the collapse of shipbuilding and other nationalised industries. Even the private sector became directly dependent on state intervention. In January 1985, a leading accountant's survey of the economy estimated that one in every five manufacturing jobs left in Northern Ireland had been saved by state subsidies in the past two years alone. The voice of British business has noted how, in the Six Counties at least, the Tories have been forced to tone down their hostility to state interference and spending:

'Government, in the sixth year of generally non-interventionist Tory administration, is everywhere—owning, underpinning, supporting, sponsoring, pump-priming or just plain pumping.' (*Financial Times,* 24 April 1984)

Government money has rescued private and public industries and provided resources for the employment of Loyalist workers. Yet it has done little to alter Loyalist control over the labour market.

Many British people believe that anti-Catholic discrimination has declined since Westminster took direct responsibility for running Northern Ireland in March 1972. But in fact discrimination has got worse in the recession. The government figures reproduced below show that in 1971, before the arrival of either direct rule or economic crisis, male unemployment for Catholics in Northern Ireland stood at 17.3 per cent, while for Protestants it ran at 6.6 per cent. By 1984, despite Northern Ireland secretary Douglas Hurd's boasts about having 'broken the back' of discrimination, the figures were 35 and 15 per cent respectively. Not only has total unemployment soared under direct rule, but the difference between Catholic and Protestant male unemployment has *almost doubled* since Britain took charge of running Northern Ireland. Protestant male unemployment today is still significantly lower than it was for Catholics 15 years ago! Little wonder that, though times may be hard for all in Northern Ireland, Loyalists still look to the link with Britain to give them a better chance of a job than their Catholic neighbours.

Religion and unemployment rate in Northern Ireland

	% Protestant workless			% Catholic workless		
	male	female	total	male	female	total
1971	6.6	3.6	**5.6**	17.3	7.0	**13.9**
1981	12.4	7.4	**10.2**	30.2	17.1	**25.5**
1982-84	15.0	11.0	**13.0**	35.0	17.0	**28.0**

Sources: *1971 Population Census,* Religion Tables;
1981 Population Census, Religion Tables; 1983-84 CHS 1985

Even the British government's high-profile 'equal opportunities' programmes are just hot air. The state has subsidised Harland and Wolff's shipyards throughout the period of direct rule, despite the fact that no Catholics are to be found among the firm's skilled engineers and fitters.

Britain has paid out thousands of pounds for every one of 6000 jobs left at Short Brothers' aircraft factory in Belfast, where just five per cent of those jobs belong to Catholics. The factory is a bastion of Loyalism in East Belfast. An Orange arch spans the shop floor and the walls are bedecked with flags displaying the red hand of Ulster and with assorted emblems of Loyalist groups. Short's is typical of what is left of Northern Ireland's manufacturing industry, a place where whether or not you get a job depends more on where you live and what school you went to than on your aptitude for the post. Short's has been targeted for privatisation by the end of the eighties, but government support will always be essential to its sectarian set-up. In February 1985 Short's chairman came to London to argue that an RAF contract should be granted to his company in Belfast rather than to British Aerospace in Surrey, not because Short's could do a better job, but because 'the important thing is where it is going to be built.' And, he might have added, which workers it was going to provide jobs for. Needless to say the British government rewarded Short's sectarian set-up by giving it the contract.

Ulster's 'Fair Employment Agency'

The supposedly non-sectarian institutions Britain has established since the seventies have themselves become part of the sectarian system. The Fair Employment Agency (FEA), founded in 1976 to investigate claims of discrimination and give British rule a non-sectarian public image, is just for show. It has done nothing to remove the Loyalists' monopoly on jobs. Indeed, the FEA has been forced to concede the truth itself—that discrimination has got worse under direct rule. The Agency's reports are suppressed, doctored and diluted to ensure that they don't rock the boat.

The FEA's first report, published in 1978, showed that 72.5 per cent of all industrial workers in the Six Counties were Protestants. In vehicles the figure rose to 80 per cent, and in shipbuilding to 90 per cent. Catholics were concentrated in the unskilled and semi-skilled jobs. Later FEA reports revealed wide discrimination against Catholic school-leavers, regardless of their qualifications. Because the publication of such material became embarrassing for Britain, subsequent FEA investigations were commissioned secretly. One such report, into the highly sensitive area of employment in the civil service, was completed in July 1981 and subsequently 'leaked' to the press. The civil service had doubled in size since 1972. On the surface it appeared that the total number of Catholics employed had increased significantly. But the FEA's breakdown of the occupation and salary grades of 19 604 civil servants revealed clear and continuing discrimination.

The December 1982 FEA report on the Northern Ireland Electricity Service confirmed the traditional pattern. Of the 291 senior directors and managers, two and a half per cent and four per cent respectively were Catholics. Less than 10 per cent of the engineers were Catholics. And of the administration, fewer than 12.5 per cent came from the nationalist community (*An Phoblacht/Republican News,* 16 December 1982).

Occupational profile of Catholic and Protestant populations (%)

	Catholic	Protestant
1. Professional/managerial	12	15
2. Non manual	19	26
3. Skilled manual	17	19
4. Semi-skilled manual	27	25
5. Unskilled/unemployed	25	15
	100	100

(FEA, *An Industrial and Occupational Profile of the Two Sectors of the Population of Northern Ireland,* Belfast 1978)

The FEA has proved unwilling and unable to act on this information. It is staffed by academics, businessmen, trade union leaders and—from 1976 to 1981—Glen Barr of the sectarian UDA murder gang. It has launched occasional prosecutions of individual employers, but none of its cases have been successful. Even this level of activity, however, has proved too much for the British state. In 1978, an inquiry into discrimination at the Ford Autolite company in Belfast was dropped on the insistence of Labour minister Don

Civil service salary grades by religion

	% Protestant	% Catholic
Senior Principal or higher	87.3	12.7
Principal & Deputy Principal	83.2	16.8
Staff Officer	82.7	17.3
Executive Officer 1	76.4	23.6
Executive Officer 2	71.7	28.3
Clerk	63.8	36.2
Electrical assistant	63.6	36.4

(See 'The FEA', *Iris*, November 1982)

Concannon, who warned that it might cause 'security problems'. In other words, sectarian employment practices must be left untouched to ensure stability in the North.

When the FEA does publish adverse findings, they serve only to illustrate Britain's inability to act against sectarianism. The agency's November 1985 report on the ambulance services found that Catholics were under-represented in all four of Northern Ireland's health and social services boards, and that 'the unsatisfactory position in respect of the representation of Roman Catholics is more marked in the senior grades, where only 10 of the 71 leading ambulancemen and two of the 45 ambulance officers were assessed by the agency as Roman Catholic...there are no satisfactory reasons.' The only reason why such discrimination could continue in the British state sector is that the British state allows it to. Yet the FEA, the soft face of the British state in Ireland, concluded that there was no evidence of 'malpractice or wilful discrimination'.

The same kind of whitewash serves to hide discrimination in the private sector. The FEA's March 1986 report into employment practices in nine Northern Ireland building societies revealed that, in total, the staff of the different firms was 78 per cent Protestant, 17 per cent Roman Catholic and five per cent 'other'. Roman Catholic representation was an astonishing eight per cent at the Leeds Permanent and as low as four per cent at the Progressive. The report held that many societies 'had not afforded equality of opportunity', but added a let-out clause: 'A finding of inequality of opportunity is not a conclusion that an employer, organisation or workforce has consciously or deliberately discriminated against an individual or a section of the community.'

British aid to foreign investors has also been dependent on their willingness to shore up sectarianism in employment. The De Lorean fiasco was launched on £90m of the state's money. De Lorean's car factory was built in a Catholic area of West Belfast. But before it opened the UDA met British officials and obtained assurances that at least half the workforce would be Protestant. The government then had to spend more money—on a new road to allow the skilled Loyalist workers to get across Belfast into the De Lorean plant. The company finally collapsed in 1983 as its charismatic founder faced charges of cocaine dealing in an American court. An embarrassed British government was left to pick up the bill.

Britain has conspired with Loyalist employers and unions to suppress FEA revelations when they threatened foreign contracts for Northern Ireland firms. Through 1983 and 1984 an American air force contract for Short's was put in jeopardy by Irish-American protests over FEA reports of the firm's sectarian employment policy. Assisted by Tory ministers and Irish premier FitzGerald, British diplomats in America launched a campaign to popularise Short's mythical equal opportunities programme. State officials in Belfast circulated a letter from Short's Loyalist shop stewards 'categorically denying' the allegations of discrimination. The contract was saved and Short's sectarianism remained intact.

In recent years the FEA has tried to prove that discrimination in employment is a tit-for-tat game which works against Protestants as well as Catholics. Under pressure from Loyalist politicians, the FEA launched an investigation into discrimination against Protestants in Derry. The agency selected firms situated in Catholic areas of the city where it would be surprising to find significant numbers of Protestant workers. When the investigation showed some of the firms had made efforts to attract Protestants, FEA chair Bob Cooper re-wrote the conclusions to give the impression that anti-Protestant discrimination was prevalent (*Iris*, July 1983). The FEA ignored the preliminary figures it had received from the department of employment in 1980, which indicated that discrimination against Catholics was still the defining feature of the Derry jobs market (see table).

Population and unemployment by religion in Derry

AREA	POPULATION		MALE UNEMPLOYMENT	
	Protestant	Catholic	Protestant	Catholic
Faughan	80	19	5.2	15
North-west Bank, Urban	7	92	8.2	23.6
Mid-west Bank, Urban	23	75	12.3	17
South-west Bank, Urban	1	98	-	24
Bogside	1	99	-	13.6
East Bank, Urban	64	34	10.2	14
West Bank, Rural	61	39	13	20
East Bank, Rural	50	49	10	23
West Bank, Village	64	34	6	14
East Bank, Village	51	45	7	16.4

Department of employment statistics, in *Iris,* July 1983

The deepening crisis of capitalism creates immense problems for British rule in Ireland. Westminster can no longer simply pump money into the Six Counties to protect Loyalist workers. The Tories' Industrial Development Board, set up to attract investment and jobs, flopped. In 1983 it created only 500 jobs, a mere quarter of the target it had set. In 1984 its budget was cut by almost 10 per cent. The government has invested massively in failed job creation schemes. By the end of 1984 Britain had gambled £50m on the Learfan jet project in Belfast. With a projected job target of 2000, Learfan employed a total of 30. In May 1985 it collapsed altogether. Britain cannot buy Northern Ireland out of recession. In 1978 there were already 55 registered unemployed for every vacancy in Northern Ireland. By 1983 the ratio was 68 to one.

The impoverishment of the Six Counties gives Westminster less and less room to manoeuvre. Attempts at 'normalisation' and economic development must give way to more repression. Whatever jobs remain will go to the Loyalists. Nationalist workers can only expect more poverty and coercion. The one growth sector in the Six Counties economy remains the 'security industry'. In December 1984, in the middle of a spate of factory closures, the government announced plans to spend another £6.6m on recruiting 500 extra RUC men. The security sector already supplies one in every 10 Six Counties jobs.

Loyal to Britain, not the working class

The oppression built into the Six Counties state means that most social conflict takes the form of nationalist resistance against Loyalist fiat. The Protestant working class has no political existence as a class—it acts and fights as part of the Loyalist community. Discrimination in jobs, housing and social services ensures that Loyalist workers have a direct stake in the British connection and in the oppression of the nationalist community. Unity between Protestant and Catholic workers is impossible while the link with Britain remains intact. The main objective of Loyalist workers' organisations has always been to block Catholic access to jobs and state services.

British imperialism is prepared to support Loyalist privilege and even accept the restrictive practices of Loyalist workers. This uncharacteristic tolerance of working class interference in the labour market arises because Britain knows that its domination of Ireland depends on the continued support of Loyalist workers.

The main mechanism through which Protestant privileges are sustained is the official trade union movement, which, in Northern Ireland, is little more than a Loyalist labour exchange. In the Six Counties, trade unions do not exist to protect workers' wages and conditions. They exist to protect Protestant living standards at the expense of Catholic ones. The expulsion of Catholic workers from the shipyards and industry in 1920 was organised through the unions. In the aftermath, Vigilance Committees were established at workplaces to prevent the return of Catholic workers. In more recent times, it is true, mass intimidation by Protestants has been used more rarely. Yet as we have earlier noted, many Catholics were driven out of industrial jobs in Belfast in the early seventies.

In Northern Ireland the Protestant unions institutionalise sectarian discrimination: they control the allocation of apprentice-ships through Protestant-only closed shops. In February 1984 the general and municipal workers' union, GMBU, behaved so outrageously towards a Catholic member that the FEA was forced to initiate its first ever prosecution for discrimination. Harland and Wolff shipyard had an agreement with the GMBU that its unemployed members would be hired first. Yet a Catholic worker laid off from the yard spent two years on the dole while the GMBU allowed 105 other workers to be taken on, 60 of whom were not members of the union.

Institutionalised discrimination at the place of work gives Loyalist workers a strong stake in the maintenance of the Union. Thus their immediate interests are realised through strengthening the Loyalist community and the British connection. This directly contradicts the interests of Catholic workers whose aspirations can only be realised through a united Ireland. Partition, therefore, not only divides the working class, but also prevents Protestant workers from acting as a class. Partition forces the Protestants to become agents of British imperialism.

Although workers in the Six Counties are highly unionised, class issues—even basic industrial issues—have always been overshadowed by sectarian divisions. In the first half of the seventies, the Six Counties lost, through each year's strikes, an average of only 486 days per 1000 workers, compared to 1146 per 1000 in Britain. The gap had closed by 1980, but only because of the decline in trade union militancy in England, Scotland and Wales.

When union disputes do occur in the Six Counties, they often serve only to underline the sectarian, anti-working class roots of the labour movement. In August 1986 management and unions at Short's united to condemn sectarianism on the shop floor, after Loyalist thugs destroyed the clocking-on cards of Catholic workers. But they stressed that their concern was with the bad publicity the firm was getting, not with the plight of Catholic workers. As the Confederation of Shipbuilding and Engineering Unions said, such overt displays of anti-Catholic bigotry provide nationalists 'with all the kind of propaganda they require in order to try to damage the interests of the company'. To damage the interests of Catholics on the shop floor is OK by Northern Ireland's sectarian labour movement. Loyalists can go on bullying as long as they do it on the quiet.

Paper unity

The unions' inability to confront sectarianism means that a labour movement which claims to unite workers 'across the sectarian divide' exists only on paper. The divisions imposed by partition mean that even the most elementary forms of trade union unity disintegrate under the pressure of sectarianism. In the end, only one question counts for Northern Ireland workers—which side are you on in the Irish War?

In 1984 the Northern Ireland Committee of the Irish Congress of Trade Unions appealed to the government not to introduce into

HARRY MURRAY, ORGANISER OF THE ULSTER WORKERS' COUNCIL STRIKE, 1974

Northern Ireland legislation directed against the closed shop. Its spokesman Terry Carlin argued that preventing union leaders from signing closed shop deals with employers could 'split the movement along sectarian lines':

'It would allow groups to break with their colleagues over something they didn't like and we wouldn't be able to use the closed shop to prevent it. Any destabilisation of existing arrangements could be exploited by outside forces and this could be divisive.' (*Irish Times*, 2 August 1984)

If the paper unity of the closed shop is removed, trade unionists in the North could divide according to where they stand on the Irish War and line up with the 'outside forces' of Loyalism or republicanism.

The fragility of the official labour movement in Northern Ireland explains why neither the British Labour Party, nor organisations modelled on it like the Northern Ireland Labour Party, have ever had any strong support in the Six Counties. In recent years the lobby calling for the Labour Party to set up branches in Northern Ireland has become increasingly vocal. But its chances of success are nil. Amalgamated Transport and General Workers' Union secretary John Freeman summed up the local union leaders' opposition to the idea at the 1984 Labour Party conference:

'Transplanting the organisation of the British working class into Northern Ireland...would inflict further divisions rather than assist in the development of democratic politics.' (*Morning Star*, 4 October 1984)

In other words any political initiative—even a modest proposal to establish Labour Party branches—threatens to upset the delicate sectarian balance and expose the fiction of trade union unity. The prospects are equally gloomy for any Northern Ireland-based Labour Party. The old Northern Ireland Labour Party has been reduced to a Unionist rump by its inability to unite workers divided by the Border and the war. Its 1984 conference discussed only two motions relating to Northern Ireland—one about drug abuse, and another concerning the affairs of the party's Belfast social club.

In 1984 the Northern Ireland Public Service Alliance, a civil servants' union, was forced to withdraw a donation to the UDR benevolent fund after Catholic members threatened to resign in protest. Such incidents indicate that the official labour movement in the Six Counties can survive only as long as it remains aloof from day-to-day political conflict and especially from the war. A real labour movement in the Six Counties can only be built through challenging the existing structures of oppression and discrimination on which the present labour movement is based.

4. The unfree state

In January 1987, on the eve of a general election in the Twenty-six Counties, revelations that British Signals Intelligence (SIGINT) had been intercepting top secret despatches sent between Ireland's London embassy and Dublin ever since the signing of the Anglo-Irish deal in November 1985 came as an embarrassment to the outgoing Fine Gael/Labour coalition government. But as the *Irish Times* commented, 'It is hardly something to be greatly surprised about.' Details of the surveillance operation exposed how London's deal with Dublin has brought the Irish Republic under much closer British supervision. A month later *Phoenix,* the Dublin equivalent of *Private Eye,* brought to light a secret security agreement, concluded as part of the Anglo-Irish deal, allowing British troops to operate South of the Border 'as of right'. In effect the arrangement allows British military or intelligence personnel to cross the Border in 'hot pursuit'—and without giving advance notice. Since the signing of the London-Dublin accord it is becoming clearer by the day that the Free State is little more than a satellite of Westminster. Likewise its security forces are little more than an extension of the British war machine in Ireland.

Voice of the people

Irish people do not generally like Britain, and like it even less when it interferes in Ireland. The history of British control over Ireland is littered with revolts against the London establishment. Gaelic clansmen crossed swords with Elizabethan mercenaries. The peasant 'Whiteboys' attacked colonial landlords in the nineteenth century. The youth of Monaghan petrol-bombed Irish police cars in protest at the extradition of republicans in 1984. People throughout Ireland have always directed their hatred against Britain and its agents. Today, hostility to all things British is much more muted than before, but Dublin pubs still cheered to the rafters when Argentina beat England in the 1986 World Cup in Mexico.

Britain's partition of Ireland in 1921 and the creation of what is now called the Republic, could not contain the Irish people's yearning for national unity and independence from Westminster. The Irish have nursed a persistent grievance over the unresolved 'national question' and over the enduring influence of the British authorities in their country. In the twenties thousands of republicans in the South took up arms against those of their comrades who had signed the partition treaty. In the thirties there was a popular campaign to end the Free State's payment of land annuities to Britain. In the forties the Anti-Partition League mobilised nationalists who hoped to create a united, free Ireland out of the turmoil of the post-war period. In 1957, 50 000 Irish citizens followed the Limerick funeral of IRA volunteer Sean South, killed attacking an RUC station in the North. In the same year Sinn Fein won 65 000 votes and four seats in elections to the Dail, the South's parliament.

Since 1969, the fierce war raging in the North has made people in the South still more resentful of British tyranny. A significant minority of people in the South, especially those living along the Border, are bitter about today's bloody British occupation of Irish cities like Belfast and Derry. The high points of British barbarity over the past 18 years have provoked angry and violent reaction in the Republic. In August 1969 Loyalist assaults on Catholic ghettos prompted Dubliners to riot, demanding that guns be sent to defend Northern nationalists. After the Bloody Sunday massacre of January 1972, Southern workers struck in protest and a furious crowd of 30 000 burnt down the British embassy in Dublin. During the 1981 republican hunger-strike in the H-Blocks, Southern youth again attacked the British embassy and two hunger-strikers were elected to the Dail.

Today few Dubliners would disagree with the idea of a united Ireland. But fewer still seem prepared to do much about uniting it. This apparent passivity is the legacy of Britain's partition of Ireland 66 years ago and the way that Dublin's rulers have since held nationalist aspirations in check.

The Free State was no sooner created than Irish politicians began to play up to popular nationalist sentiment for fear of being whipped at the polls. The policy of making nationalist gestures—'playing the green card'—was perfected by the founder of today's Fianna Fail party, Eamon de Valera. A former IRA commander, de Valera used a blend of republican rhetoric and carefully staged diplomatic rows with London to cohere nationalist support for his party. He rewrote the Free State constitution to end the Dail's formal subjugation to Westminster, tried to free the Irish economy from direct British control, and kept the South out of the Second World War. It was de Valera who did most to establish a consensus which accepted the Free State as an independent country.

To keep the Free State stable, de Valera's successors have had to make gestures about a united Ireland. During the Loyalist pogroms of 1969, Fianna Fail premier Jack Lynch was forced to criticise the British authorities and set up field hospitals and refugee camps along the Border. After the riots and strikes which followed Bloody Sunday, Lynch had to declare the day of the victims' funerals an occasion of national mourning. Dublin politicians were again obliged to voice public hostility to the intransigence of the British authorities during the H-Block hunger-strike of 1981. Again, the negotiations over the Anglo-Irish accord had statesmen from all the parties of the South trying to disguise their collusion in crafting more cross-Border collaboration by speaking out against Britain's use of supergrasses and shoot-to-kill squads in the North.

Britain's puppet

As well as responding to popular pressure at home, Irish politicians have to respond to pressure from London. The Dublin elite was installed by Westminster and it still relies on the British state to guarantee its authority.

When all of Ireland was under Crown rule in the nineteenth century, Britain stunted the growth of the Irish economy and held back the development of an independent capitalist class. London wiped out Southern industry with a flood of cheap imports and turned most of Ireland into a farm supplying British needs. In the

FIANNA FAIL'S FOUNDING FATHER EAMON DE VALERA

1840s, a potato blight brought famine to Ireland, killing a million people and forcing twice as many out of the country. Meanwhile Irish grain was shipped to Britain.

The weak Irish capitalist class objected to Britain's destruction of Irish industry, but lacked the strength to force London to relinquish its grip. The mass of the Irish people, by contrast, were less wary of confronting British power. By 1921, after two years of the Tan War for independence, they had made much of Ireland ungovernable. When Britain sought to maintain its hold over Ireland by partitioning the country and setting up a puppet Free State regime in the South, it found a willing partner in the establishment wing of the republican movement.

Ireland's feeble capitalists had opposed the Act of Union but were willing to accept British supervision on more advantageous terms. They wanted formal independence to give them room to develop an economic base, yet accepted that they were too weak to run their own affairs without Westminster's support. The treaty left the Free State as a dominion within the British Empire. As we have seen, Britain maintained control of four vital Irish ports and all members of the Dail had to swear allegiance to the Crown.

The British establishment could stitch up a dirty deal with the aspiring business classes of Dublin. But it still had to settle accounts with Irish workers and peasants, who would accept nothing less than unity and independence. Westminster offered to support the satellite Free State regime in return for full cooperation against those who were fighting on for Irish freedom. When the Dail narrowly accepted the treaty in January 1922 (the vote was 64 to 57), Churchill warned Dublin that the only hope of friendly settlement between Britain and Ireland lay in 'a clear line being drawn between the treaty party and the republicans' (Jones, *Whitehall Diary*). The British government gave the Free State regime the money and guns it needed to draw a clear line in the blood of the republican movement.

The Irish Civil War of 1922-23 was ostensibly fought between the pro-treaty forces and the stalwarts of the IRA under Eamon de Valera. But it was no internal Irish affair. A British artillery piece fired the first official shot in the war, when Free State forces levelled the IRA's Dublin HQ in June 1922. British guns, planes and armoured cars guaranteed the success of the pro-treaty forces' decisive drive south. In the autumn of 1922, Free State rulers considered borrowing the island of St Helena from Britain as an internment camp for their 10 000 republican prisoners of war. By May 1923 the British-backed troops had defeated the republicans, executing 27 of their leaders in the process. Westminster had used partition to split the national liberation movement; now its new Dublin proxies finished the war against the IRA. While British troops no longer marched in Kerry or Cork, the defeat of the republican forces meant that the whole of Ireland effectively remained under British control.

Since the Civil War, the Irish establishment has only been able to control the 26 counties allotted to it by Westminster as a result of the divisions imposed through partition and the continued British presence in the North. Partition has divided the Irish working class and slowed its development as a coherent political force. As a result, anti-capitalist revolt has been constrained enough for the fragile Dublin elite to keep a slender grip on the South. Meanwhile, the British occupation of the North has defused some of the republican challenge to the status quo.

These conditions must be maintained today. Despite occasional nationalist posturing on the floor of the Dail, the survival of the Irish authorities depends on continued British rule in Northern Ireland and close cooperation with the imperialists to smash the IRA. The Free State relies on the patronage of the British ruling class for its future. Dublin is completely subservient to Westminster.

Cross-Border warfare

Dublin politicians know that the national liberation struggle poses a threat to every British-built institution in Ireland, North and South. In opposing partition, the struggle challenges the divisions which the Dublin elite has exploited to retain power for more than 60 years. The agents of the Free State have played a full part in Britain's war against the republican movement. They have never shirked their responsibility for banning, jailing or hanging Irish freedom fighters. The Free State's original 1922 constitution allowed for the imposition of martial law and military courts. A succession of Public Safety, Offences Against the State, and Emergency Powers Acts have, at various times of crisis, given Dublin regimes power to execute or intern republicans, proscribe republican organisations and censor republican propaganda. The Republic has established a long record of political trials, convictions and executions. In recent years the military detention centre at the Curragh makes Ireland the only country in Western Europe with convicted civilian prisoners guarded by troops.

The Southern rulers' legal offensive against the national liberation movement has got worse, not better, over the past 18 years of war. The 1972 Offences against the State Act, with its draconian Section 30, gave the garda a free hand to arrest and interrogate anybody suspected of a political offence. Between 1975 and 1985, 14 000 people were arrested under Section 30, 500 people were charged and less than two per cent of those arrested were convicted under the Act. A Special Criminal Court now operates in Dublin to deal with republicans. Both the IRA and Inla are banned, and anybody can be jailed for up to seven years for membership, simply on the word of a chief superintendent.

Police can hold suspects for a week without charge. The infamous Section 31 of the Broadcasting Authority Act bans any 'subversives'—that is republicans—from appearing on Irish television or radio: it was used to full effect against Sinn Fein candidates in the February 1987 general election. The Criminal Law Jurisdiction Act allows republicans to be tried in Dublin for offences committed in Belfast or London. Today new anti-republican laws pass through the Dail on the nod when needed. In February 1985 the government empowered itself to seize £1.5m of alleged IRA funds held in the Bank of Ireland. In March 1986 the Fine Gael/Labour coalition government signed the European Convention on Terrorism, which provides for extradition for political offences, going on to pass their own Extradition Act before the year was out.

For more than 60 years extradition was the one legal measure which Southern courts fought shy of. The Irish constitution does not allow the extradition of prisoners wanted in the North for political offences, and the 1965 Extradition Act specifically prohibited extradition for 'political' offences. But under intense pressure from the British, the Southern establishment has redefined political offences to exclude any military activities by republicans. Extradition is now a powerful weapon in the hands of Britain and its Dublin allies.

In March 1984 Inla commander Dominic McGlinchey was handed over the Border and into a British jail, to be followed by republican Seamus Shannon in August that year. Both their cases eventually collapsed in the Northern courts due to lack of evidence. In March 1985 Dublin's chief justice Finlay ruled that membership of the IRA or of Inla should be a reason *for* extradition rather than a defence against it: he returned Inla member John Quinn to London for trial on fraud offences which Quinn claimed were connected with his republican activities. In March 1986 there were red faces all round when the extradition of Evelyn Glenholmes was bungled in public.

IRISH GARDAI HAND OVER CAPTURED INLA LEADER DOMINIC McGLINCHEY TO RUC ON ST PATRICK'S DAY, 17 MARCH 1984

After the courts released her, Glenholmes was hounded through the streets by gardai gone berserk. One demented detective wildly fired shots in a crowded city centre street, while his colleagues arrested Glenholmes, only to be forced to release her later by the court. After a stern rebuke from the British, Dublin resolved to tighten up. In January 1987 the high court in Dublin upheld the judicial authority of a Northern Ireland justice of the peace who had signed and issued warrants for the return of Maze prison escapee Robert Russell from the Republic.

Apart from judicial collaboration with the British, the Free State has an equally traitorous record of military manoeuvres with Britain. Irish security forces have hunted down IRA men and allowed British troops to operate with impunity South of the Border. Recently published cabinet minutes reveal that in 1922, while Free State forces were using British guns to win the Civil War, the newly 'independent' Dublin regime allowed 1000 British troops to occupy the villages of Belleek and Pettigo to stabilise the Border. Less formal arrangements have allowed British forces to roam the Republic since the seventies. In April 1984 Dublin requested and got an apology from London when an RUC assassin admitted in court that he had been ordered to cover up the details of a shoot-to-kill attack in order to conceal British operations in the South. Such diplomatic niceties aside, the Free State regime keeps open house for Crown gunmen. In 1974 Southern authorities released two carloads of SAS men arrested in Omeath and believed to be en route to assassinate an Inla leader living in a caravan in the area.

The 1985 London-Dublin accord put the legal seal on closer security cooperation between the two anti-republican regimes. Indeed, in the house of commons debate on the deal, all the talk was about Article 9, which, as Thatcher spelt out, steps up cooperation in the fight against terrorism, 'cooperation which goes beyond the Borders of Northern Ireland' (*Hansard,* 26 November 1985). While Westminster prevaricated about passing even token 'reforms', such as the repeal of the Flags and Emblems Act, it wasted no time at all getting down to its dirty business across the Border. The first officially approved Border crossing by British troops was made near Aughnacloy in the summer of 1986, after a verbal clearance had been given by Irish Taoiseach Garret FitzGerald. On that occasion uniformed British soldiers entered County Monaghan, bringing with them electronic equipment which, codenamed 'DUBLOON', is used to detect bomb-firing circuits. The British Army team worked alongside an Irish Army explosives ordnance officer and his support section from Monaghan barracks (*Phoenix,* 13 February 1987).

Dublin largely uses its own troops and police to seal off the Republic from the war in the North. The Free State Army has been built up from 8000 in 1969 to almost twice that today. Alone among European armies, it is designed solely for internal use. The Republic spends, per head, three times as much as Britain on policing partition. In December 1984 the Irish defence minister admitted that only the Irish Army stood between the IRA and control of the Border.

Britain has welcomed the move towards more overt cross-Border collaboration. It is a great improvement on the past, when Westminster often felt the need to criticise its pawns in Dublin for the inefficiency of their security system. By the end of 1983, the garda's farcical attempts to capture McGlinchey had only resulted in him tying up seven officers and taking their trousers away too. Equally, a running gun-battle between a handful of IRA volunteers and scores of Irish police and troops in December wound up with two deaths on the Free State side: the republicans eventually escaped through the back door of a Ballinamore house just as gardai charged in through the front one. A furious James Prior flew to Dublin to tell Irish justice minister Michael Noonan to get his act together. Noonan immediately announced that the Rangers—the Free State's SAS—would run all future anti-terrorist operations.

On other occasions the British authorities have dispensed with the middlemen in Dublin altogether and taken direct charge of Irish security forces. In September 1984 garda chiefs congratulated themselves on capturing the trawler *Marita Anne* off Kerry with eight tonnes of republican guns from America on board. It later transpired that the whole operation had been supervised from Whitehall. Such incidents make it obvious that the Republic's security forces operate as little more than an extension of the British state machine.

Dublin statesmen understand that they are responsible to their masters in Westminster and have a duty to stamp on the republican movement. Every Irish minister who has made gestures of resistance to British interference has also bloodied his hands in the Irish War. During the Second World War, de Valera took time off from a furious row with Churchill over Irish neutrality to borrow the British hangman and execute some IRA volunteers. Jack Lynch lost his republican reputation and his position as Fianna Fail leader when he toyed publicly with the idea of granting British helicopter gunships a 'hot pursuit' corridor through Irish airspace. Fianna Fail leader, Charles Haughey, is remembered by nationalists for his alleged role in plans to run guns from Dublin to the IRA in the North during 1970. But in 1982, Haughey's government set a legal precedent by running escaped IRA man Gerard Tuite into an Irish jail for planting bombs in London.

Free State politicians have long manipulated anti-British sentiment, the better to secure the support of Southerners who still aspire to Irish unity. Yet every Dublin government has proved willing to jail, shoot and hang those who oppose in practice the phoney independence of the Free State. This double-dealing policy has helped sustain the illusion that the Twenty-six Counties is an independent entity—that it has been the success story of partition. But in the eighties the Free State has had its hands fuller than ever before. It has to restore the credibility of constitutional nationalism through closer cooperation with Britain. And it has to stave off the collapse of the Southern economy, by attacking the working class. These two tasks threaten to shatter the fragile Free State regime. Certainly the parlous condition of the Southern economy has sparked off a political and social crisis which is pulling the Republic apart. In 1987, the Southern establishment is more embattled than at any time since the Civil War.

As a junior partner to London, the Irish capitalist class is too weak to maintain even a semblance of political coherence. Parliamentary politics consists of an ever-changing series of coalitions and no single party inspires popular enthusiasm. To preserve its rule the capitalist class relies on past traditions—and above all on the Church—to strengthen a conservative mood. As a result the backward and bigoted mentality associated with Loyalist reaction finds an expression South of the Border.

Church and state in crisis

In January 1987 controversy on condoms threw Ireland into turmoil for the second time in as many years. This time the question was whether the Church should approve the use of condoms as a safeguard against the spread of Aids. A statement issued by the Standing Committee of the Bishops' Conference ruled that the only safeguards against the disease were chastity and self-denial:

'Apart from other moral considerations, there is the grave danger that the promotion of condoms will give further encouragement to permissiveness and this in itself would contribute to a further spread of the disease. The only reliable safeguard against contracting the virus by sexual

means is through faithfulness to one's partner in marriage and through
self-denial and self-restraint outside of marriage. It is vital that this be
made crystal clear.'

As far as the bishops are concerned, it would appear, condoms are a
graver threat to the fabric of society than Aids itself.

The first furore on condoms came in February 1985, when the
Fine Gael/Labour government defied the Catholic hierarchy and
legalised the sale of contraceptives to unmarried adults. The fact
that a form of contraception in common use in most advanced
industrial nations for about a century could become a major issue of
debate in the South showed how British domination has held back
cultural development in Ireland. The distorting influence of
partition has allowed reactionary moral ideas to go unchallenged
and given the Catholic Church power and status. But the popular
support for FitzGerald's condom Bill indicated the declining
influence of Ireland's moral guardians. It showed that the
traditional standards which have long united most Irish people
behind the establishment are increasingly being brought into
question by the crisis in modern Ireland.

Ireland's 'moral decline' has caused panic in Dublin and London.
The historical strength of Catholic belief among the majority of
Irish people stems, not from some flaw in the Gaelic character, but
from British domination. Britain's interference has denied Ireland
the chance to develop into a mature capitalist nation. Just as the
Irish economy lags behind international developments, so many
ideas, opinions and lifestyles in Ireland are rooted in the past.

Britain has long recognised religion as a useful means of
controlling Ireland. The power of the Catholic hierarchy guards
against the spread of progressive ideas, and allegiance to the Church
ensures the unity of the Catholic population across class lines.
Despite the early anti-Catholic laws it imposed on Ireland,
Westminster realised by the mid-nineteenth century that it had
much to gain from making the Church a pillar of the pro-British
establishment. In 1845 Catholic orator Richard Lalor Shiel told the
house of commons of the benefits it would gain from funding a
Catholic college for Irish priests at Maynooth:

'You must not take the Catholic clergy into your pay, but you can take
the Catholic clergy under your care....Are not lectures at Maynooth
cheaper than state prosecutions? Are not professors less costly than Crown
solicitors? Is not a large standing army and a great constabulary force more

expensive than the moral police with which by the priesthood of Ireland you can be thirstily and efficaciously supplied?' (Quoted in P Beresford Ellis, *A History of the Irish Working Class*)

Since the nineteenth century, Church spokesmen have acted as Britain's moral police in Ireland. Catholic bishops and cardinals have been particularly active in condemning the actions of the IRA as 'ungodly'.

Irish women have suffered a harsh fate at the hands of Britain and its local agents in the Church and the state. The degraded position of women is summed up in the legal right the South gives to the husband to sue his wife's lover for financial compensation for loss of sexual services. Abortion is illegal and many other rights are denied women. The feeble Southern establishment cannot afford to give the female sex basic health and social services. And Westminster is keen to discourage ideas of social equality in a state whose foundations rest on inequality and domination.

The institutionalised oppression of women and sanctification of the family have underpinned the whole of Irish society. The public campaign around the 1983 referendum, which outlawed abortion through the Free State's constitution, confirmed the role of religious bigotry and women's oppression as stabilising forces in Ireland. The ban on abortion forces an estimated 10 000 women to go to England for abortions every year (the real figure is probably much higher, since many Irish women give English addresses). Even this avenue to abortion has now been curtailed since a Dublin high court ruling in December 1986 prohibited two clinics in the city from giving details of abortion facilities in Britain. The Church has also come out against female sterilisation, which is not illegal but not easily available either, after an increase in demand from desperate women. In August 1985 the Bishop of Galway, Dr Casey, sent a letter to all doctors in the area reminding them that sterilisation is 'repugnant to Christian teaching'.

In 1986 reaction won the day against those campaigning for more freedom and secularism in the South, gaining a big referendum majority in favour of retaining the constitutional ban on divorce. Popular wisdom has it that divorce has been a dirty word in Ireland for centuries. In fact, divorce only became illegal under the Free State constitution of 1937. Article 41, which bans divorce, begins with these two clauses:

'The state recognises the family as the natural, primary and fundamental unit group of society, and as a moral institution possessing inalienable and imprescriptable rights, antecedent and superior to all positive laws.

'The state recognises that by her life in the home, woman gives to the state a support without which the common good cannot be achieved. The state shall therefore endeavour to ensure that mothers shall not be obliged by economic necessity to engage in labour to the neglect of their duties in the home.'

For the past 50 years, the constitutional endorsement of Catholic views on the family has helped the Free State regime keep the lid on Irish society by keeping women at the bottom.

The problem Britain faces today is that the steadying hand of the Catholic hierarchy has a less and less firm grip on Irish opinion. Even the 1986 divorce debate illustrated how fluid things have become in modern Ireland. The Church appealed successfully to a widespread sense of economic insecurity to sway many women against divorce. Among the people, divisions of generation, social standing and moral values have grown as change blunts the direct power of the Catholic Church. Contraception is only one of the previously unmentionable issues which have become the talk of every Irish town. Through late 1984 and into 1985, an inquiry into the killing of unwanted babies in Kerry kept taboo subjects like extra-marital sex and infanticide on the front pages of all the Irish papers. Scares and panics about crime waves and drug epidemics are rife in Dublin, and violence is on the increase in every corner of the Republic. Inner-city ghettos are patrolled by vigilante squads, organised by everybody from parents hunting for drug pushers to grasping slum landlords protecting their property. Villages in country areas like County Meath have been taken over by armed gangs reminiscent of Jesse James.

Respect for the teachings of the Church is at an all-time low, even in the rural strongholds of Irish Catholicism and especially among the youth who make up half the Republic's inhabitants. The traditional standards which have kept Ireland safe for imperialism are in decline. Yet so long as every powerful political force remains tied to the institutions of the Free State, the moralists can carry the day. Capital cannot survive in the South of Ireland without the help of Catholicism. With economics still controlled by foreign investors, and its political power dependent on the backing of British imperialism, the Dublin establishment lacks authority. In today's crisis, it needs pro-family propaganda more than ever before.

THE CHURCH APPEALED SUCCESSFULLY TO A WIDESPREAD SENSE OF ECONOMIC INSECURITY TO SWAY MANY WOMEN AGAINST DIVORCE

The social fabric of the Free State is cracking up. Behind the
social crisis lies the collapse of the Irish economy. A lengthening list
of factory closures has pushed official unemployment close to 20 per
cent and pushed a third of the population on to the welfare roll. In
the hardest-hit regions, unemployment stands at more than 50 per
cent. The Free State is in no condition to deal with its mounting
economic problems. In 1987 its borrowing, a legacy of industrial
development in the sixties and seventies and profligate public
spending in the eighties meant the highest national debt per head in
the world: servicing it absorbed every penny of Ireland's massive
income taxes. The image of a prosperous democracy, so central to
the boom years, has gone forever. Once more the spectre of
emigration has returned to haunt the Irish people, who are leaving
at the rate of 30 000 a year.

The Free State's economy has always been buffeted by the ebb
and flow of the international market. Its lack of any independent
strength has left the Dublin establishment swayed by every
movement of foreign capital in and out of Ireland. For almost 40
years the Free State tried to build a manufacturing base of its own.
The result was permanent unemployment, urban poverty and rural
destitution. Thousands of young Irish men and women left their
country for the greener pastures of England, Scotland and the USA.

Between 1956 and 1961 about a quarter of a million people
emigrated to escape the depression in Ireland. Close to despair, the
Fianna Fail government threw the Irish economy open to foreign
investors—an admission that the Free State could not operate
independently of imperialism. The government spent millions on
tax incentives and infrastructure—transport, communications—to
coax the money-men in. The 'open door' policy seemed to produce
results. Industrial output shot up by 47 per cent between 1957 and
1963. Ireland's entry into the EEC in 1973 encouraged Japanese and
American investment, bringing the Free State rates of economic
growth worthy of any in Europe. Dublin hailed what it called an
'economic miracle'. But behind the spectacular statistics, the pattern
of Ireland's development confirmed its backward status.

Foreign investors were more interested in making a fast buck out
of the Irish working class than in building an industrial base for the
Dublin elite. They put their money into low-skill operations
assembling kits produced elsewhere for export to the EEC. The Free
State's traditional industries continued to stagnate. This uneven
pattern of industrialisation meant that unemployment never fell
below eight per cent. Farming retained a central place in the

economy; meanwhile, Dublin accumulated massive foreign debts.

The recession of the eighties has put a stop to all talk of miracles and exposed the Republic of Ireland as a European outpost of the third world. Foreign investors are off in search of new havens: though today they account for half of the Free State's 200 000 manufacturing jobs and 80 per cent of its industrial exports, tomorrow most of them may be gone. Those which have already pulled out have left little behind. In 1986 foreign investors repatriated vast profits without even informing the Dublin government.

Closures of foreign firms are turning newly industrialised areas like County Cork into wastelands. As for the Free State's debts, these now form a chain binding the country to the dictates of imperialism. In 1987 the Republic's foreign commitments were the biggest in the world, outstripping even notorious debtors such as Mexico and Brazil.

The politics of the past

Like the economy, many of the political props supporting the Free State over the years are beginning to slide away. Public confidence in the institutions, conventions and politicians of the past is at an all-time low. Political life in Dublin is dogged by uncertainty and a lack of belief in the established parties. The hung Dail which emerged from the February 1987 general election, in which Fianna Fail was unable for the fourth time in a row to get an overall majority, exposed the shaky political set-up that passes for a party system in the Republic. The fudged outcome of the election was nothing new. Since 1973, every election has produced a change of government, indicating the lacklustre standing of the two main parties in the eyes of the Irish electorate. The last round of indecisive voting in the early eighties resulted in a narrow defeat for Haughey in May 1981, an equally narrow defeat for FitzGerald in January 1982, and a majority for the Fine Gael-Labour coalition in November 1982. Three elections in 18 months revealed the impasse of establishment politics in the South, which the inconclusive 1987 result failed to break.

Both major Irish parties reflect the Free State's preoccupation with past traditions. Fine Gael and Fianna Fail are still identified by the part they played in the Civil War. This historical difference obscures the almost identical character of their policies for ruling modern Ireland:

Southern stalemate

The inconclusive outcome of the February 1987 general election in the Twenty-six Counties revealed the instability of Southern politics and the fragmentation of traditional voting patterns.

Final state of the parties: seats in Dail

	Post-election	Pre-election	Change	% of vote	% change
Fianna Fail	81	71	+10	44	-1
Fine Gail	51	68	-17	27	-12
Labour Party	12	14	-2	6.4	-3
Progressive Democrats	14	5	+9	11.8	+5
Workers Party	4	2	+2	3.8	—
Sinn Fein	0	0	0	1.9	—
Others	4	6	-2	4.8	

Fianna Fail, led by Charles Haughey, won the largest number of seats in the Dail, but fell three short of the number needed to win an absolute majority. Fianna Fail's election performance, following four years of austerity under the Fine Gael/Labour coalition, was poor. It won its fifth lowest share of the vote ever (it did worse only in 1943, 1948, 1954 and 1961). Its vote increased in only about half of all constituencies. It remains strong in Connaught and Ulster—counties to the north and west, where its traditional republicanism still commands support. Its other successes were in working class areas in Dublin.

Fine Gael, led by Garret FitzGerald, did badly, as was expected after four years in an unpopular alliance with Labour. It won its lowest share of the poll since 1957, losing votes to the Progressive Democrats more than to Fianna Fail. The government's unpopularity was largely the result of its failure to arrest Ireland's slide into economic ruin. FitzGerald's secularising campaigns—on abortion and divorce—also led to serious setbacks. He resigned as leader of the party and Alan Dukes took over.

The Progressive Democrats, formed by Desmond O'Malley in January 1986, failed to break the mould of Irish politics, but achieved a creditable result in winning 14 seats. The Progressive Democrats are the party of the emerging Irish middle classes, a layer which has expanded rapidly since the seventies—particularly in the urban public sector. They are conservative on economic issues and liberal on social ones. Their narrow social base is evident from the geographical spread of their support.

The Labour Party fared badly, suffering from the low esteem in which the electorate held the outgoing government. Its leader, Dick Spring, scraped in by a few votes after several recounts. Labour could have done a good deal worse and, in the circumstances, the loss of only two seats was not such a bad result. The Workers Party, the degeneration product of the old Official IRA, gained some support at the expense of the Labour Party and doubled its seats from two to four. Sinn Fein's first electoral contest since abandoning the policy of abstentionism in the South revealed its low level of support. Sinn Fein stood 27 candidates in 24 seats, winning a total of 32 573 votes or 1.9 per cent of the poll. This compared badly with the party's vote of six per cent in the 1984 Euro-elections.

The final outcome of the election left Haughey relying on votes from four independent TDs (MPs) to make him Taoiseach. Haughey does not enjoy a majority in the Dail, a fact which points toward another period of unstable government for the Republic.

'The main contest in the Republic's politics has lain between two major parties, undifferentiated by solid class interests or competing ideologies, springing from the two sides in a long extinct Civil War, sustained as much by dynastic ambition as by any coherent programme.' (*The Times*, 28 January 1983)

Fine Gael, which emerged out of the pro-partition forces of the early days of the Free State, has traditionally been associated with big farmers and the middle classes. While it has grown in stature at the polls as the middle classes have come to carry more weight, Fine Gael has always proved unable to mobilise enough popular support to form a majority government. Its success has always been restricted by its reputation as the pro-British party of the aspiring professionals and landowners who agreed to partition in 1921. All its brief spells in office have been in unstable coalitions—usually with the Labour Party. Now it has to compete with the Progressive Democrats for the same professional constituency. After four years of austerity, unemployment and repression, it went down to a devastating defeat in the 1987 election.

Fianna Fail, which claims the republican mantle of the forces which originally opposed the partition treaty, has long looked to the small farmers of Ulster and Connaught for its support. It is strongest among the declining groups of the rural outback; weakest in the swanky suburbs of Dublin southside. Fianna Fail's populist appeal to nationalist Ireland has kept it in power for most of the Free State's history. But population shifts from the rural west to the urban east, together with the growth of the working class and the middle classes, have altered the composition of the Dail and altered Fianna Fail's chances of commanding a majority as well. The party shares Fine Gael's middle class approach to righting the economy through austerity measures imposed at workers' expense. Its leader Haughey has toned down his nationalist rhetoric as the national question has lost its old importance to the life of the South.

The Free State has always had the parliamentary trappings of a European democracy on the British model. But its political wrangles often have more in common with the affairs of a Latin American or African dictatorship. The British media likes to poke fun at the parochial and corrupt style of politics in the Republic. Irish statesmen electioneering outside Sunday mass from the back of a tractor, cabinet ministers caught up in bribery scandals and the odd murder inquiry—these episodes are often contrasted to the sophisticated world of Westminster. But London newspapers fail to

FIANNA FAIL LEADER CHARLES HAUGHEY

FINE GAEL LEADER ALAN DUKES

point out that such features of Free State politics are the consequence of imperialist domination.

Britain's retarding influence on the Southern economy has left the Irish establishment with a narrow base for capital accumulation. As a consequence, the Irish capitalist class lacks confidence and authority. It is unable to impose its will on society and retains only a slender hold on power. Dublin relies on a clique of middle class politicians to keep up a semblance of order. Lacking any solid class base of their own, these statesmen rule through cobbling together a series of compromises with the major forces in Irish society—British imperialism, the Irish working class, the Catholic Church, the farming community. The fragility of capitalist relations in the Republic ensures permanent political instability, gives added prominence to the rural constituencies, and leaves ample scope for graft and corruption.

The Irish parliament's low standing in British eyes is due to its uncertain ability to keep the peace. This problem has been made acute by the social breakdown brought on by recession. The unstable state of Irish politics reflects a broader problem of growing disrespect for the agencies of the Free State. Dublin's guardians of order and democracy have been rocked by a succession of scandals involving sex, violence and bribery. A series of inquiries and court cases about garda brutality has also discredited the police force.

The climate of public hostility towards the establishment and its agents has encouraged the spread of violence and law-breaking and the drift away from traditional loyalties to Church and state. The Republic's phoney democracy is under pressure within Ireland, and the Dublin establishment is under pressure from Britain to put its house in order. The unusual prominence the British press gave to the February 1987 general election showed Whitehall's worries about what goes on across the Irish Sea. Most media commentators greeted the collapse of the faltering Fine Gael-Labour coalition as a merciful release and prayed for a majority government. The *Financial Times* indulged in wishful thinking, musing that the Republic 'could benefit from having a healthy left-wing party'. Anything that could help contain the threat to the established order in the South—even a socialist alternative to the mainstream parties—is OK by Britain.

The Anglo-Irish agreement is, in part, an attempt to restore credibility to the beleaguered Irish bourgeoisie and so batten down the hatches against growing popular dissent. It has won the backing of all the establishment parties in Ireland, each of which is as desperate as Downing Street to stop the rot. But, while the accord has proved popular among passive nationalists South of the Border, the national question no longer commands enough interest in the Free State for it to be used successfully to stabilise society.

The South goes North

The Dublin government has always been keen to have some say in Northern Ireland affairs so as to boost its status with Southern nationalists and to make sure that the conflict did not sneak across the Border. Its previous advances have long been rebuffed by the British state: 'Northern Ireland is none of your business' said Tory prime minister Edward Heath's telegram to Dublin in 1972. But by the eighties all the Southern parties were desperate to do a deal on the North. The accelerating social crisis in the Free State made sure of that.

Economic havoc, the loss of public respect and the alienation of Irish youth have all combined to throw the Free State regime into a panic. It became desperate to halt the rise of Sinn Fein after the hunger-strikes and to revive the fortunes of its Northern ally, the Social Democratic and Labour Party. Dublin's concern over the welfare of the SDLP reflected a crisis of confidence about the future of constitutional nationalism throughout the island. It needed some confirmation that there was a role for the representatives of Irish capitalism in Britain's plans for Ireland, and was prepared to pay almost any price to obtain it. This was the thinking behind the year-long New Ireland Forum which came with three proposals for a negotiated Anglo-Irish solution: a unitary Irish state, a federal Ireland, and joint authority over Northern Ireland to be shared by the Dail and the British parliament.

The progress of talks about the agreement reflected the South's subservience to Britain. In November 1984 Thatcher declared that the Forum report's tame proposals were 'Out, out, out'. A year later she signed a deal with Dublin without altering her opinion one iota. Every idea the Irish put forward, from abolishing the UDR to having Southern judges sitting in Northern courts, was thrown out. The final settlement was written entirely by the British. SDLP leader John Hume declared the agreement would be 'a stepping stone'; but these were the same words that Michael Collins used about the 1921 treaty, which guarantees partition, in Tom King's words, 'in perpetuity'.

Cracking down on republicanism is crucial for Dublin. But it is also dangerous. Overt collaboration in the Irish War threatens to expose the real relationship between Britain and the Republic, and so open the way for the Irish working class to take up the struggle against Britain. Yet the political legacy of partition still holds Irish workers back from joining their brothers and sisters in the North.

Workers' independence and Irish freedom

Every aspect of Irish workers' lives is influenced by Britain's domination of their country. The capitalist recession has brought mass unemployment and a sustained government offensive on workers' wages and rights. The labour movement itself is continually torn by competition for members between Irish and British-based unions. Yet British oppression is not an issue of debate in the official institutions of the Irish working class. The Irish labour movement has stood on the sidelines of the national liberation struggle for more than 60 years.

The last time the working class took an independent stand in the fight for Irish freedom was in the Easter Rising of 1916. James Connolly's Irish Citizen Army, originally formed as a workers' militia to protect striking dockers, led the fighting against British troops in Dublin. But the working class was too weak to sustain its leading role. After the defeat of the Rising and the execution of Connolly, the prime position in the national struggle passed to the middle class leaders of the early republican movement.

Irish workers played a vital part in the independence war, both as volunteers in the IRA and as strikers disrupting the British war effort. On 23 April 1918, the unions staged a one-day total stoppage in protest against the threat of conscription in Ireland. Elsewhere transport workers interfered with Britain's supply lines. But the political path taken by the battle against British oppression was dictated by middle class compromisers. In the 1918 general election, which was fought on the issue of Irish independence, the Irish Labour Party abstained; and abstention has defined the official labour movement's attitude to the fight for Irish freedom ever since. As a consequence, the reactionary politicians of Fianna Fail have been able to monopolise the nationalist aspirations of the Irish working class.

In the forties the Irish Trade Union Congress temporarily split along national lines. The Irish Transport and General Workers Union and a number of small craft unions protested at British

MONAGHAN, MAY 1987: AN IRISH GARDA OPENS FIRE ON MOURNERS AT THE FUNERAL OF JAMES LYNAGH, ONE OF EIGHT IRA VOLUNTEERS KILLED IN AN SAS AMBUSH AT LOUGHGALL

interference in the Irish labour movement and formed a breakaway Congress of Irish Unions. The British-based unions, with a heavy Loyalist membership in Northern Ireland, stayed with the ITUC. But the split had more to do with personality clashes and recruitment squabbles than the emergence of any anti-imperialist trend among Southern trade unions. The supposedly nationalist CIU remained under the influence of Fianna Fail's Catholic constitutional nationalism. In 1950, when the Pope celebrated Holy Year, the CIU sent two representatives to Rome, 'to convey to the Holy Father the loyalty and homage of the Irish working class'.

Until the sixties, the Irish labour movement was a weak force in the Free State. But the rapid industrialisation and expansion of the state sector which followed the influx of foreign capital changed all that. For the first time, the working class moved to the centre of Irish society. Workers used their newfound power to fight for improved wages and working conditions. Throughout the seventies the Republic was always one of Western Europe's three most strike-prone countries.

The upsurge of economic militancy among Irish workers coincided with the outbreak of war across the Border. Yet the two events might have been on opposite sides of the world. Apart from angry outbursts after outrages such as Bloody Sunday, the Irish working class has failed to throw its power behind the nationalist community in the North.

While many workers in the South sympathise with the plight of their Northern cousins, they do not regard the division of Ireland as a practical problem for people in the Twenty-six Counties. Sympathy alone is rarely enough to make people throw themselves into a struggle. The submerged character of the national question in the Republic means that it scarcely figures as a subject of political debate. Ask anybody on the streets of Dublin what they are concerned about, and issues such as unemployment or taxation come to mind long before the Anglo-Irish agreement. Indeed the Progressive Democrats won widespread support when they were first formed by calling for more discussion on modern issues and 'an end to Civil War politics'. When Dubliners do get round to mentioning the agreement, they are more than likely to tell you it's a good thing.

Speaking at a January 1984 rally in Dublin, Matt Merrigan, vice-president of the Irish Congress of Trade Unions, bemoaned the continuing dominance of middle class politics within the labour movement:

'I don't see 200 000 people on the streets today. FitzGerald and Haughey have more influence with the working class than the trade union movement has.' (*An Phoblacht/Republican News*, 26 January 1984)

Union officials like Merrigan may complain about the lack of any distinct labour movement politics in Ireland. But they carry a large share of the blame for it. Official labour movement spokesmen have echoed Fianna Fail's support for the phoney independence of the Free State. The nationalism they espouse is purely of the economic variety, directed against foreign multinationals rather than the British imperialists who guarantee Ireland's economic subjugation. Thus the vice-president of Ireland's largest union, the transport workers', opposes the pay policies of American firms because 'the Irish people have not struggled for centuries to achieve political freedom only to exchange it for economic slavery.' The same tendency to direct workers' anger against the wrong targets afflicts all the political parties identified with the Irish labour movement.

Workers and youth in the Free State have staged angry protests against the interference of foreign powers in their country. There have been countless strikes and occupations against overseas firms which invest in Ireland, then pull out as soon as their profits take a tumble. 'EEC out, jobs in' graffiti are plastered around the urban areas. But the anger is directed only against the faceless financiers of 'multinational capitalism'. Such narrow economic protests miss the prime political target—the British state.

What passes for working class politics in the Free State is only a more radical presentation of the same middle class ideas which dominate the Dail. The major left-wing parties in the Republic are the Irish Labour Party and the Workers Party, the rump of the old Official republican movement which gave up fighting Britain in the early seventies. In coalition with Fine Gael from 1982 to 1987, the Labour Party presided over mass unemployment and huge cuts in welfare spending. Labour's Dick Spring admits that his party has never had any difficulty in demanding that workers make concessions to support the Free State. The left wing of the Labour Party and the Workers Party lack any concept of independent working class action. Their most radical proposals are for minor reforms to the Free State's taxation system—hardly a programme to break workers from Fianna Fail or Fine Gael.

The radicals' plans for governing Ireland are all based on the institutions of the Free State. Thus they share the established parties' hatred of republican freedom fighters. The Labour Party protests at the economic consequences of British domination, but appreciates that such matters come second to supporting the political division Westminster has imposed on Ireland. In September 1984 the Tory government pulled out of the deal to pump natural gas from the Republic to Northern Ireland. Dick Spring declared his outrage, but insisted that London's move would not affect cross-Border collaboration against the republican threat:

'The Northern Ireland situation is so serious that upsets in normal business, normal commercial deals, even if they have major socio-economic implications for Ireland as a whole, can't be allowed to distract from the major problem.'

The former republicans of the Workers Party share this desire to smash the liberation struggle—to the extent of supporting Section 31 of the Broadcasting Authority Act, which notoriously keeps republicans off the airwaves. The Workers Party has complained at the ruling parties' harsh economic measures, not because they destroy workers' living standards, but because they make Ireland a 'perfect breeding ground for anti-democratic forces'—that is, for those struggling for national democratic rights.

The pre-eminence of middle class politics in the South has led to a division between economic militancy and political passivity among Irish workers. Many working class people in the South are willing to fight their employers over jobs and wages, and to express support for the liberation of the North. But the two struggles are seen as separate. No political force yet exists in Ireland to show workers in the Free State that their problems stem from the same source as the difficulties facing nationalists in the Six Counties—Britain. This state of affairs remains the guarantee of London rule in Belfast, and of London's lackeys' control in Dublin.

5. Judicial terror

'We have absolute confidence in the judiciary in Northern Ireland,' declared Margaret Thatcher during the parliamentary debate on the Anglo-Irish agreement:

'Indeed the integrity and courage which they have shown in recent years in maintaining high standards of judicial impartiality have been outstanding.' (*Hansard,* 26 November 1985)

Perhaps Thatcher was referring to Lord Justice Gibson. In June 1984 Gibson commended three members of the RUC, men who two years previously had pumped 100 bullets into three unarmed republicans, for what he called their 'courage and determination' in bringing the three men 'to justice, in this case the final court of justice'. Such is the impartiality of British law and order in Northern Ireland.

The British Army justifies its presence in Ireland on the grounds that it defends law and order. The government, the press and the Army itself all go to great lengths to preserve this image of keeping the peace. *The Times* has warned that the security forces cannot afford to be seen to be acting outside the framework of the law:

'For if suspicion were converted to belief, and belief into knowledge, that the civil power in Northern Ireland has resorted to countering the armed subversion of lawful order by its own perversion of lawful means, then not only would the confidence of the nationalist community be lost for ever, the moral basis for Britain's presence in the province would vanish.' (5 January 1983)

The Times need not worry. In the Six Counties the law operates in such a flexible way that virtually any crime committed by the security forces is interpreted as legal. More than 250 murders by the security forces have led to less than a dozen prosecutions. Two soldiers are serving life sentences for the 'Pitchfork Murders', an act of British Army savagery in October 1972 that still shocks the farming community of County Fermanagh. Mickey Naan, a local farmer and civil rights activist, and Andrew Murray, who worked for Naan, were pitchforked to death in the farmyard. Locals thought that Loyalists had done it, but nobody suspected the British Army. The truth would never have come out but for the Yorkshire Ripper. An ex-soldier in Britain who read about the Ripper thought he had the same style as the pitchfork murderers. He knew the guilty soldiers and feared one might be the Ripper, so he walked into a police station and told the story. The British authorities always claimed the murderers—Argyle and Sutherland Highlanders—were off-duty. But locals maintain they were on patrol and were briefed about which 'suspects' to see.

In December 1984, after 15 years of the Irish War, Private Ian Thain became the first British soldier to be found guilty of murder while on duty. Thain was convicted because his victim, Thomas 'Kidso' Reilly, was a pop group road manager well-known in Britain. Reilly's murder attracted far more embarrassing publicity than other shoot-to-kill incidents, and the British authorities felt compelled to make a gesture. The decision did nothing to alter the courts' general approach to British murder in Ireland. On the same day that he sentenced Thain, Justice Higgins found UDR Corporal David Baird not guilty of the murder or manslaughter of Armagh teenager Martin Malone. Higgins considered that 'in the light of the situation', Baird's failure to check his safety catch was not 'reckless'. For the British courts, gunning down Irish youth is never reckless.

The only RUC man to be convicted of the murder of a nationalist in Northern Ireland was sentenced to life imprisonment in September 1985. Thomas Andrews was off-duty and drunk when he stopped his car in the Short Strand area of East Belfast, pulled out his personal issue Ruger gun and shot dead 18-year old Tony

Dawson. Every single RUC man *in uniform* who has gunned down
Irish nationalists has done so with impunity. In September 1986
RUC reservist Neil Hegarty, who killed John Downes with a plastic
bullet in front of TV cameras at an anti-internment rally in Belfast in
August 1984, walked free from the courts. Hegarty was not even
charged with murder, and was acquitted of manslaughter. The
verdict rubber-stamped the Crown forces' licence to kill.

The law is an important weapon in Britain's arsenal. Before we
turn to examine how the law has shaped the war, it is useful to
outline the peculiarities of the legal system in the Six Counties.

Colonial law

Although Northern Ireland is supposed to be part of the 'United
Kingdom', the legal system there betrays its status as a colony. Many
legal reforms passed in Westminster have never been enacted in this
corner of the 'United Kingdom'. The British government has rarely
sought to impose legal changes in the Six Counties in the face of
Loyalist resistance.

Between partition and the outbreak of the war in 1969, the only
legal measure that Britain imposed in the face of Loyalist opposition
was the National Assistance Act of 1948, which established the
framework for the welfare state. It was passed, despite vehement
opposition from Unionist MPs, because Westminster saw it as a good
way of keeping the lid on unrest. The Act did little to disturb existing
political relations in the Six Counties. Indeed, the growth of the
welfare state turned out to be useful in providing jobs and services to
keep Loyalist workers in line.

Legal reforms in Britain which implied a challenge to Loyalist
ideology have largely been kept out of Northern Ireland. Most of
these measures were introduced from the late sixties up to the mid-
seventies, when the last benefits of the post-war boom allowed the
state to implement a few reforms. Reforms concerning the legal
position of women and the family met the fiercest Loyalist opposition.

The Loyalist commitment to the Protestant way of life elevates
religion to a state philosophy. The cross-class alliance on which
Loyalist control rests requires continuous vigilance over morality,
the celebration of the family unit and the assertion of the inferior role
of women in society. One of the most important British laws kept out
of Northern Ireland by Loyalism is the 1967 Abortion Act. In Britain
the main aim of this legislation was to prevent the few thousand
women the state considered incapable of motherhood from having

children. In Northern Ireland even that was far too much. The illegality of abortion has a vital disciplining role to play, uniting the Loyalist community around an issue that cuts across diverging class interests.

The 1975 Children's Act proposed to establish a comprehensive adoption service. This too was repugnant to Loyalism: even the illegitimate off-spring of Protestants had to be guaranteed a Protestant upbringing. The Act has never reached the statute books in the Six Counties. Other reforms of the late sixties and seventies have reached the Six Counties, but usually they have appeared late and often diluted or distorted in form. Their eventual introduction coincided with Britain's efforts to 'normalise' the Six Counties, efforts which included bringing the law into line with the rest of the 'United Kingdom' and the EEC.

The 1969 Divorce Reform Act arrived in the Six Counties in 1978, without the original provision for postal divorces. The 1976 Domestic Violence and Matrimonial Proceedings Act had to wait until 1980 to become the Domestic Proceedings Order in the Six Counties. In Britain the Act provided for the exclusion of a violent husband or male cohabitee from their home. Because God-fearing Protestants do not cohabit, Loyalists modified the law to give legal protection only to legally married women.

The most bitter struggle of all concerned the 1967 Sexual Offences Act, which supposedly legalised homosexuality for consenting male adults. Attempts to introduce the Act into Northern Ireland met with Ian Paisley's 'Save Ulster from Sodomy' campaign. The Act was finally brought in as the Homosexual Offences (Northern Ireland) Order in October 1982—15 years after its introduction in Britain. Paisley's reaction to this setback summed up the Loyalist attitude to liberal legislation. Claiming—probably correctly—that 23 of the 26 councils in the Six Counties opposed the Order, he said that the move would 'attack the family', which was the 'cement of society....Those of us who believe in the moral power of the home must voice their opposition' (*The Voice of Ulster,* November 1982).

The Six Counties has rejected laws which might benefit workers—particularly nationalist workers—to the detriment of Loyalist landlords or local councils. The 1974 Rent Act, which granted tenants some powers to prevent rent rises, and the 1977 Homeless Persons Act, which gave local authorities a legal duty to provide for the homeless, are two examples of this.

The fact that the Loyalists have resisted legal reform does not mean that Westminster has a progressive role to play in Ireland. It indicates only that imperialist domination stirs up the most reactionary prejudices. British rule in Northern Ireland encourages the degrading ideology of Loyalism and its ritual displays of allegiance to the British Crown to pull together a carefully contrived majority in favour of the British connection. A legal apparatus which spews bigotry and prejudice from every courtroom in the Six Counties under the seal of the British monarch is a true monument to Britain's 'progressive' influence in Northern Ireland.

Another name for oppression

The legal system of the Six Counties has been specially refined to institutionalise oppression and maintain Loyalist privilege. Some law—'emergency' or otherwise—is always at hand to legitimise the repression of nationalists. Through the years after partition, the 1922 Special Powers Act provided the legal mechanism for terrorising opponents of the new state. The Act was originally introduced as an emergency measure to deal with the republican movement in the early twenties. Like all such laws in Ireland, it remained in force long after the immediate crisis had passed. It was renewed annually until 1928; then it was renewed for five years. It was made permanent in 1933, and remained on the statute books for another 40 years.

The Special Powers Act gave Stormont unlimited powers. It allowed for arrest without warrant, internment without trial, execution, the prohibition of inquests into the cause of death, flogging, the destruction of buildings, the requisitioning of land and property, and the banning of meetings, organisations and publications. The minister of home affairs was given the authority to delegate the powers of the Act to anybody he felt needed them. A catch-all provision empowered him to legislate against anything not specifically dealt with but 'calculated to be prejudicial' to the stability of Northern Ireland. Anything the Loyalists needed to contain nationalist opposition could be encompassed by the Act.

Internment hung over the nationalists as a constant threat. It was in force between 1922 and 1924, in 1925, and from 1938 to 1946 during the republican campaign in the Second World War. Internment was reintroduced during the IRA's Border campaign between 1956 and 1961, and again from 1971 to 1975. The Special Powers Act was replaced by the Emergency Provisions Act in 1973. The new Act was simply a refinement of its predecessor, providing a framework for successive British governments to manipulate Northern Ireland law.

The law is flexible enough to deal with all the changing forms of nationalist struggle. In 1933, for example, more than 40 republican activists were detained. Though these individuals were considered a threat, the general level of unrest was not sufficient to justify the introduction of internment. Using the Special Powers Act 'catch-all' clause, the minister of home affairs created an offence for them: that of refusing to answer incriminating questions before a magistrates court. The detained republicans were all found guilty and sent to prison for breaking a law introduced after their arrest.

The law was again modified in 1971, when, after 20 000 nationalists began a rent and rate strike in protest against internment, Stormont rushed through the Payment of Debts Act. The Act allowed for rent and rate charges to be deducted directly from supplementary benefits. It was later extended to cover electricity and gas charges, and to allow for the removal of money directly from public sector workers' wages. Since most Catholics in the Six Counties are either on the dole or working for the state, the Act was on target.

In another move to keep the law in line with the needs of British imperialism, a 1981 Order barred prisoners from standing in elections. This was designed to prevent any repeat of the embarrassment Britain suffered when Bobby Sands was elected to Westminster. In addition, following Sinn Fein's success at the polls in the May 1985 local elections, Tom King called for the introduction of a 'peace oath', to force election candidates to 'renounce violence', as well as a new rule to extend the period of disqualification from office for candidates with a criminal record from 15 to 20 years.

Until the Irish War broke out in 1969, Stormont was left to its own devices in imposing law and order. In the very year the troops invaded, Britain's house of lords made it clear that it was up to the Loyalists to decide what was 'subversive'. After Britain imposed direct rule in 1972, however, the old Loyalist legal machinery was revamped. It was too crude and too closely associated with 50 years of discrimination. To find an alternative, the British appointed Lord Diplock to head a commission in 1972.

Concentration camp law

Diplock's brief was to come up with 'arrangements for the administration of justice in Northern Ireland...otherwise than by internment by the executive' (Haldane Society, *Diplock and the Assault on Civil Liberties,* 1980). Diplock's recommendations became the 1973 Emergency Provisions Act, which has been renewed every six months ever since. It was refined and extended further in 1978.

The Emergency Provisions Act became central to the strategy of Ulsterisation. Under the Act, internment without trial was still possible but largely unnecessary. Diplock's emphasis was on making the mass imprisonment of republicans respectable by maximising the number of convictions gained in the courts. To assist this, the new Act established what became notorious as 'conveyor-belt' justice.

Although political status has been officially abolished, the Emergency Provisions Act allows for the special treatment of 'scheduled offenders'—that is, republican political prisoners. The conveyor belt begins with the detention of these offenders by the police or the Army. The Act allows for an initial detention period of 72 hours. To justify such treatment it is only necessary to have a 'suspicion' that the detainee is involved in a scheduled offence. Unlike other emergency legislation—such as the Prevention of Terrorism Act—the Emergency Provisions Act does not stipulate that the suspicion should be 'reasonable'.

Thousands of detainees have been subjected to brutal interrogation under Diplock. The object is often solely to extract information: often, no charges are brought. The Bennett Commission revealed in 1979 that only 33.5 per cent of the 2814 people detained between September 1977 and September 1978 were charged. By 1980, while the detentions had increased to 3868, the percentage charged had dropped to just 8.6 per cent (*Hansard,* December 1980). For detainees singled out for the conveyor belt, interrogations are geared toward obtaining confessions.

The Emergency Provisions Act established no-jury courts—known as Diplock courts after their inventor. These have become little more than rubber stamps for police 'evidence'. A written confession virtually guarantees conviction by the single judges who preside over these courts. In discussions around the Anglo-Irish deal, the Dublin government and other bodies lobbied for the replacement of the Diplock system by three sitting judges. King categorically rejected this in December 1986, arguing that the Diplock procedures had 'maintained successfully the highest standards of justice'. Most Irish nationalists cannot see the advantage in getting three doses of anti-nationalist bigotry instead of one.

Extracting confessions has become the RUC's top priority. The judiciary is not too concerned about the methods it uses to get them. The Diplock report found that the rules regarding the way statements were obtained were 'hampering the cause of justice in the

● *The conveyor belt*

Arrest:	A nationalist is detained for 72 hours on 'suspicion' of terrorism.
Interrogation:	Police terrorise their chosen victim into 'confessing'.
Trial:	A single Loyalist official acts as judge and jury and doles out a heavy sentence on the strength of the 'confession'.
Jail:	The nationalist is sent to British concentration camps where prisoners are outnumbered three to one by brutal wardens and subjected to beatings, harassment and strip-searches.

case of terrorist crimes' (paragraph 87). The Emergency Provisions Act implicitly accepts the need for torturing detainees to get confessions: psychological torture was explicitly condoned by Diplock. The RUC made the few adjustments necessary to get away with physical torture. The only barriers to this were the Judges Rules, the guidelines for the treatment of prisoners during 'interviews'.

During his time as boss of the RUC, Kenneth Newman established two categories of questioning. There were 'interviews', during which the Judges Rules would apply, and 'interrogations', during which they would not. In interrogation centres such as Castlereagh, opened in 1977, prisoners suffered beatings, electric shock treatment and sensory deprivation. Some were put to death in the drive to force them to sign pre-written confessions. Not surprisingly, many confessed and subsequent conviction rates were high.

Once convicted, sentences are heavy. Immediately after the implementation of the Emergency Provisions Act, the number of prisoners serving more than eight years in prison rose dramatically. Harsh sentencing emphasises the seriousness of the 'crimes', and is intended to act as a deterrent. It has also allowed the state to appear more liberal by granting up to 50 per cent remission in the Six Counties compared with 33 per cent in Britain. Despite this, prisoners in the Six Counties serve longer sentences on average than those in Britain.

Supergrasses and showtrials

Once condemned by international courts for its methods of extracting confessions, Britain claimed to have shut down its torture centres. But the RUC still does as it likes behind closed doors. Patricia Moore, a 23-year old nationalist from Derry, walked free from court in October 1986 after a year on remand, charged with IRA membership and bombing offences on the uncorroborated word of police informer Angela Whoriskey. During her detention at the pleasure of the Crown, Moore went through the ritual degradation that awaits every republican suspect. She was threatened with being shot by the SAS and was constantly strip-searched, even when she was too ill to stand. When she underwent an operation for a ruptured ovarian cyst, her jailers gave her a 15-minute sit down in the hospital recovery room before rushing her back to jail. The British authorities freed Moore after they finally had to admit that they could no longer bully Whoriskey, a vulnerable single parent and psychiatric patient, into shape as a credible witness.

In the early eighties the authorities supplemented traditional brutality against republicans with a new tactic: supergrasses. (The term originated from the use of inside informers against armed robbery gangs in London in the seventies, a practice which British courts subsequently ruled out of order as unreliable and disreputable.) At least in the short term, supergrasses proved highly effective in putting nationalists behind bars.

In November 1981 the RUC produced its first supergrass—former Belfast IRA man Christopher Black. In return for immunity from prosecution, a new life abroad and permanent protection at British expense, Black told all about his past in the IRA and informed on his former comrades. The showtrial of the 33 men and five women charged on Black's word began in Belfast Crown court on 2 December 1982 and ended, 117 days later, with 35 convictions and sentences totalling more than 4000 years. The Black case was a model supergrass showtrial. There was the large-scale round-up of named suspects, the prolonged periods in custody awaiting trial, the showtrial with a few dozen defendants in the dock, the summary convictions based solely on the informant's evidence, lengthy sentences imposed by a Diplock judge. However, the final outcome of the trial also took a standard form. In July 1986 appeal courts quashed the convictions against 18 of the 22 defendants who appealed. But by the time the appeal began, 13 of the 22 had already served their sentence: indeed five of those who went free had already served the equivalent of a 10-year sentence by the time they were released.

It is more than five years since the first supergrass caused a media sensation. More than two dozen supergrasses and 600 arrests later, the showtrial system seems to have run out of steam. But it has been a big success story for the British state. At the height of the supergrass scare, it only took a whisper to send the security forces on sweeping raids in nationalist areas. Every nationalist was a suspect. Graffiti on a Derry wall summed it up: 'I knew Raymond Gilmour—thank fuck he didn't know me.' The system soon earned the name 'internment on remand'. The rising scale of arrests under Special Powers legislation (and particularly under the section of the Prevention of Terrorism Act which allows 'suspects' to be held for seven days) is testimony to the savage sweep of the supergrass system. Nearly 500 people were detained under the PTA in 1981, 828 in 1982, and 1175 in 1983. In previous years PTA detentions had never exceeded 250.

The RUC managed to imprison hundeds of people for periods ranging from months to years without even the formality of a trial.

Following a long history of harassment by the RUC, Kevin Mulgrew was one of the defendants convicted on the word of IRA informer Christopher Black in August 1983.

●

The story of Kevin Mulgrew

October 1972: Arrested and charged with 'attempted membership' of the IRA. Charge dismissed.

October 1976: Arrested and held for seven days in Castlereagh. Required hospital treatment. Later received compensation for injuries inflicted while in custody. Charged with causing an explosion and held for five months in custody before being released without explanation in February 1977.

October 1979: Arrested on the word of Stephen McWilliams (an informer in the pay of the British Army). Held in custody for seven months before original charge was dropped for lack of evidence. Kept in custody on a further charge of 'possession' which was finally heard before Judge Kelly in October 1980. Kelly acquitted Mulgrew but implied that he was 'lucky to get off'. He got no apology for the 13 months he spent on remand.

November 1981: Arrested on the word of Christopher Black. Held in custody until the end of the trial in August 1983. Sentenced to life imprisonment solely on Black's word. By the time Mulgrew's appeal was heard he had served the equivalent of a 14-year sentence.

In a letter to the Stop the Showtrials Committee in 1983, Mulgrew told how British laws had taken away his life:

'I am 28 years old. I have no previous convictions. I have been sentenced to life imprisonment on the uncorroborated word of a paid perjuror, Christopher Black. This is just another method used by the government to "put people away"—it should be opposed as vehemently as internment.'

Kevin Mulgrew was freed on appeal in July 1986.

Prisoners on remand were subjected to physical and psychological abuse. Women remand prisoners were forced to submit to humiliating strip-searches in Armagh jail, which itself became notorious for its barbarous techniques. Republican women prisoners have now been moved to the modern Maghaberry prison, but the strip-searches have moved with them. Two defendants in the Black case were strip-searched 120 times each.

The showtrials had an extraordinary impact. They removed many republican activists from the streets and spread an insidious suspicion of informers through the ranks of the republican movement. While the system is on its last legs, scores of nationalists are still suffering under the scourge of the supergrass.

To give the showtrial system an air of even-handedness, Britain used supergrasses to detain Loyalist paramilitaries as well as republican suspects. But this ploy was little more than a public relations exercise. In April 1983 the first trial ended, when 14 Loyalists were jailed on the word of Ulster Volunteer Force informer Joseph Bennett. In December 1984 all were freed on appeal. Over the next three months more than 20 Loyalists were released from prison as UVF supergrasses James Crockard and John Gibson retracted their evidence. By mid-1985 not a single Loyalist was serving a prison sentence as a result of a supergrass.

The collapse of the Loyalist cases underlined some of the problems of the supergrass system for the British authorities. Crockard withdrew his evidence after the UVF had followed his family to the 'safe house' in Carlisle in which his paymasters had installed him. Despite the fact that the British government admitted to running a supergrass slush fund worth £1.3 million, supergrasses and their minders lived in constant fear of retribution.

The role of supergrasses as informers and traitors made them unstable and unreliable. In October 1983, Dungannon republican Patrick McGurk retracted his evidence, making the authorities release seven alleged IRA men. In the Kevin McGrady case, which followed Bennett and Black, Lord Chief Justice Lowry threw out most of the major charges based on McGrady's allegations, and acquitted three defendants. He then went on to convict three other defendants (including leading Sinn Fein member Jim Gibney) on the same evidence he had previously dismissed as 'contradictory, bizarre and incredible'. The remaining four defendants were convicted on this evidence, plus 'statements' made during interrogation. Two other republican supergrasses—Jackie Grimley and Raymond Gilmour—provided evidence that was so contentious that even

Northern Ireland's judges had to throw their cases out. At the end of 1984, when Lowry freed on appeal the 12 men earlier convicted on the word of Bennett, he stated, in defence of the original prosecution, that 'even the uncorroborated evidence of an accomplice of bad character could be accepted by the courts'—a fact that by this time the nationalist community was well aware of. By 1985 the blatant corruption of justice surrounding the supergrass system was the cause of growing embarrassment to the British government.

After Jackie Grimley was discredited as an inveterate liar with chronic psychiatric problems, the RUC's enthusiasm for supergrasses cooled. Revelations that the RUC had advance knowledge and complicity in republican operations which endangered the security forces caused a furore. The RUC brought forward only two more supergrasses in the following 18 months, both of whom withdrew their evidence within weeks. After four years it seemed like the supergrass system was on its way out. Of 25 supergrasses, 15 had retracted, and of 450 people detained, 260 had won release. In October 1986 the director of public prosecutions dropped the charges against two people in the Angela Whoriskey case. In December 1986 24 Belfast men convicted on the word of Inla supergrass Harry Kirkpatrick were freed after their convictions were quashed by the court of appeal.

The storm of criticism roused by supergrasses and shoot-to-kill squads in the early eighties reflected Britain's increasing difficulties in disguising the Irish War as a law and order problem. The mask of legality frequently slipped to reveal the brutal face of British terror. In May 1984, 21 of the defendants in the Kirkpatrick showtrial were injured when the RUC baton-charged them in the dock. Three months later the coroner for Armagh resigned rather than hold an inquest into the deaths of republicans Seamus Grew and Roddy Carroll, shot by the RUC in November 1982. The coroner said that he could not reconcile the real circumstances of the slaughter with the RUC version, accepted by the court which acquitted police of the murders in April 1984.

To shore up British law and order in Ireland, the government appointed the Right Honourable Sir George Baker OBE to conduct a review of the Emergency Provisions Act. Baker's April 1984 report recommended that no major changes were required in the conduct of the supergrass trials, and that there was 'no objection to the principle of accomplice evidence'. But the report proposed that the name of the law be changed to the 'Protection of the People's Act', because the label 'Emergency Provisions' gave the game away:

Supergrass victim speaks out

In December 1986 Terry Robson, a three-time victim of the supergrass showtrials, flew over from Derry to speak to an Irish Freedom Movement rally in London and to expose the truth about British justice in Northern Ireland.

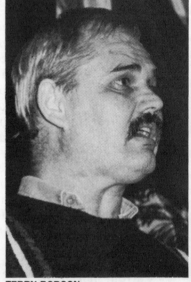

'I was first arrested in 1970, charged with incitement to riot and sentenced to six months. Since then I've been incarcerated 10 times in Castlereagh and Gough barracks. I've received 10 seven-day orders, and I can't count the number of three-day orders—maybe 30 or 40. When they came for me in February 1982 I thought it was just another seven-day order. But I was held for two years and 10 months on the evidence of paid perjurors.

'There were 200 people on our wing of Crumlin Road jail, and 180 of them were held under supergrass evidence. They were the middle leadership of the republican movement.

TERRY ROBSON

'The security forces come into your house at 5am, turn it over, get the kids out of bed, and take you out. For several years we woke up automatically at 5am, waiting for them to arrive. It was only when it got light and people started moving around that we felt safe enough to go back to sleep for a while.

'You get used to it—like you get used to staying in a cell by yourself. I spent nearly three years in solitary confinement. You learn to cope with the isolation. The technique is based on the recognition that it's a common struggle. When we had the opportunity, we would engage in debates, shouting through the doors, trying to keep people aware. Then we had the antagonism of the screws and the RUC. It kept our blood boiling and our minds active. It was much more difficult for our wives and friends, who had to go back home, not knowing how to deal with a situation that was beyond their control.'

AN UNDEFEATED ARMY: IRA SOLDIERS ON PARADE

'GET OUT OF OUR GARDEN, AND OUR COUNTRY'

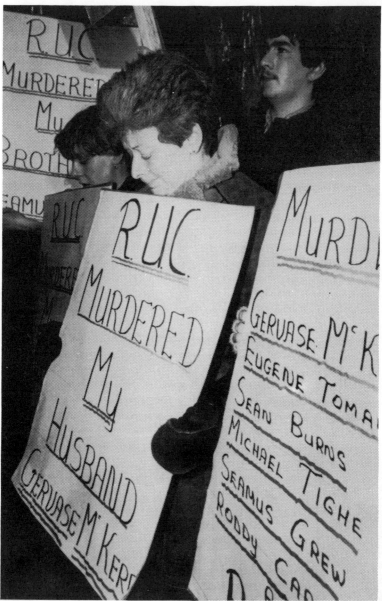

ELEANOR McKERR, WIFE OF ARMAGH IRA LEADER GERVAIS McKERR WHO WAS SHOT DEAD BY A CRACK RUC SHOOT-TO-KILL SQUAD IN NOVEMBER 1982, ON A PROTEST IN JANUARY 1983

BLACK FLAGS AT HALF-MAST IN DERRY AFTER THE SAS SHOT DEAD EIGHT IRA
VOLUNTEERS AT LOUGHGALL, COUNTY ARMAGH, MAY 1987

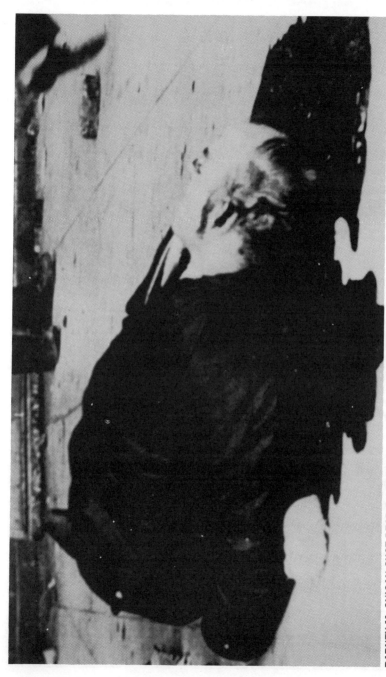

BARNEY McGUIGAN SHOT DEAD BY BRITISH PARATROOPERS IN DERRY, BLOODY SUNDAY, 30 JANUARY 1972

THOUSANDS FOLLOWED IRA VOLUNTEER PATRICK KELLY'S COFFIN THROUGH DUNGANNON, AFTER HE WAS SHOT DEAD BY THE SAS AT LOUGHGALL

'To many outside Northern Ireland the title conveys nothing, or worse it conveys a false impression of widespread civil strife or uprisings against the government involving large sections of the population.' (*Review of the Operation of the Northern Ireland Emergency Provisions Act 1978*)

Baker's plans revealed the aim of the law in Northern Ireland: to channel the Irish War into the courts and so uphold the sanctity of British rule. In December 1986 a Bill, based on Baker's report and amending the 1978 Emergency Provisions Act, had its second reading in the house of commons. In the spirit of duplicity that Baker intended, the new provisions have been presented as a move to protect the rights of people suspected or accused of 'terrorist' offences. In reality, they strengthen the authorities as against the nationalist community. The Baker Bill maintains the Diplock system of no-jury courts and its powers. It proposes to make the security forces prove 'reasonable grounds of suspicion' before detaining people without charge. But, as every British soldier, Loyalist policeman and Lord Justice knows, being an Irish nationalist is 'reasonable' enough grounds for arrest—or worse—in occupied Ireland.

In 1979 Labour's Northern Ireland secretary Roy Mason summed up on the 'law' in Northern Ireland today:

'All Northern Ireland courts and the Northern Ireland judiciary are completely independent of government control...and they are an integral part of the legal system in the UK. The courts play a fundamental role in the protection of human rights in Northern Ireland....No one is imprisoned for his political beliefs, and there are no political prisoners in Northern Ireland.' (Roy Mason, *Protecting Human Rights in Northern Ireland*)

The judiciary which Mason is at pains to distance from politics has traditionally been monopolised by reactionary Loyalist politicians. A 1971 study revealed that of the 20 judges appointed to the high court since partition, 15 had been influential members of the Unionist Party. Such good men and true have a clear view of what British justice means. In April 1984 Mr Justice MacDonald presided over the trial of RUC undercover officer John Robinson, who was involved in the shoot-to-kill deaths of Seamus Grew and Roddy Carroll in Armagh City in 1982. MacDonald acquitted Robinson and praised him for his 'sharp shooting'. The only justice Britain can offer the Irish is the justice of the executioner.

The law is the law even if it is deployed to frame, maim, torture and murder. Anyone who challenges this judicial terror is labelled a

● *The justice of the executioner*

On 11 November 1982 Gervais McKerr was driving through Lurgan, County Armagh, with Eugene Toman and Sean Burns. An RUC patrol opened fire on his car, killing all its occupants. Eugene Toman was half out of the passenger door when he was killed. All three men were unarmed.

The RUC issued a statement claiming that the car accelerated through a check-point, that the police opened fire, that the car careered off the road and that, when officers went to examine it, the occupants were all dead. Later police claimed that shots were fired from the car.

Local people said that there was no road-block and that the car was found 300 yards from the alleged check-point. They emphasised that some 40 bullet holes were found in and around the driver's door. McKerr had suffered devastating injuries, which would have made it impossible for him to drive 300 yards along the winding road past the supposed check-point. All the signs pointed to an ambush and assassination.

Almost a year after the killings, three RUC officers were charged with the murder of Eugene Toman. There was no charge in relation to either McKerr or Burns. The trial took place in a Diplock court before Lord Justice Gibson in June 1984. An RUC chief told the court that the three men were part of the undercover E4A surveillance unit, trained by the SAS in 'firepower, speed and aggression'. The three officers were not even called to give evidence. At the close of the prosecution case, Gibson made clear his grounds for acquitting all three men:

'I wish to make it clear that having heard the Crown case I regard each of the accused as absolutely blameless in this matter. That finding should be put on record along with my own commendation for their courage and determination in bringing the three deceased men to justice, in this case, the final court of justice.

'The case is going to have a more widespread effect among other members of the security forces generally. When a policeman or soldier is ordered to arrest a dangerous criminal and on the basis of that order to bring him back dead or alive, how is he to consider his conduct now?'

The verdict gave the go-ahead for more shoot-to-kill murders.

criminal. Bobby Sands, the freedom fighter, was vilified as a criminal and forced to die by the upholders of the law. In a situation where every form of repression can be justified by the state and its judiciary, thousands of Irish men or women are proud to be law-breakers, and rightly so.

6. War on the home front

In October 1986, two years after the Brighton bomb, the Tories did their best to create a bomb scare at the party conference in Bournemouth. First there were front-page stories about the 'gunman' caught at Thatcher's hotel. He turned out to be a friend of the chef, returning his mate's broken starting pistol. Then there was the man arrested under the PTA for lurking outside the conference centre with wires and batteries. He turned out to be the loon who holds one-man anti-smoking protests at all party conferences: the electrical gear was for lighting his signs at night, but the police still threatened to blow up his pushbike. The police, indeed, did manage to blow up a number of other harmless objects in Bournemouth, even blasting to bits a brand-new Jaguar because it had a tell-tale copy of the *Irish Times* on the back seat. They and their Tory allies in government and in the media will go to any lengths to invent a 'terrorist threat' and so bolster support for their war against the Irish people.

The British establishment fights the Irish War on two fronts—in Ireland and in Britain. To strengthen its hand in Ireland, the British state needs to ensure a solid base of support at home. A consensus of approval for government policy is essential if the armed forces are to have a free hand to crush resistance. Here it must be noted that the British ruling class has been strikingly successful. While criminalisation has failed in Northern Ireland, it continues to influence public opinion in Britain.

Since 1969, the British authorities have been trying to win a war in Ireland while pretending they are not even fighting one. They have carefully manipulated the media presentation of the war. Wide endorsement for repression has created an atmosphere in which anti-Irish propaganda finds a ready audience. Given that even the left wing of the Labour Party regards the republican movement as a terrorist conspiracy, the authorities' big hype about IRA 'criminals' has few critics in Britain.

Because the stakes in the Irish War are so high, the ruling class has left nothing to chance. In 1969 the British propaganda machine was unprepared for the outbreak of war, with the result that early media coverage revealed the brutality of the British and Loyalist forces too vividly for establishment tastes. Thus in April 1971, the ministry of defence took over responsibility for publicity in Northern Ireland. Ministry officials soon announced that they intended to vet journalists before granting access to military briefings. The Army established a monopoly over war news. Journalists would simply wait for the military to tell them what was happening. The media dutifully portrayed the soldiers as 'peace-keepers' and the freedom fighters as 'terrorists'. Most journalists spent more time in the bar of the Hotel Europa than on the streets of Belfast. The republican movement expressed its opinion of the media by turning the Europa into Europe's most bombed building.

British news coverage of the Irish War supports the British establishment. The republican movement's aims and activities are mercilessly caricatured and distorted. On the other hand, Army and Loyalist raids and atrocities are presented neutrally and often condoned. Since Ulsterisation, there has been a deliberate policy to cut down on news about the war and ignore many of the activities of the resistance movement. Even liberal criticism of official policy receives short shrift.

Television documentaries have been the hardest hit. The Prevention of Terrorism Act has made it illegal to interview members of the IRA. But the PTA is scarcely necessary, since all British television channels have been only too ready to impose self-censorship.

When the Army tightened up on media coverage in 1971, the heads of both television networks declared their willingness to cooperate. Lord Hill of the BBC assured the government that 'between the British Army and the gunmen, the BBC is not and cannot be neutral.' Lord Aylestone of the ITA was even more direct. 'As far as I'm concerned,' he announced, 'Britain is at war with the IRA in Ulster and the IRA will get no more coverage than the Nazis would have done in the last war' (L Curtis, *Ireland: The Propaganda War*). The broadcasting schedules of the last 16 years are littered with last-minute replacements of advertised programmes on Northern Ireland.

In July 1985 censorship reached new levels when the government itself intervened to force the BBC to drop the now famous documentary *At the Edge of the Union*—part of its *Real Lives* series. Thatcher called for voluntary self-censorship by journalists, to 'deprive terrorists of the oxygen of publicity'. The banned programme was a day-in-the-life study of two members of the Ulster assembly from Derry. It contrasted Martin McGuinness of Sinn Fein, a leading supporter of the IRA's fight against British rule in Ireland, with Gregory Campbell of the Democratic Unionist Party, a virulent opponent of the IRA and upholder of the Union with Britain. The programme was unacceptable to the British authorities because it would have undermined the public image of people like Martin McGuinness as crazed killers—an image which British governments have spent the last 18 years perfecting.

The BBC was forced to agree with the Tories that this was not the sort of propaganda they should be producing on Northern Ireland. Lady Faulkner, the retiring BBC governor for 'the province', said that she was appalled that the film should portray McGuinness as 'domesticated, sanitised and a rather likeable sort of chap'. She said the ban had been imposed because the programme gave 'a distorted view' of what republicans were like. She meant that it had gone too far in exposing the 'distorted view' of Irish freedom fighters popularised by the British government.

The ban caused a constitutional crisis at the BBC and provoked the one-day strike which stopped almost all news broadcasts and put the BBC world service off the air for the first time. The decision of the BBC board of governors to ditch the programme and so go along with the home secretary of the day, Leon Brittan, brought howls of protest from BBC management, broadcasting unions and the Labour Party. But while they disagreed with the ban, they all agreed

IRISH FREEDOM MOVEMENT SUPPORTERS PROTEST AT BBC CENSORSHIP ON IRELAND

with Brittan on the need to keep the message of Irish freedom out of British politics. Labour leader Neil Kinnock wrote to Thatcher objecting to the government's interference in BBC affairs. But he added an obligatory patriotic rider to his note: 'Obviously there can be no reasonable person among those who have voiced criticism of these actions who has anything but loathing for terrorism and determination to defeat violence.' As a consequence the Tories won the key debate on the programme.

The *Real Lives* documentary was finally televised after substantial footage of IRA violence had been added to emphasise McGuinness' supposed 'terrorist' connections. But it was not to be the last ban at the BBC. In February 1987 a new BBC drama series, scheduled to start on 6 March, was referred back to senior management for 'editing' after the BBC controller of programmes in the North, James Hawthorne, complained that it was 'not close enough to reality' and showed the IRA in too sympathetic a manner to be acceptable. The British authorities have always tailored the 'reality' of its war in Ireland before issuing it for mass consumption.

Judicial cover-ups

Britain's attempts to whitewash its role in Ireland go far beyond state interference in the media. Successive governments have sponsored investigations under eminent judges. The aim has been to show that they were seriously concerned about the problems of Northern Ireland and were earnestly seeking alternative solutions.

The earliest reports (Hunt, Scarman) made criticisms of the RUC's sectarianism during the 1968 and 1969 disturbances. Here the state presented itself as a neutral agency standing above the conflict. Later reports dealing with the activities of the Army and police also made mild criticisms, but always contained a 'let-out' clause for British policy. Sir Edward Compton's 1971 investigation into the treatment of internees concluded that they had not been tortured. Torture, according to Sir Edward, had to be enjoyed by its perpetrators. The troops and RUC men he had interviewed had not enjoyed beating up nationalists, and were therefore innocent of torture.

Lord Widgery's report on Bloody Sunday in 1972 admitted that the 14 dead Catholics had been unarmed and innocent. For Widgery, however, this indicated only that the Army had been 'mistaken' in shooting them. There was no question of murder. More recently, Britain has been found guilty of torture by the European Court of Human Rights. But the liberal political prisoners organisation

Amnesty International came to the rescue. Amnesty's 1978 report on the treatment of detainees in Castlereagh interrogation centre distinguished between 'maltreatment' and 'torture'. The RUC had maltreated its prisoners but never tortured them. This revelation came, no doubt, as a relief to those at the wrong end of the 'maltreaters'.

When the RUC attacked a Belfast anti-internment rally in front of millions of British television viewers in August 1984, Lord Hunt called for a repeat of his 1969 inquiry into the police. He claimed that the RUC would 'come out very well' and that the inquiry would remove 'the general kind of prejudice against the police' which could otherwise spread.

Following an outcry about assassination squads in Armagh in 1982, RUC chief constable John Hermon called in the deputy chief constable of Greater Manchester, John Stalker, to head an investigation into the shoot-to-kill claims. On 11 November 1982 a crack RUC squad pumped 109 bullets into IRA volunteers Gervais McKerr, Eugene Toman and Sean Burns in a pre-planned ambush in Armagh. On 24 November they shot dead 17-year old Michael Tighe and maimed his friend Martin McCauley, who had the misfortune to chance upon a cache of ancient rifles at a farmhouse near Lurgan. On 12 December the squad ambushed and shot to pieces republicans Roddy Carroll and Seamus Grew at Mullacreevie estate outside Armagh City.

None of the shoot-to-kill victims were armed. After the killings came the reports, the inquiries and the cover-up. The British authorities went to great lengths to conceal the truth. First, the RUC issued lying statements about what happened. Then four of the RUC killers were charged with murder, and let off after being complimented from the bench for their marksmanship. But when these court cases revealed the extent of illegal and undercover RUC activities, the authorities thought it best to bring in an outside officer—Stalker—to run a mock investigation. Stalker's inquiry was intended to bolster the public image of the police, and to delay inquests into the deaths. But when his report was completed in 1986, its conclusions included some embarrassing observations on how the RUC killing machine operates. The British government agreed with the RUC that something had to be done to blacken his name and undermine the inquiry. Stalker was pushed off the job, suspended from the Manchester force after allegations of corruption and, finally, was edged out of the police force altogether.

The British media moaned about Stalker being 'the victim of a conspiracy'. Yet nobody made the most obvious point about the 1982 shootings: the Irish people are the victims of a dirty colonial war being waged by the British security forces. Given the scandal that surrounded the silencing of Stalker the scene is set for a few token prosecutions, but the RUC officers responsible have already been acquitted of murder charges in no-jury courts.

The British establishment has used black propaganda against republicans for 150 years. Political commentators and cartoonists have been given free rein to attribute bestial, sub-human characteristics to those who challenge British rule. In 1985 *Sunday Express* editor Sir John Junor enquired of his readers 'Wouldn't you rather admit to being a pig than Irish?' It is standard imperialist practice to denigrate oppressed peoples around the world. But the black propaganda aimed against the republican movement is far more sinister than Jak's vicious cartoons in London's *Standard.*

In their attempts to undermine the resolve of the nationalist community, soldiers posing as IRA volunteers have shot innocent Catholics at random. Undercover units have planted bombs, moved republican explosives to areas where they will cause most damage, and deliberately ignored IRA warnings that bombs would be going off. Many civilians have died as a result of these attempts to portray republicans as heartless killers and thus break nationalist support for the armed struggle.

The British state and its allies have been careful to suppress any propaganda that runs counter to their cause. Irish solidarity demonstrations are banned from London's Trafalgar Square. The Trades Union Congress has made a special contribution to British rule in Ireland: it has clamped down on several trades councils for holding discussions in opposition to the official pro-government line on Ireland. In February 1983, the TUC intervened to stop a showing of an Irish Freedom Movement video entitled *No British Solution.*

The Prevention of Terrorism Act

The Prevention of Terrorism (Temporary Provisions) Act was introduced in 1974 and amended and extended in 1976. It was further refined and institutionalised in March 1984. The Act allows for the proscription of 'terrorist' organisations, and for the detention and exclusion without charge of individuals suspected of 'terrorism'. Up to the end of 1986, 6400 people had been detained under the Act. Only 181 of these detainees—two and a half per cent—were charged with an offence under the PTA.

The PTA was never meant to convict IRA bombers—existing criminal law is more than adequate for this task. The role of the PTA is to criminalise the republican movement and its supporters, and to prevent the emergence of an anti-imperialist movement in England, Scotland and Wales. Convictions are irrelevant. What matters is the creation of a climate of fear—especially inside the Irish community in Britain.

In 1974 Labour home secretary Roy Jenkins, now a leading member of the Social Democratic Party, explained why his government introduced the PTA. Labour's object was 'to stem the infection from Ireland'. The government wanted 'to keep people out, to send people back if they in any way encourage terrorist activity'. The pretext for the introduction of the PTA was provided by the Birmingham pub bombings.

On Thursday 21 November 1974 the Mulberry Bush and the Tavern in the Town pubs in Birmingham city centre were wrecked by bombs. The explosions killed 21 people and maimed and injured more than 100 others. Television reports broadcast the carnage into every home in the country. The public outcry over the bombings was quickly matched by the Labour government. Eight days later the PTA was law. It passed through parliament without even the formality of a vote. All political parties were unanimous in their approval for what Jenkins himself described as 'a draconian measure'.

Police chiefs objected. For them, such extraordinary powers of detention, and of deportation without trial, were an unnecessary embarrassment. The PTA would only make public existing Special Branch practice. Months before its introduction, Scotland Yard held Irishmen accused of bombing London's Old Bailey incommunicado and without charge for four days. But the political establishment was motivated by broader concerns than the technicalities of police work. It passed the PTA as an ideological weapon to insulate British politics from the destabilising effects of the Irish War and to silence the Irish community within Britain.

For more than 18 months before the Birmingham bombings, sporadic protests against the war rocked areas with large Irish communities such as London and the Midlands. After Bloody Sunday in 1972 thousands of Irish people protesting in London clashed violently with police in Downing Street. In the week before the pub bombings Birmingham was hit by a row over plans for a march to commemorate IRA volunteer James McDaid, killed during a bomb attack in Coventry. Labour home secretary Jenkins banned the march and bussed in 1300 extra police to contain

Birmingham's Irish community. The PTA was introduced against this background. The pub bombings provided the excuse for the PTA, but not its cause. Westminster wanted a legal measure which could help win the war on the home front by branding its opponents as criminals and so making their repression a universally desired goal.

An unnoticed exchange of government letters from 1974 illustrates the thinking behind the PTA. Three weeks before the Act became law, the ministry of defence wrote to Alford council in Lincolnshire requesting that the name of a local soldier killed in Northern Ireland be removed from the town's war memorial. The ministry argued that 'Army action in support of civil authority should not be confused with war.' It warned against the consequences of admitting that British troops were not civil peace-keepers but foreign aggressors in Ireland:

'If one war memorial is added to in this way other towns may follow the example, and in areas where there is a large Irish connection it may promote partisan action.' (*The Times,* 9 November 1974)

Whitehall's fears were never realised. The PTA has stamped on any 'partisan action' in support of Irish freedom.

The Act in detail

The Prevention of Terrorism Acts of 1974, 1976 and 1984 contain three main powers. The Act gives the state powers to ban organisations, and to deport or detain individuals.

The original PTA gave the home secretary the power to *proscribe* any organisation 'appearing' to be involved in 'terrorism'. The Act itself named the IRA as proscribed and it became an offence to raise funds, support or hold meetings for the IRA. It soon became clear that this provision was too specific. It limited the scope for harassing the Irish community in Britain to those directly supporting the republican movement.

The 1976 Act broadened the state's powers of proscription. It made it an offence for anybody to raise support for 'terrorism' in general, rather for named organisations. It is left up to the police to decide what constitutes raising support for terrorism in general. In March 1987 Bob Geldof's former manager Fachtna O Ceallaigh was convicted under the PTA for wearing a badge bearing the inscription 'Out of the ashes arose the Provisionals'. The judge declared

O Ceallaigh guilty of supporting the IRA and fined him £75. Other offences under this section can include selling anti-imperialist propaganda or collecting money for the relatives of republican prisoners. In an unprecedented step, taken in 1985, police arrested a 77-year old Irish solidarity activist from Scotland on the charge that he 'carried and displayed a document entitled "Ireland's War" in such a way and in such circumstances as to arouse reasonable apprehension that he was a member or supporter of a proscribed organisation—namely the IRA—contrary to Section 2 of the Prevention of Terrorism (Temporary Provisions) Act 1976.' This was the first time that the anti-Irish law had been used in this way. The most common 'offence', however, is merely being Irish. The scale of terror against the Irish community under this provision rose significantly after the 1976 amendment.

The second part of the PTA provides the home secretary with the powers of *exclusion*. Anybody the home secretary 'believes' to be involved in terrorism can be excluded from Great Britain to Northern Ireland. It was under this clause that a Sinn Fein delegation was prevented from visiting London in December 1982. As a sop to Loyalist complaints that Northern Ireland was being used as a dumping ground for undesirables, the 1976 amendment to the Act also provided for exclusion from Northern Ireland to Britain. This provision has never yet been used. The last thing the British authorities want is to import republicans from Northern Ireland.

The object of the Act is to allow the government to kick out Irish people at will. The threat of deportation hangs over the heads of thousands of Irish men and women in Britain and of all Irish people trying to come here. The Act is a warning to those who sympathise with Irish unity: 'When in Britain behave like a decent Briton and do not question what the British government does in Ireland.' Up to December 1986, 284 people had been deported from Britain on an exclusion order.

Under the original PTA the only safeguards against exclusion were to have lived in Britain since birth, or to have been here continuously for 20 years—not counting time spent in prison. The 1984 Act reduced the necessary time of residence from 20 years to three. This was no liberal concession, but merely a recognition of the Act's past successes. Most of the long-term Irish residents in Britain whom the state would have wanted to be rid of are either already deported, dead, imprisoned or have been terrorised into silence. The vast majority of exclusion orders in recent years have been served at ports against those travelling from Ireland. Irish political prisoners

● *The PTA—The Powers*

Proscription: The IRA and Inla are banned. It is an offence to raise support for them, dress like them, or to support 'terrorism' of any kind.

Detention: Police can lock up anybody they 'reasonably suspect' of terrorism for up to a week without charge, without access to a solicitor, and without the right to silence.

Exclusion: The authorities can kick Irish people out of Britain without any explanation, unless they have lived here continuously for three years—excluding time spent in jail.

recently released from British jails are the British 'residents' most likely to be kicked out today. Because time spent in prison does not count, the new PTA's three-year resident requirement is normally enough to send former prisoners of war straight back to Belfast.

Exclusion orders can be served without any charges being brought, without any trial or semblance of legal procedure. Such orders cannot be challenged in court. Those who are ordered out can appeal for an oral hearing of their case, but this is granted only at the home secretary's discretion. Even if they are granted a hearing, the 'defendants' have little chance of winning. They are expected to rebut the allegations made against them without even knowing what they are or from what sources they come.

Under the 1984 Act exclusion orders run out after three years. But they can be renewed indefinitely at the whim of the home office. In practice those kicked out are likely to be out for the duration of the Irish War.

Part three of the Act deals with powers of *detention*. Under the PTA, arrests can be made without a warrant. Those arrested under the Act can be held for 48 hours without charges being brought against them. When that time is up, the police can apply to the home secretary for a further five days' detention, again without making any charge. Once in custody, a prisoner can be photographed and fingerprinted without consent.

The 1976 Act added another element of legalised terror to detention. It made it an offence not to pass on any information that would help prevent 'acts of terrorism' or 'catching terrorists'. In effect, this removes the defendant's right of silence. In March 1986, at the end of an 18-day conspiracy trial, Peter Lynch was sentenced to 400 days for withholding information, but he was freed having already served his time on remand.

In addition the PTA gives the police the right to stop and search anybody they suspect of involvement with terrorism. Since 1974 more than half a million people—mainly Irish—have been stopped, searched and questioned under the PTA (West Midlands PTA Project). Any premises can be raided on the order of a police superintendent if he judges that 'immediate action is necessary in the interests of the state.' Of course many of these methods are used by the police unofficially to deal with all sorts of crimes. But the PTA legitimises them in connection with the war in Northern Ireland. The PTA gives the police official sanction to abandon all legal niceties when it comes to suppressing any support for the Irish liberation struggle.

The 1984 Act extended the powers of detention to cover 'international terrorists' operating in Britain. When Britain met with a series of violent incidents involving agents and refugees from the Middle East, the British establishment took full advantage of the episode to stir up chauvinist sentiments and to familiarise the public with paramilitary police operations. A number of Libyans were arrested under the PTA in 1984, and more were deported in the wake of the joint US/British air-strike against Libya in 1986. However, the use of the PTA against 'foreign terrorists' remains a sideshow to the main purpose of the Act. Middle East nationals shooting at each other in London's West End embassy belt are an irritant to the British authorities. But unlike the Irish liberation movement they are not a mortal threat to the British state. The PTA remains essentially anti-Irish.

What is terrorism?

The PTA defines terrorism as 'the use of violence for political ends (including) the use of violence for the purpose of putting the public or any section of the public in fear'. In practice the definition is strictly qualified. The state does not object to 'the use of violence for political ends' if the political ends benefit the British ruling class. The British Army's use of violence in maintaining British rule in Ireland is not covered by the Act. Nor, for the most part, is the Loyalist paramilitaries' use of violence to put a 'section of the public in fear' by terrorising the nationalist community. The PTA aims specifically to criminalise the anti-imperialist resistance of the republican movement.

In 1974 when the PTA proscribed the IRA, the Ulster Volunteer Force was regarded benignly as having a part to play in 'normalisation'. Hence the UVF was legalised and encouraged to take part in the 1974 elections in Northern Ireland. Inla was proscribed under the PTA in 1979 after its assassination of Tory MP Airey Neave. But the Loyalist Ulster Defence Association, responsible for many sectarian murders, remains a legal organisation.

Under the PTA 'terrorism' means anti-imperialism. Yet the prime targets of the Act are not the active service units that carry out the republican movement's acts of war on the British mainland. Throughout the bombing campaign which preceded the Birmingham explosions of 1974, the police assured the Labour government that no special legislation was required. They were making arrests under the 1833 Explosive Substances Act and the 1968 Firearms Act. The PTA plays only a subsidiary role in dealing with 'terrorists'. It often merely provides the excuse for the initial arrest.

The central role of the PTA is to isolate the republican movement from any potential support in Britain. Its central target is the Irish community in Britain.

'Stemming the infection'

To keep the Irish republican infection out of Britain, the government devotes considerable resources to policing British ports and airports. More than two thirds of all detentions under the PTA have taken place at Liverpool, Stranraer and London. The police at ports and airports are particularly efficient Irish-catchers. In Liverpool, where more than a quarter of all detentions take place, there are permanent anti-terrorist squads at the port, the airport and the railway station. The Bridewell police station in the city has cells specially designed for PTA detainees.

Detention at a point of entry brings the threat of immediate exclusion. No Irish traveller is safe. Known republican sympathisers are special targets. The identities of republican speakers coming over for British marches or meetings have to be kept secret for as long as possible to avoid their exclusion on the way. Even if they get into Britain, they are unlikely to get home again without being detained and threatened with an exclusion order to prevent future visits. A typical example was the detention of Teresa and Patsy Moore from Derry's campaign against the supergrass showtrials. They were picked up, interrogated, and threatened with being banned on their way home from a Liverpool Irish Freedom Movement conference against the PTA in November 1983. In February 1987, Sinn Fein councillor Tommy Maguire was arrested under the PTA when he arrived in Liverpool for a cultural visit at the invitation of the Welsh Language Society. Most victims of the PTA, however, are not involved in the struggle against British rule.

The Irish Freedom Movement has supported many people who were picked up at points of entry and excluded under the Act. In July 1983 Seamus Reid, a 41-year old father of four from Belfast, arrived in Liverpool on his first trip to Britain to buy a taxi for his father's firm. He was detained for six days and then deported. His crime was to be one of several hundred nationalists interned 12 years previously. In December 1983 Martin McAllister arrived at Birmingham airport on a business trip for his double-glazing firm in the republican stronghold of Crossmaglen. He was locked up for a week and excluded under the PTA because his cousin Jim McAllister was elected to the Ulster assembly on the Sinn Fein ticket.

The PTA can turn a short trip to Northern Ireland into an enforced repatriation. In 1980 three Irish men living and working in Barnsley returned to the North for a friend's wedding. On the way back they were detained at Liverpool, and two of them were sent back—for good. Cases such as these are enough to discourage many Irish residents in Britain from maintaining close links with the North. Some victims of exclusion orders have had no closer link with Northern Ireland than the accident of having been born there. During a wave of mass arrests and raids on the Irish community in December 1979, James Martin was arrested and detained for seven days. Born in Northern Ireland, his only safeguard against exclusion would have been 20 years' residence in Britain. Yet he had lived here for only 19 years. Despite the fact that his three children had been born in Britain, he was banished to Northern Ireland. He lost his job and his council house. On arrival in Northern Ireland the housing executive refused to rehouse the family.

The power of exclusion is also used to good effect in dealing with individuals whom the police suspect of involvement in the war, but against whom they have insufficient evidence to obtain a conviction. Edward Forest appeared in Clerkenwell magistrates court in January 1976, charged with possessing nitro-glycerine. His case was dismissed. As he left the court, he was re-arrested, whisked off to Brixton police station and served with an exclusion order. Two days later he was dumped in Belfast.

None of the outrages carried out under the PTA should be interpreted as the police 'abusing' their powers. They are merely terrorising the Irish community as the Act intended. The state is fully aware of the fact that the majority of those excluded have nothing to do with the Irish War. The RUC has long since given up bothering to detain or question those excluded on their arrival in Northern Ireland. The Northern Ireland office has made it clear that it does not consider the victims of exclusion orders to be responsible for the continued violence in the North. In Ireland, an excluded person is just another nationalist. But in the context of trying to maintain stability in Britain, any Irish man can be an extremist, liable to be excluded to Northern Ireland as an example to others.

The power of detention is the most widely used and best known face of the PTA. Pick-ups are carried out in a manner designed to produce maximum intimidation. Victims' doors are kicked in by armed anti-terrorist squad police in the early hours of the morning, their homes are ransacked and their families threatened. Once they are taken into custody, without a warrant, all of the norms of British justice are suspended. Detainees may have their hands swabbed for traces of explosives, and their fingerprints and photographs taken. 'Reasonable force' can be used by the police to obtain any of these. They may be stripped and left naked in a cold and dirty cell, and will almost certainly be denied access to a solicitor.

Detainees face intensive interrogation over seven days. Physical threats, denial of sleep or washing facilities, production of false evidence: all are used to extract information. Techniques of intimidation are often interspersed with periods of affable conversation, offers of clean clothes, food, etc, to break the victim psychologically. British methods of combining inducements with coercion have been refined in Northern Ireland, where they were officially sanctioned by Lord Diplock.

Because the Act makes it an offence to withhold information about 'terrorism', in practice this means that detainees failing to fully cooperate with the police are liable to prosecution. The police demand information not just about republican activities, but about the social activities and movements of the detainee's acquaintances. Detailed evidence is built up for possible future use. The intimidation of the Irish community is a systematic process.

Detention and interrogation under the PTA is a traumatic experience. It has left many Irish people in fear of voicing any opinion about events in Ireland. It has destroyed others completely. Leo O'Neill came to Britain from Newry in the mid-seventies and took up a trade union studies course at Middlesex Polytechnic. In late 1981 he was one of a group of Irish Republican Socialist Party supporters arrested under the PTA. During a seven-day detention ordeal in Rochester Row police station, he was beaten up and had his food drugged. He never recovered from his experience of the PTA. After his release he suffered a mental and physical deterioration, his marriage broke up and he quit college. He returned to Newry where, in May 1984, he jumped to his death from a block of flats—murdered by the Prevention of Terrorism Act.

The PTA is used to foster a mood of suspicion and anti-Irish hysteria in Britain—a mood on which the state depends for its freedom to act against the Irish people. In response to every bombing in Britain, the authorities and the media make a big fuss about how Irish people are potential terrorists. The police circulate Identikit pictures of suspected bombers. They issue warnings on radio and television stations alerting the public to be on the lookout for suspicious Irish people inquiring about flats or buying radio parts. Public buildings, buses and trains are plastered with warning posters about Irish suspects and unattended packages.

The PTA gives legitimacy to the treatment of all things Irish as a potential threat to the British people. Every bombing is followed by raids on the Irish community. After the Harrods bombing in December 1983 police used the PTA to rampage through Irish homes in London, Glasgow, Birmingham, Liverpool, North Wales and Manchester. In London they arrested four Irish men with no known republican connections. In Wales they surrounded the home of a couple in their sixties. In Manchester police picked up former Irish prisoner Gerry Small at dawn. Press headlines condemned him as 'the Birmingham pub bomber', although he had been in police custody at the time of the 1974 explosions. Police used tracker dogs and explosives experts to put the frighteners on Gerry Small's girlfriend. They made sure that her neighbours knew about her alleged (though non-existent) connections with the Harrods bombing. Small spent Christmas with the Special Branch before being deported to Northern Ireland. No charges were brought against him or his girlfriend. His case indicates how the PTA is used to spread suspicion and anti-Irish prejudice among British workers. The raids and arrests are largely a propaganda exercise.

In the absence of a bombing campaign, police and press make one up. In June 1985, around the same time as police finally charged Patrick Magee with responsibility for the Brighton bombing, the authorities launched a major terrorist alert. The pretext was the round-up of an alleged IRA active service unit and the exposure of a supposed plot to bomb 12 seaside resorts over the summer holiday season. The object of the elaborate exercise was to create wider public sympathy for measures of state repression against Irish people. For a week the press speculated that the police had smashed the IRA unit responsible for every bombing in Britain over the previous five years, not to mention kidnappings and jailbreaks in Ireland. The media even succeeded in dragging that symbol of the unity of the British people—the Queen—into the bomb scare. Her Majesty made clear her courageous determination to go ahead with a visit to Great Yarmouth...in several months' time. The message of the media charade was clear: the IRA is the enemy of us all, we must be vigilant, we must be united in defiance.

The police know that most of their PTA detainees have nothing to do with bombing campaigns. In 1975 two Irish women visiting

St Paul's Cathedral were detained under the Act because they unknowingly parked their car—with a Northern Ireland registration number—near the Old Bailey, where the Guildford pub bombing trial was being heard. Their arrest caused a public furore about a possible car bomb attack on the court. But the police knew better. The two women were not even questioned once during their six-day detention.

On occasion the police have pushed the PTA's powers further, to victimise and frame Irish solidarity activists. In January 1985, Maire O'Shea, a doctor and well-known Irish activist, was arrested under the PTA in Liverpool and charged, along with five others, with conspiring to cause explosions. After an 18-day conspiracy trial in March 1986, O'Shea and her co-defendant Patrick Brazil were acquitted. Peter Jordan and William Graves got 14 and 10 years in prison respectively for conspiracy to cause an explosion. Peter Lynch was freed having already served his 400-day sentence for withholding information on remand.

The PTA has also played its part in ensuring that the media present only the establishment view of the Irish War. In 1976 both the BBC and ITV conducted long interviews with the Prisoners' Aid Committee about the fate of prisoner of war Frank Stagg. Stagg died while being force-fed at Wakefield jail after a prolonged hunger-strike. When senior figures in the Labour government heard about the impending broadcast, they let it be known that a film which revealed the reality of Britain's treatment of Irish political prisoners could be construed as supportive of the IRA. Threatened with prosecution under the PTA, the BBC ditched the project and ITV screened it only after savage editing. In 1980 a BBC film of an IRA road-block in Northern Ireland was referred to the director of public prosecutions for consideration. Attorney General Sir Michael Havers announced that the government was determined to deal with such coverage of the Irish War. From the shop floor to the BBC boardroom, the PTA provides the framework for criminalising opponents of the Irish War in Britain.

The critics

The arbitrary character of the PTA and its flagrant violation of basic civil liberties have provoked criticism from liberal quarters. To accommodate the critics, governments periodically hold parliamentary reviews of the PTA. The last was carried out by Lord Jellicoe in 1983, and some of its recommendations were introduced in the 1984 Act. The most significant reform was to drop the phrase 'temporary provisions' from the title of the Act.

Since February 1983, the Labour Party—which introduced the PTA in 1974—has called for the repeal of the Act on the grounds that its indiscriminate powers are likely to turn more Irish people against Britain. Labour's attempts to challenge the Act in parliament have noted that, in the opinion of some of Northern Ireland's 'most distinguished opponents of terrorism', it would give 'nothing but support to the terrorists'.

Labour wants merely to come up with a less arbitrary method of suppressing the Irish liberation struggle. Its narrow, legalistic opposition to the PTA is a cynical manoeuvre, motivated solely by the party's need to develop alternative policies to the Tories. The Labour Party maintains its longstanding support for criminalisation and still identifies terrorists as the problem. In the February 1986 parliamentary debate on the PTA, shadow home secretary Gerald Kaufman declared that terrorism is 'a horror and a plague and we should unite in using all legitimate weapons to combat and defeat it'. The best a future Labour government could achieve would be to replace the PTA with an Act which is just as repressive but slightly less indiscriminate.

The National Council for Civil Liberties opposes the PTA in equally ineffective terms. When its former general secretary, Larry Gostin, complained about a wave of PTA detentions in January 1985, he stressed that the NCCL was 'unequivocally opposed to terrorist activity' because it provides 'justification for drastic curtailment of traditional liberties'. In other words, the NCCL blames the IRA for the PTA. When the official NCCL report on the 1984-85 miners' strike blamed striking miners for picket-line violence, its members rebelled and forced Gostin to resign. Yet there has been no revolt against the leadership line on the PTA. Liberal critics of the PTA who accept that Irish freedom fighters are terrorists will never be able to fight the PTA successfully.

Irish prisoners

Wedding days are normally happy occasions. Tommy Quigley's was a nightmare. On 31 January 1986, Quigley married Geraldine Bailey in Albany prison on the Isle of Wight. The wedding had already been postponed for several weeks after Quigley was held in solitary confinement with no explanation. The couple had arranged to have a religious ceremony, but, minutes before it was due to begin, the prison priest refused to do it. In addition the authorities threatened to cancel the wedding unless Quigley paid a further £30. Contravening accepted practice, the prison governor refused to allow Bailey's family to take photographs. A prison officer took a few snaps, none of which were sent to the family. More than a dozen wardens were present to intimidate the family: Quigley's elderly mother collapsed and required medical attention. During their few days on the Isle of Wight, the wedding party was kept under constant surveillance by the Special Branch. Mary, Roy and Betty Quigley were arrested under the PTA and held for an hour at Liverpool as they made their way back to Belfast. The prison authorities had certainly given Irish POW Quigley a day to remember.

Irish political prisoners in Britain suffer the full force of criminalisation. Although they are labelled as ordinary criminals, the treatment they get sets them apart from other prisoners. From their arrest to their release, Irish political prisoners are given an unofficial special-category status. They receive all the penalties of political status, but none of the benefits.

The majority of the 46 Irish political prisoners are convicted members of the republican movement. But there are also those (11 in early 1987) who have nothing to do with the nationalist struggle. These people are victims of frame-ups. Yet to protest their innocence is to accept that republican prisoners are 'guilty' of 'crimes'. In the eyes of the state, to be Irish in Britain is guilt enough. All Irish people are liable to harassment under the PTA and, when circumstances demand it, all Irish people are in danger of imprisonment. Opposition to the treatment of Irish political prisoners can only be effective if based on defending the rights of all the prisoners.

Republican prisoners are victims of the trial procedures of kangaroo courts. More than 80 per cent are tried for conspiracy—a charge so open to definition that little or no evidence is required for it to be proved. The onus is always on the defendant to prove innocence. The state goes to great lengths to create the kind of anti-Irish climate which can guarantee a conviction. In December 1983 and March 1984, joint RUC/Scotland Yard snatch squads grabbed Tommy Quigley and Paul Kavanagh from Belfast. Amid hysterical publicity the RAF flew them to London's top-security Paddington Green police station. Whenever they appeared in court, the press ran 'Harrods bombers' headlines, even though neither had been charged with that attack. Armed police prowled the courts to add extra atmosphere. Such carnivals of reaction allow police to get convictions on little or no evidence. Quigley and Kavanagh were sentenced to life imprisonment in March 1985.

In June 1986, in the infamous Brighton bomb trial, seven Irish people were convicted of explosives offences at the Old Bailey. Newspapers tried to outdo each other. Patrick Magee, the man branded as the Brighton bomber, was variously labelled 'the Chancer', 'Mad Pat' and 'the Mechanic'. Peter Sherry was 'the Jackal', 'the Butcher' and 'the Armalite kid' but, if we are to believe the *Star,* 'the Admirable Crichton'. Then there were the two women convicted of conspiracy, Ella O'Dwyer and Martina Anderson, lumped together under the tag 'the Angels of Death', and there was Gerard McDonnell, whom the *Sun* credited with the unlikely title of 'the Blurp'. As 'Mad Pat meets the Blurp', the make-believe world of the Saturday morning pictures becomes hard copy for the hysterical hyenas of the British press. It might be rude to call people names, but then the general idea behind the coverage of the bomb trial was to convince the British public that Irish republicans are not people at all, but beasts and animals. All the defendants got life sentences.

The 'evidence' is often farcical. The most infamous frame-up was that of Annie Maguire in 1976. At the trial of four people accused of the Guildford and Woolwich pub bombings, a bomb factory run by an anonymous 'Aunt Annie' was mentioned. The press seized on this, demanding that 'Aunt Annie' be caught. Annie Maguire was picked out as the target for the witch-hunt. She had lived in Britain for 20 years, was a member of Paddington Conservative club, and the flags on her children's bedroom wall were British Union Jacks, not Irish tricolours. But she was from Belfast and was visited by friends from Belfast. That was enough to make her guilty. Her house was raided, and she and seven friends and relatives were arrested. They were all found guilty of running a bomb factory and received sentences ranging from four to 14 years.

The only piece of evidence offered at the Maguire trial was a rubber glove. Forensic tests had shown this glove to have traces of explosives on it. This was presented as unquestionable proof of guilt, and eight Irish people went to jail. Evidence produced later showed that the forensic tests had been improperly conducted and that the 'explosive' traces found could just as easily have been left by cigarette smoke.

Today six Irishmen are serving life sentences for the Birmingham pub bombings. They have consistently denied any involvement. The 'Birmingham Six' were convicted on the strength of confessions beaten out of them so severely that the state was forced to go through the motions of charging their jailers. The warders were acquitted

● *Irish showtrials*

From the Fenian fighters for Irish freedom to the volunteers of the
Irish Republican Army, the British authorities have made out that
Irish republicans are not people at all, but beasts and animals.

The Brighton bomb trial, 1986

'The men on trial sat in front. Determined men with unyielding
eyes. Sitting in cool isolation Patrick Magee replied in a firm and
unmistakably Northern Ireland accent....He stared coldly at the press
bench. Just stared. It was a cold stare. A bit frightening. And the two
girls nudged one another. But still looked chic with it.'
P Callan, *The Mirror,* 7 May 1986

The Clerkenwell bomb trial, 1868

'Only Barrett stood out; he had not been in jail as long as the others
and his clothes were in better condition. The dark flashing eyes of Ann
Justice roved around the court, taking in the brilliant robes and
uniforms. Barrett looked around with interest but the other men
seemed cowed by the court.'
P Quinlivan and P Rose, *The Fenians in England: 1865-1872*

after claiming that the six were already maimed when they left police custody. The prisoners' attempts to start a private prosecution against their torturers were stamped on by Lord Denning, who made it clear that no British court could take the side of Irish people against the agents of the state:

'If the six men win, it will mean that the police were guilty of perjury, that they were guilty of violence and threats, that the confessions were involuntary and improperly admitted in evidence and that the convictions were erroneous. That would mean the home secretary would either have to recommend they be pardoned or would have to remit the case to the court of appeal. This is such an appalling vista that every sensible person in the land would say: "It cannot be right that these actions should go any further." '

In January 1987 Tory home secretary Douglas Hurd finally reopened the case of the Birmingham Six, who have languished in jail for 13 years. For this to happen, it took long and mounting pressure from relatives, experts discrediting the forensic evidence produced at the trial, a former police officer testifying that the Six were beaten, threatened with guns and deprived of food and drink before signing their 'confessions', two *World in Action* documentaries and Chris Mullin's book, *Error of Judgement.* Hurd referred the case to the appeal court. He refused to reopen the case of the Guildford Four, or the Maguires who are still trying to clear their name, or the case of Judith Ward, framed for the M62 coach bombing which killed nine soldiers and three civilians in February 1974. Two months later Hurd agreed to look at fresh evidence in the Guildford Four case after Yorkshire TV's *First Tuesday* programme found a new witness who insisted that Paul Hill, one of the four, was at her house on the night of the Woolwich explosion.

The Guildford Four are three Irishmen—Paul Hill, Patrick Armstrong and Gerard Conlon—and Armstrong's English girlfriend, Carole Richardson. They have spent nearly 13 years in British jails after being convicted of planting the Guildford pub bombs which killed four soldiers and one civilian in October 1974. The prisoners and their families have insisted throughout their imprisonment that they had nothing to do with the attacks. The only evidence against the Guildford Four is statements made when they were being beaten and bullied in police custody. All of them are riddled with inaccuracies and inconsistencies. The idea that these statements are factual becomes even more ridiculous when they are compared to the detailed versions given by the IRA volunteers who have admitted that *they* planted the bombs—the famous 'Balcombe

Street' unit, who bombed the Surrey pubs as part of a campaign which continued after the Guildford Four were arrested.

During their 12 years in prison, the Guildford Four have received the typical treatment reserved for Irish political prisoners. Paul Hill, jailed for his natural life, has been singled out for special persecution. He has spent around four years in solitary confinement, and often suffered beatings. His health has been destroyed. He has been shunted from prison to prison 42 times, spending time in Hull—the grimmest of jails, and one where the authorities have borne a grudge against Hill ever since he successfully protested against the beatings he received after the riots there more than 10 years ago. Today Paul Hill still suffers every harassment imaginable at the hands of his British jailers. If he has a jug of water overnight, they spit in it. If he has a pen, they put a dud refill in it. If he has a radio, they play it until the batteries wear out. But they have not worn out his determination to be free.

In his speech from the dock during the Balcombe Street trial, IRA volunteer Joe O'Connell exposed the tricks of the legal trade through which the court had 'proved' the Guildford Four were bombers: 'This shifty manoeuvring typifies what we, as Irish republicans, have come to understand by the words "British justice".' He ended by savaging the 'independence' of the legal system, saying his unit had 'fought to free our oppressed nation from its bondage to British imperialism, of which this court is an integral part'. Paul Hill had nothing to do with the Balcombe Street volunteers or the Guildford pub bombings. But it is doubtful whether he, or his three co-defendants, or the Maguires, or the Birmingham Six, or Judith Ward, would disagree with O'Connell's description of 'British justice' for the Irish.

Turning the screws

British prison regulations require that all prisoners be categorised according to security risk. Apart from categories A through to D, an additional category E is used for prisoners who are thought keen to escape: extra security arrangements are made for them. There are around 400 A prisoners out of a prison population in England and Wales of 44 000. All but a handful of Irish political prisoners are category A and many are AE.

The application of category A status to republicans is the British state's way of singling out these prisoners for special treatment, while maintaining the lie that there are no political prisoners in England. In fact, all Irish political prisoners are treated as special cases. Category A republicans are singled out for especially strict treatment. There exists a 'Special A' or 'Irish A' category. This status is designed to impose maximum isolation on Irish prisoners: they are not allowed to mix freely with others.

GOD works in mysterious ways. All prisoners are liable to have an experience with GOD, but Irish prisoners are particularly favoured. GOD (Rule 43—Good Order and Discipline) is a temporary order by which a prisoner can be placed in solitary confinement for up to 28 days. Although 'temporary', it is renewable indefinitely and some republican prisoners have spent years in solitary confinement. The 'lie down' rule under GOD entails a 23-hour lock-up with only a bucket in the room during the day and bedding thrown in at night. Appeals against GOD can only be made to the home office, which normally takes a leisurely six months to consider the case. Just as the home office refuses to recognise the existence of political prisoners, so it refuses to admit that such solitary imprisonment exists: the prisoners are merely being held in 'cellular confinement'.

Visiting restrictions are tight for A prisoners and tighter still for those designated AE. Irish political prisoners are likely to have additional restrictions on their visits. In 1977, there were 92 prisoners in England whose visits come under 'especially secure' restrictions. All but 10 of these were Irish republicans. Visiting restrictions and security procedures are designed to break Irish prisoners from regular contact with friends and family. In January 1987 the governor of Long Lartin prison, together with the home office, announced his intention of implementing a new booking system for visits, designed to prevent more than two visits occurring on the same day.

During visits conducted under 'especially secure' conditions, conversation takes place through glass or a wire mesh. Everything is recorded by closed-circuit television cameras. Warders are present to prevent physical contact and to make notes of the conversation. Ordinary prisoners do not have wardens sitting in on their visits—but, in Durham prison, Ella O'Dwyer and Martina Anderson have three. Prisoners are strip-searched before and after the visit. Visitors are also searched. The distress and aggravation that visits entail has meant that many potential contacts are denied to Irish political prisoners. In December 1986, Judith Ward described the conditions facing women like O'Dwyer and Anderson in Durham's 'H' wing, the same wing where she has served most of her life sentence:

'Our main priority here at the moment is the strip-searching. Over the last nine months the amount of strip and rub-down searches (body searches) has attained ridiculous proportions. At the very minimum each girl is subjected to six body searches a day! This is before entering and after leaving the workroom twice a day and before entering and leaving the exercise yard....Besides all these unnecessary and futile searches, we are subjected to body searches before a visit and a full strip-search after a visit, whether it be a social or legal visit.'

However, the degrading conditions of visits are not the main barrier facing prisoners anxious to maintain contacts with family and friends. Although it is official home office policy to locate all prisoners as near to their families as possible, this policy does not apply to Irish political prisoners. The immediate families of most Irish prisoners live in Ireland, and the distance is too great for many people to be able to make a visit very often.

Even when a visit is arranged, the prison authorities often interfere. Republicans are transferred around different prisons more frequently than most prisoners. In 1986 Vincent Donnelly was moved no less than 10 times. This kind of regime is designed to increase isolation and disorientation. Transfers are often timed to coincide with arranged visits. Relatives sometimes arrive at a prison to find that their son or brother has been moved to the other end of the country a few hours before.

Prisoners who cause trouble are moved as a form of punishment. Eddie Byrne, whose family lives in Birmingham, was moved from Gartree prison to the Isle of Wight more than 100 miles away, as a result of his campaign against the use of drugs to control the prison population in Gartree.

Prison authorities like to play sick jokes with prisoners' transfer requests. Pat Guilfoyle had constantly asked to be moved from Wormwood Scrubs to a prison in the Midlands in order to be closer to his elderly parents in Birmingham. Early in 1982, shortly after both his parents died, the prison authorities announced that they would grant his longstanding request, and they moved him to Gartree. Like most Irish political prisoners, Guilfoyle was denied compassionate parole to attend his parents' funeral.

Apart from the distress caused by visiting conditions and cancelled visits, the families and friends of Irish prisoners are themselves subject to harassment. The most famous example is that of Guiseppe Conlon, who was arrested under the PTA when he came from Ireland to visit his son. He was sentenced to 12 years, and subsequently died in a prison hospital on 22 January 1980.

Screw brutality

Irish political prisoners suffer ill treatment in different ways. There are many accounts of beatings after protests against ill treatment or in solidarity with the Irish struggle. The prisoners' rights group—PROP—has exposed the existence of a special squad to deal with problems of prison order: republican prisoners have suffered particularly at its hands. It is known as the MUFTI (Minimum Use of Force Tactical Intervention) squad. Many letters from Irish prisoners have given detailed accounts of the beatings and brutalities meted out in the prisons. The press and prison governors try to make out that injuries sustained by Irish political prisoners are inflicted by other prisoners.

Irish prisoners suffer sensory deprivation and other psychological tortures in the infamous control units. These British torture chambers have officially been closed after a public outcry against them. But the authorities merely changed the labels—to 'F-wing' in Wakefield jail and to 'segregation unit' in Gartree—and put them back into operation. Irish POWs have been kept in these hell-holes for up to three months. As a result they suffer dizziness, disorientation and speech difficulties (Irish Republican POW campaign pamphlet).

Drugs are used against Irish prisoners and other 'politically conscious' and 'non-conforming' prisoners. Parkhurst, Gartree and Hull are particularly known for the use of drugs. The screws forcibly administered addictive barbiturates to Eddie Byrne at Gartree.

In October 1984 British prisons' minister Lord Elton, infamous for condemning Irish prisoners as 'subversives' intent on undermining prison regimes, announced government plans for new special control units. The new system would make a 'much more definite connection between a prisoner's behaviour and the privileges he enjoys':

'Men who are persistently disruptive should be removed from long-term prisons and returned to the sentence-planning units for a short period of assessment.' (*Irish Times,* 2 October 1984)

Irish prisoners in Britain have long experience of what such 'assessment' of their resistance will mean at the hands of brutal British jailers. After the May 1983 Albany prison riots, Paul Norney was held in a Durham strip cell for nine months. Other prisoners were robbed of up to 670 days' remission after a kangaroo court convicted them of mutiny.

Prison brutality does not end with bruised minds and bodies. Five Irish political prisoners have been killed in prison. On 3 June 1974, Michael Gaughan died after being force-fed in Parkhurst at the end of a long hunger-strike. On 12 February 1976, Frank Stagg died on hunger-strike in Wakefield after a three-year struggle against criminalisation in solitary confinement. On 9 October 1976, Noel Jenkinson died in mysterious circumstances in the special security block at Leicester prison. He had spent six months in solitary and had been badly beaten on three occasions. Guiseppe Conlon was the fourth to die. The fifth was Sean O'Connell, who died of cancer at Parkhurst in October 1977 after being treated with aspirin and alcohol rubs. His condition, which had been ignored by the prison authorities, was only diagnosed by an independent autopsy.

The main demand of Irish political prisoners is for repatriation to Ireland. According to Instrument 388 of Prison Rule 31 issued in 1964, all prisoners in the United Kingdom should be located as near to their families as possible. But although more than 60 British soldiers have been transferred from the Six Counties to English jails after 'crimes committed in the course of duty', only five Irish prisoners have ever been transferred to Ireland. Marian Price, Dolours Price, Hugh Feeney and Gerard Kelly were transferred only when they were on the verge of death after a 205-day hunger-strike in 1974. The only republican prisoner to have been repatriated in recent years was Shane O'Doherty from Derry, who discovered religion and renounced his previous views and actions.

In a candid admission of the fact that republicans are members of a political organisation, Tory junior Northern Ireland minister Lord Gowrie rejected any comparison between soldiers of HM armed forces and soldiers of the IRA:

'As regards the transfer of soldiers who have been sentenced to imprisonment for offences committed in Northern Ireland the minister can only repeat his view that persons sent to the province in the course of their duty cannot be compared with persons who have set out to commit offences on behalf of organisations whose public and declared aim is to challenge, by means of terrorism, including pre-planned murder, the authority of the elected government.'

Demands for repatriation have been taken up by humanitarian organisations and individuals, who centre their campaigns on the suffering and harassment prisoners' relatives go through when visiting. Several Liberal and Labour MPs have supported such campaigns by writing to the home office, but former home secretary

William Whitelaw dismissed their efforts. He admitted to breaking statutory obligation, but insisted that such methods were necessary to prevent terrorists receiving 'heroes' welcomes' in Ireland. No liberal can successfully counter such statements without opposing the strategy of criminalisation and admitting the reality of the Irish War. The prisoners themselves are clear about the issues at stake in demanding repatriation. They want political status, not humanitarian concessions:

'Whether we spend 20 years in prison in England or 20 years in prison in Ireland is irrelevant to us: what is relevant is that we never plead or apologise to people who for years have done their utmost to break us and criminalise our nation and our national aspirations.' (Sinn Fein, *Prisoner of War,* May 1982)

Prisoners are especially keen to distance themselves from representations made on their behalf by pro-imperialists such as John Hume of the SDLP or Father Faul of the Catholic Church.

Despite all the obstacles, the Irish political prisoners have established a remarkable record of resistance to all attempts to criminalise them. Roof-top protests have been one effective way of drawing public attention to their cause. On 26 April, 1981, at Wormwood Scrubs, and from 4 to 11 May at Long Lartin, republican prisoners demonstrated on the roofs with flags and painted slogans. They shouted messages of support to their comrades on hunger-strike in the H-Blocks. Hunger-strikes have been used to protest against ill treatment and criminalisation.

Several prisoners have organised blanket protests. Despite many risks, Irish political prisoners have organised themselves under their own discipline. Their solidarity was clearly displayed in February 1983, when republican prisoners organised a solid one-day national strike from all prison work to publicise their demand for repatriation. Little of this ever gets reported, of course, because there are no political prisoners in English jails.

7. Britain – the way forward

For anybody living in Britain who wants to end the war in Ireland the main question must be: 'Why is there no serious solidarity movement working on the streets of London, Manchester or Glasgow?' Why is it that during the past decade demonstrations protesting against Britain's war in Ireland have attracted only a couple of thousand people, while those protesting against nuclear weapons or apartheid have mobilised 10, 20 or even 50 times as many people?

Solidarity work in Britain has always been a story of evasions and excuses. The main excuse promoted by the British left is that the working class has no interest in Ireland or, alternatively, that it is anti-Irish. It is true that anti-Irish views have acquired a widespread resonance in Britain. But such prejudices, which have existed throughout this century, did not prevent hundreds of thousands of workers from demonstrating in favour of Irish freedom in the early twenties. Nor is anti-Irish feeling so strong today that nothing can be done. One indication is the far from hostile response to the IRA bombing of the Tory Party conference in Brighton in 1984: 'pity they missed' was the verdict of many striking miners. Within days jokes about the bombing were circulating in working class communities. While it would be an exaggeration to say that the Brighton bomb converted the British working class to the cause of Irish freedom, nevertheless many ordinary people recognised that the IRA was attacking a common enemy. At the very least this experience showed that building an effective solidarity movement in Britain is not beyond the realm of possibility.

An examination of the mainstream of the British solidarity movement reveals that it has never tried to win a working class audience for its views. It also reveals a more sordid truth: the mainstream solidarity movement has singularly failed to question the right of the British state to determine the affairs of the Irish people. Organisations like the Troops Out Movement and the Labour Committee on Ireland are not even prepared to agitate around demands like 'Troops out now!' At the April 1987 LCI conference delegates agreed that 'Troops out now!' was too extreme, and voted instead to call for 'withdrawal within the lifetime of a Labour government'.

This decision was a significant modification of the demand for 'Troops out now!' By giving a future Labour government the initiative, it implies that the British state could play a progressive role. More to the point, it makes the question of Irish self-determination *negotiable,* a perspective which negates the very idea of self-determination. Either the Irish people have the right to self-determination or they do not—there is no middle ground. The LCI position suggests there can be a British solution to a conflict created and sustained by Britain. British intervention is the problem, not the solution. Incidentally, by putting off the fight for Irish freedom until a Labour government has been elected, the LCI is admitting that it takes a long, a very long, view of ending imperialist oppression in Ireland.

For most solidarity groups, work on the Irish question is synonymous with working through the Labour Party. But how reliable is this strategy given Labour's record on Ireland?

The cause of Labour or the cause of Ireland?

'We want a massive majority for the agreement,' declared Labour's deputy Northern Ireland spokesman Stuart Bell during the parliamentary debate on the Anglo-Irish accord in November 1985, 'not because it is bipartisan, but because it is right for the people of Northern Ireland, the United Kingdom and the ultimate aspirations of the Labour Party' (*Hansard,* 26 November 1985).

With these words Bell rallied Labour's forces to give a vote of approval to the agreement which reinforces the partition of Ireland and strengthens Britain's repressive forces against Irish freedom fighters.

The Labour Party has had nothing to say against Thatcher's Anglo-Irish agreement. As Kinnock put it, he had a debt to the British security forces and fully and freely recognised Thatcher's achievement in imposing her plan on Ireland. Kinnock saved all his anger for those fighting for Irish unity and independence. Unless the agreement succeeded in smashing the republican movement, Kinnock warned, nationalists would 'continue with the noxious insincerity of their bullet and ballot strategy to sustain insecurity throughout the province'. Former Labour Northern Ireland secretary Roy Mason hailed the accord as 'the most progressive and historic step...since partition' and spelt out what the new deal with Dublin must mean: 'joint police board operations, covering chases across the frontiers, hot pursuits across the Border, helicopter patrols, Army liaison, and joint operations by the British and Irish armies'. In his typically blunt fashion, Mason exposed the accord as an anti-IRA device.

Kinnock's full-blooded support for the Anglo-Irish deal is an appalling display of anti-Irish feeling. But that is nothing new. Labour has always backed Britain's war in Ireland. The unity of the Tory and Labour parties on the Irish issue—bipartisanship—has survived through 18 years of struggle. At every key moment in the Irish War, the British establishment has been able to count on the Labour leaders to scab on the Irish people.

In government, Labour invaded Ireland. Out of it, in the early seventies, Labour backed Tory assaults on the nationalist community from internment to Bloody Sunday. It was left to Irish MP Bernadette Devlin to punch home secretary Reginald Maudling on the nose in parliament after his lies about the Derry massacre. Labour MPs just sat on their hands and watched Westminster's war machine stamp on the Irish.

The Labour governments of the seventies built the bloody strategy that Britain still pursues in Northern Ireland. They withdrew political status from Irish republican prisoners and criminalised them. They despatched the undercover assassins of the SAS across the Irish Sea. They introduced the Prevention of Terrorism Act. And they opened the RUC torture and interrogation centre at Castlereagh. Labour's Roy Mason distinguished himself as the most brutal British warmonger to run the Northern Ireland office, fully deserving the label 'Butcher Mason' he was given by Irish victims of his vicious regime. In opposition in the early eighties, Labour sent Northern Ireland spokesman Don Concannon to hunger-striker Bobby Sands' death cell to tell him that Labour approved of his death.

Under Kinnock the Labour Party has proved itself willing to whip up anti-Irish hysteria, to whitewash atrocities carried out by British forces, and to watch in silence as Thatcher sealed an anti-Irish settlement. By putting Britain first, Labour has put the Irish people in the firing line over and over again.

It is impossible to overestimate the importance of bipartisanship to the British war effort. The parliamentary united front on Ireland has ensured that no serious criticism of Britain's crimes against the Irish is ever aired. This has enabled the British authorities to go about their bloody business in Northern Ireland, safe in the knowledge that the home fires are being kept burning with pro-British propaganda. Bipartisanship has been the guarantee that successive governments could cope with the Irish War. It remains the most important reason why Thatcher could crack down on the republican movement after her deal with Dublin.

Most people think there is a definite difference between the Labour and Tory parties. Most Irish people who live under British rule do not. When the IRA says that 'the language of force is the only reasoning the British government understands,' it is not just talking about Thatcher. It is talking about every British government— Liberal, Labour and Conservative—that has terrorised the Irish community since Northern Ireland was created in 1921.

For more than a decade of the Irish War the left wing of the Labour Party remained silent about its leaders' support for British terror. But the events of 1981, and particularly Concannon's visit to Sands, prompted new tensions within the party. Left wingers staged a protest march in Concannon's Mansfield constituency, while the Labour right joined skinheads waving Loyalist flags on a counter-demonstration. The 1981 Labour Party conference was inundated with a record 54 motions calling for a British withdrawal from Northern Ireland.

The conference adopted a national executive statement which committed the party to the eventual reunification of Ireland. Within the framework of this policy, subsequent Labour conferences have taken a radical stance against aspects of British terror in the North. In 1982 a motion to ban the production and use of plastic bullets was passed with only a dozen dissenters. In 1984 the Labour Party conference voted to oppose Diplock courts, plastic bullets and strip-searching—against the advice of the national executive.

The Labour left has celebrated the 1981 executive statement and the conference decisions that followed it as a 'step forward': a 'break' with bipartisanship; and one which brings Labour closer to becoming the party of withdrawal. But there was nothing progressive about the statement the national executive made in the middle of the hunger-strikes for political status:

'We support the policy of treating them like other prisoners, which was introduced by the last Labour government in 1976.'

The policy hailed by the left explicitly endorses the imperialist device imposed on Northern Ireland by right-wing Labour leaders—the device of criminalisation.

Given its support for repression, Labour's apparent enthusiasm for eventual Irish reunification is meaningless. No party that condemns Irish freedom fighters as criminals can do anything to further the fight for Irish freedom. The authors of the 1981 policy outlined a three-stage plan for a British withdrawal. In the long term, Ireland would be reunited. In the medium term, authority would be transferred to a local power-sharing assembly. For the foreseeable future, Labour would 'continue with direct rule'. In practice support for direct rule in the present is the only part of the policy which matters. The interim measure of power-sharing cannot be achieved in a Northern Ireland state under British domination, while the ultimate goal of Irish unity remains a nice idea on the other side of the rainbow.

Labour Party policy for Northern Ireland today adds up to a continuation of the two central themes of British strategy over the past decade: direct rule and criminalisation. Whatever subsequent conference decisions might claim, accepting these themes means accepting all the repressive measures necessary to implement them, from plastic bullets to Diplock courts. Hence the left's policy changes present no challenge to the right. Every attempt by the left to commit Labour's conference to a withdrawal from Ireland has been overwhelmingly defeated.

Labour's policy of 'eventual Irish reunification' is an attempt to distance the party from Tory terror without hampering the state's ability to pursue its war in Ireland. Labour has a long record of similar manoeuvres, designed to placate liberal disquiet over

WAVING THE
TROOPS OFF,
LABOUR LEADER
HAROLD WILSON

● *The Labour Party's shameful record*

1921: Labour Party leader Arthur Henderson welcomed partition 'not only with joy but with great satisfaction'.

1949: Clement Attlee's Labour government passed the Northern Ireland Act, endorsing the status of the Six Counties as part of the United Kingdom.

1969: Harold Wilson's Labour regime launched the British Army's invasion of Northern Ireland.

1974: Wilson's next Labour administration passed the Prevention of Terrorism Act.

1976: Labour introduced criminalisation by withdrawing special-category status from republican prisoners and opening the H-Blocks at the Maze prison.

1977: James Callaghan's Labour government opened the RUC torture centre at Castlereagh.

1981: Labour's Northern Ireland spokesman Don Concannon told hunger-striker Bobby Sands that Labour supported his death at the hands of the Tory government.

1984: Labour leader Neil Kinnock backed Britain's shoot-to-kill campaign, endorsing the use of 'every force' against republicans.

1985: Her Majesty's loyal opposition backs the Anglo-Irish deal, a Tory scheme for securing British control over Northern Ireland.

1986: Kinnock declares that 'nobody in or associated with Sinn Fein is welcome within a million miles of the Labour Party or anything we stand for.'

Britain's Irish policy while protecting the establishment from any genuine anti-imperialist pressure.

During British protests against the Tan War in 1921, the Labour conference came out in support of an 'independent' Irish state, provided its constitution prevented Ireland 'from becoming a military or naval menace to Great Britain'. After the uproar caused by Bloody Sunday in 1972, Labour leader Harold Wilson announced that Britain should withdraw from Ireland within 15 years. This policy was more radical than the 1981 decision: it actually set a date for withdrawal, and it was fully endorsed by the Parliamentary Labour Party. But Wilson's promise of freedom in the future did not prevent him being the architect of repression in the present. Today it is obvious that Labour's support for 'eventual Irish reunification' will count for equally little sway in a Labour government's discussions on the Irish War.

Since its defeat in the 1983 general election, the Labour leadership has forgotten all about conference policy. Instead it has gone back to full-blooded support for military repression to convince the establishment of its fitness to govern. Neil Kinnock has laid down the law on matters concerning Northern Ireland and the left has fallen lamely into line.

Kinnock has endorsed the shoot-to-kill campaign against republicans. On the day that the security forces shot dead two republicans in Derry, in December 1984, Kinnock took the side of the SAS assassins: 'If there is reason to believe that people are going to commit acts of outrage, every force must be used to stop them.' The left stayed silent.

After Sinn Fein's success in the May 1985 local elections, and the IRA's success in blowing nine RUC men to pieces at Newry barracks in the same month, the British tabloids started a new anti-republican fury over plans for a Sinn Fein speaker to address a meeting in Brighton. The meeting's organiser, local Labour councillor Richard Stanton, had also made the mistake, in the eyes of the gutter press, of refusing to condemn the IRA's attack on the Tory cabinet in the town in October 1984. The *Sun* said that Stanton was 'best left undisturbed beneath a stone'. Stanton's fellow Labour councillors added their vitriol to that dispensed by Tories and Liberals: one said Stanton should be 'thrown out of the Labour Party'. Another blustered that Stanton 'has been elected to put across Labour Party policy and this is not it'. In fact, the Labour Party's real policy is to repress opponents of the Irish War—whether they are Sinn Fein members in Belfast or Labour Party members in Britain.

Shortly after the Labour Party cracked down in Brighton, the party's national agent, David Hughes, vetoed an apparently harmless motion from the London Labour Party calling for Sinn Fein members to be invited to speak in Britain. Leading Labour left winger John McDonnell attacked Hughes' action as 'an outrageous attempt at subverting democracy'. But what else can the left expect? When Labour sent the troops into Ireland in 1969, it made a still more outrageous attempt at subverting democracy, and one whose success they have supported through thick and thin.

In the run-up to Labour's 1986 party conference, after an invitation had been extended to a Sinn Fein speaker to address a fringe meeting, Kinnock announced: 'Nobody in or associated with Sinn Fein is welcome within a million miles of the Labour Party or anything we stand for.' He despatched Stuart Bell to the meeting to tell the republican speaker that Labour opposed the violence of the IRA unequivocally.

In July 1986 Labour's national executive committee refused to support the call for a national demonstration against strip-searching in November. In place of a demo, therefore, Labour Women for Ireland called a rally. But even that was too much for Kinnock's entourage: it banned Sinn Fein, the South West Africa People's Organisation, and even the Irish in Britain Representation Group from addressing the rally from the platform. The poorly attended event turned into a rambling, token affair that embarrassed its organisers. This is the price the Irish people are expected to pay for the return of a Labour government. The lesson of the last few years is that people who want to fight for Irish freedom without being banned and censored have to break with the Labour Party. But Labour left wingers are so concerned to get Kinnock into government that they are willing to forget about building a movement here that can help the Irish people get Britain out of their country.

Under Kinnock, Labour has abandoned any pretence of working towards Irish unity. Kinnock has declared that while Ireland will 'ultimately' be united, 'ultimately can be a very long way away.' After the 1983 general election Labour set up a study group to prepare a consultative document for the 1985 conference to debate and for the 1986 conference to vote on. In the event Labour wheeled on a drunken Alex Kitson to address the 1985 conference, and shelved the report before the 1986 get together.

If ever the Labour left had cause to take up the cudgels against its leaders' Irish policy, now is the time. Yet the left has lowered its

horizons so as not to upset Labour's chances of re-election. At the
Labour Coordinating Committee conference on Ireland held in
January 1987 left wingers agreed with Peter Hain that 'a demand for
immediate British withdrawal is simply not practical as it would
leave a vacuum in which violence and dissension would continue.'
They voted for Hain's proposal for withdrawal 'within the lifetime of
a Labour government'. The Labour left did not even have the guts to
oppose the Anglo-Irish deal by arguing for the only alternative—a
British withdrawal.

In places like Haringey, London, Labour left wingers have set up
Irish sections in the party. They have reduced their sights to
'campaign and lobby in the Labour Party on Irish issues'; and, more
importantly, 'to encourage Irish people to join Labour' and 'to
campaign for the Labour Party within the Irish community'. Irish
sections supporter Seamus Carey said that 'we support the Labour
Party despite its terrible record on Ireland, because it holds out the
prospect of a socialist, anti-imperialist future.' It is difficult to see the
logic of Carey's statement; it is clear, however, that the left has given
up criticising its party's Irish policy in favour of securing the Irish
vote for Labour.

Incapable of offering any alternative to the Labour leadership's
'war-as-usual' approach, the left has retreated into a dream world
where Britain pulls out of Ireland without anybody having to build a
movement to push it out. Today every left-wing statement about
Ireland begins from the assumption that the British establishment
will soon put a stop to the war. In an illuminating collection of essays
by Labour's solidarity activists, Ken Livingstone kicks off with the
thought that 'we could find withdrawal happening fairly quickly and
quite unexpectedly.' As for Tony Benn, he takes off Tommy Cooper,
insisting that if the British persuaded Dublin to join Nato, 'they
would set a date (for withdrawal) "just like that" ' (M Collins ed, *Ireland
after Britain*). Labour left stalwart Clare Short? She has taken to
complaining that Irish solidarity activists are too 'obsessed' with
opposing the Anglo-Irish deal, and stresses that the deal is 'bringing a
united Ireland closer' (*Labour and Ireland,* December/January 1987).
The logic of the left's position is that we do not have to worry too
much about building a movement for Irish freedom. We can wait for
Westminster to decide to go, while we dream of what will happen
when the Irish War is all over.

The Labour left cannot effectively challenge its leaders' anti-Irish
policy because it shares the right's view that Britain has a progressive
role to play in Ireland. Labour left wingers look to the British state to

re-unite Ireland: they want Britain to negotiate a solution with Ireland's parties. It is for this reason that the left castigates republican violence as a 'counter-productive' force which interferes with 'the political process'. In an interview given in May 1984, Ken Livingstone, then a leading figure in the Labour left's Irish campaigns, asserted that he was 'opposed to every act of violence' and called for 'a political solution and negotiations between the warring factions'. But there are only two 'factions' at war in Ireland—the republican movement and the British. The only political solution which could follow from any negotiations that take place before the military defeat of the British forces in Ireland would be a British-imposed solution. Livingstone's repudiation of the armed struggle revealed the Labour left's antagonism to the only force fighting to prevent such a solution.

Behind all the talk of new policies and radical departures, the Labour Party aims to bring the Irish War to a conclusion by British means. The only debate among Labour's right and left concerns the precise form of the final solution Britain should impose on the Irish people.

Off the fence!

The left has developed a form of solidarity work which avoids taking a stand on the Irish War. Many British socialists believe that campaigns around issues such as torture, plastic bullets or strip-searching can shock British people into opposing their government. They often present their campaigns as neutral, impartial and objective. In 1978, the 'International Tribunal on British Crimes in Ireland' changed its name to 'International Tribunal on Britain's Presence in Ireland' lest it be seen to pre-judge the issue. In February 1983 a Labour Party conference on plastic bullets sought support around the open-ended question: 'Are plastic bullets part of the solution or part of the problem?' After Irishman John Downes was killed by an RUC plastic bullet in August 1984, left-wing Labour MP Joan Maynard appealed to the British sense of fair play. She claimed that the RUC had ignored its own guidelines, and that it had shot Downes from the wrong distance in the wrong part of the body.

The left's appeals to British justice and fair play could only have any kind of effect when the Irish War was all Bloody Sundays, internment and overt British repression. This created a certain space for popularising liberal concern. But even then the left's solidarity movement was a peripheral force in British politics, with no real influence in the working class. This was because appealing to people's consciences cuts no ice in a war which demands that people take one side or the other. The left's evasion of the central issue—the war—is not only dishonest: it just doesn't work.

The British public is not like an umpire at a cricket match. People support 'our' government and 'our' soldiers in Ireland. The man in the street might have misgivings about Ireland, but in the end knows that the only alternatives are victory or defeat. People who support British rule will accept repression and torture, perhaps as unfortunate and unpleasant, but certainly as necessary and unavoidable.

At the same time as the ineffectual 'Tribunal on Britain's Presence' asked Roy Mason to make it a submission, Labour's Northern Ireland minister boasted to the Tory press of his latest gambit:

'We are squeezing the terrorists like rolling up a toothpaste tube. We are squeezing them away from their supplies of money and explosives. We are squeezing them out of society and into prison.' (*Daily Express,* 5 December 1977)

The directness of 'Butcher' Mason stands in sharp contrast to the evasions of the British left. The ruling class asks the British public straight—support our war drive. The left, for its part, demands objectivity and neutrality about a British 'presence'.

Like any war the conflict in Ireland has two protagonists. One side stands for oppression in Ireland and reaction in Britain. The other side stands for Irish freedom and a challenge to the grip of the ruling class in Britain. The battle-lines are drawn on the streets of Derry and Belfast. They cannot be redrawn by committee-room debates on British 'fair play' in Ireland.

The failure of the left's solidarity movement is the failure to take sides in the Irish War. The Labour left has searched for a middle ground occupied by people who oppose the extremes of British brutality without supporting the national liberation struggle. More than 60 years of experience have shown that on Ireland there is no middle ground in Britain. The left's search for the non-existent middle ground explains the demise of liberal solidarity movements like TOM and the LCI.

● Fighting for Irish freedom

Irish Freedom Movement campaigns to win British workers to
the cause of Irish freedom

1979 November:	LONDON: National demonstration to protest at five years of the PTA.
1980 March:	LONDON: Occupied Congress House in protest at the TUC bans on Irish solidarity.
October:	BRIXTON: Marched to support first H-Block hunger-strike and mark the sixtieth anniversary of Irish hunger-striker Terence MacSwiney's death in Brixton jail.
1981 March:	COVENTRY: Held labour movement conference in support of second H-Block hunger-strike, despite TUC threats to expel supportive labour movement bodies.
	LONDON: Two supporters narrowly prevented by police from winning London marathon carrying 'Victory to the Irish hunger-strike' banner.
September:	Organised Workers' March for Irish Freedom from Manchester to TUC conference at Blackpool, demanding support for the hunger-strikers.
1982 February:	LONDON: Won wide backing for a national labour movement conference, despite TUC instructions to union bodies 'not to associate in any way' with the campaign.
April:	BELFAST and DERRY: Led 100 young people from British cities on 'Youth for Irish Freedom' delegation.
May:	Took relatives of nationalists murdered by British and Loyalist forces on speaking tour around Britain.
June:	LEEDS: Caused furore in press and council by campaigning for a public monument to hunger-striker Bobby Sands.

1983 January: LEEDS: Dominated annual Bloody Sunday commemoration march and held conference against Britain's shoot-to-kill campaign.

March: Held national week of action against the PTA, including protests at airports where arrests are concentrated.

April: MANCHESTER: Led another struggle against TUC attempts to silence union opposition to the Irish War.

May: MIDLANDS, MERSEYSIDE, YORKSHIRE: Began campaigning for county councils to make their areas 'PTA-free zones' and cut off Special Branch funding.

June: LIVERPOOL: Backed strike by Australian seamen which won the release of an Irish shipmate arrested under PTA.

November: KENT: Put on champagne breakfast celebration to greet Irish POW outside Maidstone prison.
LIVERPOOL: Held conference against supergrass trials.
BELFAST: Took delegation of trade unionists around the war zone.

December: LONDON, MANCHESTER, LIVERPOOL, BIRMINGHAM: Organised protests outside jails and police stations after wave of PTA pick-ups.

1984 January: SHEFFIELD: Staged conference against Labour council ban on Bloody Sunday commemoration march.

March: SHEFFIELD: Organised 1200-strong national demonstration against Labour's bans on Irish solidarity.

October: BRIGHTON: Protested outside Tory party conference against PTA and for political status—two days before the IRA bombing.

November: BIRMINGHAM: Marked 10 years of the PTA with packed conference.

1985 January: LIVERPOOL: Organised a series of pickets outside magistrates court to protest at wave of PTA arrests and defied joint Loyalist/police attacks to hold an anti-PTA rally.
LONDON: Marked the anniversary of Bloody Sunday with a torchlit demonstration through North London.
SCOTLAND: IFM supporters in Scotland went to Derry for the official Bloody Sunday commemoration.
MIDLANDS: Joined a republican rally in Leicester after Leicester Labour council banned the planned Bloody Sunday commemoration march through the city, and broke the ban by marching from the rally to picket Leicester jail in support of Irish prisoners of war.

May: Held a series of rallies around the country to mark the anniversary of the death of hunger-striker Bobby Sands.

BLOODY SUNDAY, SHEFFIELD, 1987

June/July:	Organised police station pickets and street protests from Glasgow to Brighton in response to PTA pick-ups after Scotland Yard's 'seaside bombing scare'.
August:	LONDON, BIRMINGHAM, MANCHESTER: Organised protests against the BBC ban on the *Real Lives* documentary, *At the Edge of the Union,* featuring leading Irish republican Martin McGuinness.
	Challenged the censors, local councils and the police and organised showings of the banned TV documentary to packed audiences nationwide.
	LONDON: Organised major march against British terror led by the Rising Sons of Ireland flute band from Limavady, County Derry to mark the fourteenth anniversary of the introduction of internment without trial in Northern Ireland.
November:	MANCHESTER: Organised the biggest conference for a decade in support of the Irish liberation struggle, 'Ireland: Behind the Wall of Silence'.
	LONDON: Organised protests outside Paddington Green police station where four men and two women were being held after two bombs were found outside Chelsea barracks.
December:	LONDON: Protested against police and Army terrorism at London's Copex '85 arms trade exhibition.
1986 January:	LONDON: Hundreds of people packed into an eve-of-march rally entitled 'No British solution' to hear speakers remember the massacre of 14 Irishmen on Bloody Sunday 1972 and turned out the next day to make the IFM contingent the best and biggest on the annual commemoration march.
May:	LONDON: Supported pickets outside the courts in solidarity with those on trial for the Brighton bombing.
August:	LONDON: More than 2000 people joined the IFM's march through London to mark the fifteenth anniversary of Britain's introduction of internment without trial in Northern Ireland.
	STRATHCLYDE: Supported 'Free the Guildford Four' march called by the Republican Bands Alliance in Coatbridge.
December:	LONDON, SHEFFIELD: Invited Terry Robson, a victim of Britain's supergrass system, to tell the truth about the Irish War a year after the signing of the Anglo-Irish agreement.

Building an Irish solidarity movement

British terrorism is the one consistent theme which runs through hundreds of years of British rule in Ireland. Liberal, Tory and Labour governments have run Ireland under various constitutional arrangements from the 1801 Act of Union, through partition in 1921, to direct rule since 1972. Whatever its political form, British rule has always rested on the terror of British troops and Loyalist murderers.

All parties have given uncritical support to state terror in Ireland, while denouncing the 'terrorism' of the republican movement. The right wing of the Labour Party has often been even more vociferous than the Tories in its attacks on the IRA. And the left wing of the Labour Party has adapted the traditional theme of terror to suit its own purpose.

Labour left policy on Ireland has emphasised diplomacy and dialogue with the republican movement as an alternative to military repression and the armed struggle. But the left's alternative amounts to little more than the pursuit of terror by other means. The content of the dialogue sought became clear in 1983, when Labour's deputy Northern Ireland spokesman Clive Soley led a delegation of MPs to the Six Counties. Delegates put their cards on the table. At a West Belfast meeting with Sinn Fein, according to the *Irish Times,* the delegation 'raised the question of an all-Ireland police force and asked what would be the minimum conditions for a Provisional IRA ceasefire' (22 September 1983).

Since 1983, the constant theme of the left's side of the 'dialogue' with Sinn Fein has been to force a republican ceasefire. They want republicans to move away from the armed struggle against imperialism and toward British-style electoral and community politics instead. In a recent essay, Martin Collins of the Labour Committee on Ireland claimed that the 'elitism and putchism of petit-bourgeois physical force republicanism has been eroded', and he was glad of it (in *Ireland after Britain*). Ken Livingstone, who thinks that the Irish national liberation movement is becoming more like his own soft-left wing of the Labour Party, is disparaging about 'the lack of political thinking and the predominance of activities in support of the armed struggle in the early seventies' (*Tribune,* 9 January 1987).

The left has tried to achieve by force of persuasion what the British
Army has failed to achieve by force of arms. The left shares with the
Army the aim of disarming the republican movement and imposing a
British solution in Ireland. Radical Labour spokesmen have
encouraged the nationalist community to participate in the sham
assemblies and forums that Britain has set up in the Six Counties.
These institutions only exist to whitewash British terrorism. Yet the
left has urged nationalists to take them seriously and get involved in
the 'democratic process'. Labour left wingers want the Irish people to
submit to British rule without a fight.

IRA bombings in Britain underline the common ground shared by
left and right in Britain on the Irish War. The Tories condemn each
'terrorist outrage' and use the occasion to spew out anti-Irish bigotry.
The left joins in and bemoans the lost opportunities for forging
ahead with its 'dialogue' with Sinn Fein. The British establishment
calls on the government to step up repression and the left calls on
republicans to give up bombs and stick to ballots. Both sides deny the
Irish people the right to fight for their freedom. The IRA's position
on the balance between its bombs and ballot strategy is clear. After
Sinn Fein's success in winning seats in the May 1985 local council
elections Derry Sinn Fein leader Martin McGuinness put the left
straight: 'The results are good but, at the end of the day, it will be the
cutting edge of the IRA which will bring freedom.' Unlike their
would-be British advisers, republicans live in the real world of the
Irish war zone. They know the Irish people have to fight for
their rights.

IRA bombing campaigns are an extension of the armed struggle to
Britain. The nationalist community has no alternative but to fight
the terrorism of British rule. There is no future for the Irish people
while the Six Counties remain under British occupation. The history
of British terror shows that British imperialism cannot be talked out
of Ireland. This must be the starting point for any movement in
Britain in solidarity with the Irish people's struggle.

The Irish Freedom Movement supports Irish national self-
determination as a basic democratic right. And we recognise such
support must include the right to *fight* for self-determination. Our
backing for the Irish people's national rights is unconditional. This
means that we support the struggle against British imperialism,
whatever tactic the Irish people care to use. By its nature a war inflicts
violence on civilians and can have tragic consequences. This is
regrettable, but it does not alter our support for Irish freedom against
British tyranny.

The British establishment deplores the IRA's use of violence 'for political ends'. Yet when the Tories sent the task force to the Falklands in 1982, the armed forces' violence was hailed as a *defence* of democracy. British socialists decry IRA bombs in Britain as 'mindless violence'. Yet when the liberation movements of South Africa or Central America use similar tactics, their actions are applauded as blows for freedom. Clearly 'the use of violence for political ends' is not at issue. It is the political end being pursued which decides who is for or against the use of violence. British socialists who condemn IRA violence are taking sides with the state against the Irish liberation struggle.

Anti-imperialists have to challenge the widespread approval for the British state's role in Ireland. The Irish Freedom Movement is out to break the consensus that backs up Britain's war in Ireland. We want to win workers to support Irish self-determination. That means confronting the question: 'Who are the real terrorists?' Irish freedom is a political end which has to be pursued through violent resistance to British terror.

There can be no compromise solution to the Irish War. It is a fight to the finish.

Winning wider support for the cause of Irish freedom cannot be done by dodging the central issue of the war. Waffle about 'human rights' and 'fair play' will get us nowhere. We have to direct our arguments at a working class audience and convince ordinary people in Britain that their interests lie in lining up with Irish freedom fighters against the warlords of the British establishment. Winning the arguments on Ireland is part of a broader political struggle to change the way working class people see the world and their role in changing it. We have to spell out that in Ireland, as in every conflict in Britain, there are two sides—that of the ruling class and that of the working class. Ordinary people here have no more interest in agreeing with the establishment on Ireland than they would have in siding with Thatcher on wages or NHS cuts.

Seen in this light, taking sides with Irish freedom fighters against the authorities ceases to be a matter of simply sympathising with the Irish and becomes a vital part of building a movement in Britain that can stand up for itself against the employers and their state. If we can show working class people that accepting the establishment's arguments about 'our' right to rule in Ireland means allowing our class opponents to monopolise political debate, we will be well on the way to making Ireland an issue over here.

WAR FACTS

1.

War personalities

ADAMS
Gerry
President of Sinn Fein since 1983.
Born 1949, West Belfast. Founder
member of Northern Ireland Civil
Rights Association, 1967. Interned
1971. Member of Provisional IRA
delegation for secret talks with
William Whitelaw, 1972. Arrested and
imprisoned in Long Kesh in 1973 as
leading figure in Belfast IRA. Released
in 1976. Detained on remand in 1978
for seven months on charges of IRA
membership—charges subsequently
dropped. At 1979 commemoration of
Wolfe Tone he emphasised the
importance of combining a political
approach with military tactics. Elected
as Sinn Fein representative to Ulster
assembly on abstentionist ticket,
October 1982. Banned under PTA
from visiting London on Sinn Fein
delegation, December 1982. In June
1983 he defeated pro-British Catholic
Gerry Fitt, and became Sinn Fein MP
for West Belfast on abstentionist
ticket. Victim of unsuccessful
assassination attempt by Loyalist
Ulster Freedom Fighters, March 1984.
Made keynote speech at 1986 Ard
Fheis in favour of ending
abstentionism policy in the Twenty-
six Counties on the grounds that it
should be treated as a tactic. At
funeral of an IRA volunteer killed by
SAS at Loughgall, promised 'Margaret

Thatcher, Tom King and all the other rich and powerful people will be sorry in their time that Loughgall ever happened,' May 1987. Re-elected with increased share of the vote in June 1987 election.

ARCHER
Peter
Appointed Labour Party spokesman on Northern Ireland in place of Don Concannon after 1983 party conference. Former vice-chair of the Anti-Slavery Society and founder member of Amnesty International. As Solicitor General in 1974-79 Labour government he reorganised Northern Ireland's prosecution system to cope with the extra demands of criminalisation and the conveyor-belt system of imprisoning republicans. Consistently refused to support motions calling for troops out at Labour Party conferences. Led negotiations with Sinn Fein over the winter of 1986-87 in pursuit of Irish votes for Labour, but slavishly followed Kinnock's line condemning armed struggle. Called for RUC strength to be increased after IRA blew up Lord Justice Gibson, April 1987.

ATKINS
Humphrey
Secretary of State for Northern Ireland, 1979-81. Appointed by Margaret Thatcher after Tory election victory, May 1979. Got the job because of the assassination, during the election campaign, of leading contender Airey Neave. Blundered along for two years before handing over to James Prior, after presiding over the deaths of 10 hunger-strikers and the discrediting of Britain's criminalisation policy.

BARR
Glen
Loyalist paramilitary leader. Member of the Loyalist Association of Workers and the Ulster Defence Association, 1971. Chairman of the coordinating committee which ran the 1974 Ulster Workers' Council strike. Leader of Loyalist delegations in talks with Merlyn Rees, October 1974. Collaborator with William Craig's Vanguard movement, 1973-78. Prominent in the UDA's political front, the New Ulster Political Research Group, 1978. Member of Britain's 'anti-sectarian' Fair Employment Agency, 1976-81.

BARRY
Peter
Deputy leader of Fine Gael. Born in Cork, 1928, to family known as the 'merchant princes'—because of their tea-importing concern. Tried to improve his party's nationalist image, by criticising Britain's use of shoot-to-kill squads and the PTA against Irish people, and pushing for Dublin to have more say in the affairs of the North. As Irish foreign minister, 1982-87, he was the leading Irish politician involved in the negotiations over the introduction of the Anglo-Irish agreement, November 1985. With Tom King, co-chaired regular Anglo-Irish conferences. 'Peter Barry' was the stooge name Unionists put up to provide paper opposition in uncontested seats during the January 1986 anti-accord by-elections in the North.

BELL
Stuart
Appointed Labour Party deputy spokesman on Northern Ireland in 1984. Welcomed Norman Tebbit's return to parliament after the

Brighton bomb with a chorus of
'We've grown accustomed to your
style'. In a March 1985 parliamentary
debate, made clear that Labour
would condemn republican violence
'today, tomorrow and always'. Shared
platform with Sinn Fein councillor at
1986 Labour Party conference,
contrary to Kinnock's instructions, in
order to use the opportunity to
lambast Irish freedom struggle.
Joined Labour Party talks with Sinn
Fein over winter 1986-87.
Embarrassed party leaders when he
let the cat out of the bag by
promising Unionists an early review
of the Anglo-Irish accord in return for
parliamentary support for Labour,
March 1987.

BIGGS-DAVISON
Sir John
Pro-Unionist Conservative
frontbench spokesman on Northern
Ireland, 1976-79. Subsequently
chairman of the party's Northern
Ireland committee. A staunch
defender of imperialist interests,
he addressed Dublin's New Ireland
Forum in October 1983 to put the
British case against joint sovereignty.
In 1984 he co-authored a report
proposing new Anglo-Irish institutions
and more cross-Border collaboration.
Prominent in the campaign to reopen
the cases of the Birmingham Six and
Guildford Four to restore reputation of
British 'justice'.

CHICHESTER-CLARK
James
(later Lord Moyola)
Stormont prime minister, May 1969-
March 1971. Ousted Terence O'Neill,
in favour of a tougher approach to
nationalist demands for civil rights.
Requested British military invasion,
August 1969. Presided over mounting
chaos in 1971 as Loyalist

paramilitaries regrouped and nationalist resistance became more organised. Pushed out by the even more hardline Brian Faulkner.

CORRIGAN
Mairead
Co-founder in 1976 of the Peace People with Betty Williams and Ciaran McKeown. Formed the Women's Peace Movement (later Peace People) in response to the death of her sister's three children when struck by a car whose republican driver had been shot dead at the wheel by British soldiers. The nationalist community soon repudiated the Peace People when they condemned only the resistance of the republican movement, not the violence of the British state. The movement soon collapsed, discredited by winning the Nobel peace prize and the adulation of the British establishment, which lifted the ban on Irish demonstrations in Trafalgar Square for a Peace People rally in 1976.

CONCANNON
Don
Labour's junior minister in Northern Ireland under Roy Mason, 1976-79. Notorious for his visit to Bobby Sands' death-bed to inform Sands of the Labour Party's solid support for the Tory strategy of allowing the hunger-strikers to die. Also known for his patronage of entrepreneurs like John De Lorean, whom he provided with vast sums of money in return for empty promises of job creation in Northern Ireland. Spoke out against troop withdrawal motions at Labour Party conferences but was replaced as Labour's frontbench spokesman in 1983.

COSTELLO
Seamus
Founder of the Irish Republican
Socialist Party. Born Wicklow 1939,
murdered by the Official IRA, Dublin,
October 1977. Active as a teenager
in the IRA's 1956 Border campaign.
Local council activist in Wicklow in
the sixties. Prominent member of the
Official IRA after 1969-70 split with
the Provisionals. Expelled from the
Official IRA for opposing its
renunciation of the armed struggle
against British imperialism. Formed
IRSP in December 1974.

CRAIG
William
Loyalist leader. As Stormont home
affairs minister was responsible for
banning civil rights march in Derry,
which was subsequently attacked by
the RUC, October 1968. Expelled
from the Stormont cabinet in
December 1968. Staunch Loyalist
critic of what he saw as the
conciliatory approach of the Unionist
leadership, calling for even harsher
repression. Opposed direct rule,
1972, in favour of Ulster autonomy.
Attracted enormous public rallies for
his extreme Loyalist Vanguard
movement, which he arrived at in
stately black car with Hell's Angel
motorbike escorts. Backer of Ulster
Workers' Council strike, 1974. Support
collapsed when he pushed his
notions of an independent Ulster so
far as to propose some collaboration
between Loyalists and the SDLP.
Appointed to Council of Europe (and
its human rights committee!), 1977.
Lost East Belfast parliamentary seat
to Paisley's Democratic Unionist
Party, 1979. Failed to win a seat in
1982 assembly elections.

CREASEY
Lieutenant-General Sir Timothy
Army General Officer Commanding in Northern Ireland, 1977-79. Useful experience as commander of the counter-insurgency forces of the Sultan of Oman, 1972-75. The Provisional IRA is being 'suppressed, contained and isolated' he said in December 1977. But in January 1980 he admitted that the IRA could not be defeated, 'given the national will'. Returned to Oman to become commander-in-chief and chief of the defence staff, 1980-85. Personal military adviser to the Sultan of Oman, 1985. Died in 1986.

DUKES
Alan
Leader of Fine Gael party in the Republic, March 1987 to date. Born Dublin, 1945. Chief economist for Irish Farmers Association, 1972-80. Served in Brussels as IFA lobbyist, 1973-76. Elected for Kildare seat, June 1981. Made minister of agriculture on his first day in the Dail. As minister of finance, 1982-86, presided over increasingly austere budgets. Appointed minister of justice in February 1986 and steered the Extradition Act through the Dail.

FAUL
Father Denis

Catholic priest from Dungannon, critical of British repression and republican resistance. A longstanding campaigner on issues of civil rights and scrupulous documentor of brutality under interrogation and the use of plastic bullets. His attempts at mediation during the hunger-strikes and his condemnations of the armed struggle have brought him into repeated conflict with the republican movement. Claimed that active membership of IRA was a mortal sin after they blew up Lord Justice Gibson, April 1987.

FAULKNER
Brian
(later Lord Downpatrick)
Last Stormont prime minister, 1971-72. Succeeded O'Neill and Chichester-Clark as a more consistent hardliner. He had resigned from O'Neill's cabinet in January 1969 because of its concession to the nationalist community of appointing the Cameron Commission to inquire into the Derry disturbances. His attempt to crush nationalist resistance—internment in 1971 and Bloody Sunday in 1972—backfired badly and led to the collapse of Stormont and his premiership. Brief return to prominence as chief executive in the power-sharing assembly before it collapsed after a few weeks in 1974. Fell off his horse and killed himself while out hunting in 1976.

FITT
Gerry
(now Lord Fitt of Bellshill)
Longstanding pro-British Catholic statesman. Former merchant seaman; Belfast city councillor, 1958; Stormont MP, 1962; Westminster MP, 1966-83. Early civil rights campaigner and founder member of SDLP, 1970. Deputy to arch-Loyalist Brian Faulkner in 1974 power-sharing executive. Left the SDLP in 1979 claiming it was too 'green nationalist' for his taste. His condemnations of the republican movement and refusal to support the hunger-strikers lost

him the support of his West Belfast constituents. Lost his parliamentary seat to Sinn Fein's Gerry Adams in June 1983 general election, in which many of his votes were thought to have come from Unionists. House burnt out by nationalist youth a month later. Rewarded for his services to British imperialism with a seat in the house of lords. Has since tried to recoup lost support by campaigning for a review of the cases of the Birmingham Six and the Guildford Four—so that the 'real culprits' can be dealt with.

FITZGERALD
Garret

Free State premier (Taoiseach) 1981-March 1982; December 1982 to February 1987. As leader of Fine Gael party noted for his fawning admiration of British. In 1984-85 his government began extraditing republicans to stand trial in the North, hijacked IRA arms shipments and impounded supposedly republican bank deposits. Fond of mentioning his parents' role in the 1916 Rising when accused of being collaborator. Leading figure in the search for a negotiated solution through the New Ireland Forum, signed Anglo-Irish deal with Thatcher, November 1985. Popularity plummeted after four years of austerity government. Lost divorce referendum in 1986 against the combined opposition of the Church and Fianna Fail. FitzGerald's coalition government collapsed after Labour refused to back cuts budget, January 1987. Fought and lost February election on austerity platform. Resigned leadership of his party shortly afterwards.

GOULDING
Cathal
Official IRA chief of staff since closing stages of the Border campaign in 1962. Born Dublin 1922, interned during the Second World War and imprisoned with Sean MacStiofain for arms raid on an Essex school in 1953. In the sixties prominent in promoting the reformist political strategy that came to dominate the movement. Led the Official IRA in declaring its ceasefire in 1972 and in its subsequent condemnations of the Provisionals.

HATTERSLEY
Roy
The man who sent the troops in, 1969. As minister of defence for administration was responsible for the British military intervention and later for the transformation of the 'B' Specials into the UDR. As opposition defence spokesman, visited Northern Ireland to review the success of Operation Motorman, 1972. Supported the introduction of the Prevention of Terrorism Act, 1974. As shadow home secretary, opposed the renewal of the PTA in 1983, on the grounds that it was 'ineffective in dealing with terrorism'. During 1987 election campaign called for IRA to be dealt with by 'prudent, but substantial military power'. Now deputy leader of Labour Party.

HAUGHEY
Charles
Leader of the Fianna Fail party in the Republic. Irish premier (Taoiseach) December 1979—July 1981, March—December 1982, March 1987 to date. Millionaire accountant, launched his political career by marrying daughter of former premier

Sean Lemass. As minister of justice in the sixties, incarcerated IRA men in concentration camps. The Free State's leading 'green' politician, he has often clashed with Britain over its policy in the North. In 1970 was sacked from the cabinet after being charged with running guns to the North. Caused a diplomatic crisis by refusing to back EEC sanctions against Argentina during the 1982 Malvinas War. Nevertheless, Haughey appreciates the need to cooperate with Britain against the republican movement. In 1980 held a famous summit meeting with Thatcher at which he gave her a silver teapot. In 1982 presided over the jailing of republican Gerard Tuite. The great survivor of Irish politics, Haughey has fought off numerous setbacks, corruption scandals and challenges to his leadership. His dexterity was on display again when he won the February 1987 election by capitalising on the unpopularity of the FitzGerald regime, and pledging not to ditch the Anglo-Irish agreement. But for the fourth time Haughey failed to win an outright majority.

HERMON
Sir John

Chief Constable RUC, January 1980 to date. Born Larne 1928. Joined RUC in 1950. Caused a riot when he helped remove an Irish tricolour in Divis Street, West Belfast in 1964 after a complaint was made by then little-known Ian Paisley. Commandant of RUC training centre, 1969. Studied police management at New Scotland Yard, 1979. An unpopular character, has clashed with Unionists, Irish police chiefs and British ministers. In 1982 welcomed the emergence of supergrasses and denied they were under any police pressure, and

launched his Divisional Mobile Support Units—trained to act with 'speed, firepower and aggression'—on a shoot-to-kill campaign. In August 1984 he defended the RUC attack on a Belfast republican rally in which one nationalist was killed and many maimed, and rebuked Northern Ireland secretary James Prior for suggesting the police might have over-reacted. Clashed with Manchester deputy police chief John Stalker, assigned to investigate the shoot-to-kill campaign, and gave him the elbow, 1985.

HUME
John

Leader of the SDLP. Member of the Westminster and European parliaments. Early civil rights campaigner and founder member of the Social Democratic and Labour Party, 1970. Eager participant in every power-sharing or devolution initiative, executive or assembly talks or even tea-party given by the British state to promote a moderate, constitutional political approach in the nationalist community. Managed to defeat Sinn Fein candidate in 1984 Euro-elections, with the help of British government money and Unionist transfer votes. Nationalist pressures forced him to boycott the Ulster assembly. Leading light in the New Ireland Forum's attempt to restore credibility of constitutional nationalism. In March 1985 sought peace talks with the IRA to bolster his standing, but called them off after refusing to be photographed with 'terrorists'. Boosted by the Anglo-Irish agreement and his party's showing at the January 1986 Northern Ireland by-elections, Hume made several speeches praising the RUC for its attempts to restrain rampaging Loyalist mobs. Welcomed Loyalist paramilitary UDA's call for a power-sharing government in the North in early 1987.

HURD
Douglas

Tory secretary of state for Northern Ireland, September 1984 to September 1985. Earned the nickname 'Hitler Hurd' at public school for his enthusiasm for caning junior boys. Part-time author of bad novels, including one about the IRA in which he ascribes the cause of the 'troubles' to the violent influence of Irish Catholic grandmothers. A close aide to the Heath government during the attempt to introduce power-sharing in 1973-74, he met Sinn Fein leaders for unofficial talks in 1978. His background, plus his foreign office connections, made Loyalist leaders highly suspicious when he was appointed to replace Prior in 1984. But Hurd pursued the shoot-to-kill campaign with as much vigour as his predecessor. He also made efforts to draw the Dublin government into closer cooperation with the British war effort. In March 1985 he admitted that defeating the IRA was the precondition for any British political solution in Ireland. Promoted to home secretary in a cabinet reshuffle, where he sat on the cases of the Birmingham Six and Guildford Four for two years 'considering the evidence'. Referred the case of the Birmingham Six to the court of appeal, January 1986, but refused to re-open the cases of the Guildford Four and the Maguires.

KING
General Sir Frank

Army General Officer Commanding in
Northern Ireland, February 1973-75.
Famous for his refusal to follow
government instructions to crush the
Loyalist Ulster Workers' Council strike
that brought down power-sharing
assembly in 1974. His action
provided the clearest example since
the Curragh mutiny of 1914 that the
armed forces in Ireland will defy
political directives if necessary to
defend the wider interests of the
British state. Now director of private
counter-insurgency firm, Control
Risks.

KING
Tom

Northern Ireland secretary of state,
September 1985 to date. Born 1933.
Served in Kenya with King's African
Rifles in early stages of war against
the Mau-Mau freedom fighters. MP
for Bridgewater, 1970 to date. Held
various ministerial posts concerned
mainly with the economy, 1975-85.
Catapulted from dodging questions
about unemployment from docile
Labour MPs into dodging bricks flung
by hostile nationalists and
intransigent Loyalists, enraged by the
Anglo-Irish agreement in September
1985. Attacked by Loyalist mob
outside Belfast city hall on first visit
to North, November 1985. Slipped on
first of a series of banana skins in
Brussels in December when he upset
Dublin by being blunt about the
meaning of the Anglo-Irish deal: 'For
all practical purposes and into
perpetuity there will not be a united
Ireland.'

KINNOCK
Neil
Leader of the Labour Party and the opposition, 1983 to date. Born in Wales, 1942. MP for Bedwellty, 1970-83. MP for Islwyn, 1983 to date. Aide to Labour's secretary of state for education, Shirley Williams, 1974-75. Youthful radicalism faded quickly. Has relished proving his loyalty to the establishment on Irish War. In December 1984, backed the use of 'every force' against republicans after SAS had shot dead two republicans. During Anglo-Irish debate in parliament condemned IRA 'terrorism and the noxious insincerity of their bullet and ballot strategy'. At the Blackpool 1986 Labour Party conference he told Irish activists that 'Nobody in or associated with Sinn Fein is welcome within a million miles of the Labour Party or anything we stand for.' In November 1986, Kinnock met Loyalist leaders Ian Paisley and James Molyneaux for secret talks on the prospects for the Anglo-Irish accord under a future Labour government. On visit to North in January 1987 Kinnock despatched his boys to tell Sinn Fein that Labour disapproved of its 'dual strategy' of the ballot and the armalite. Confirmed his admiration for Britain's elite terrorists when, after they had murdered eight IRA volunteers and one nationalist at Loughgall, he applauded the SAS death squads for having won 'a significant victory over the men of violence', May 1987.

KITSON
General Sir Frank
Former commander-in-chief, United Kingdom land forces. Infantry brigade commander in Northern Ireland, 1970-72. Old hand at imposing

imperialist terror in Kenya, Malaya, Cyprus and Oman. During his tour of Northern Ireland, put into practice the ideas in his *Low Intensity Operations: Subversion, Insurgency and Counter-Insurgency* (1971). Laid the basis for the Army's use of 'psy-ops' — psychological operations and black propaganda aimed at undermining nationalist morale in the Six Counties. Retired 1985, but published controversial book critical of geriatric Army leadership in 1987.

LIVINGSTONE
Ken

Left-wing leader of Labour Greater London Council, 1981-85. President of radical Labour Committee on Ireland. Initially supported British invasion of North in 1969. Changed his view to support Irish unity, but retained illusions in Britain's potentially progressive role in Northern Ireland. Invited Gerry Adams to London in December 1982 to discuss how to negotiate a British solution to the war, but vociferously condemned the Ballykelly bombing which the Tories used as an excuse to ban the republican visit. Visited Belfast and condemned the armed struggle, February 1983. Played down his interest in Ireland to cultivate a respectable image in campaigning against the abolition of the GLC, but continued pouring money into Irish community quangos to win the support of Irish people in London for Labour. Chaired fringe meeting at 1986 Labour Party conference addressed by Sinn Fein councillor to keep Labour's 'dialogue' with Sinn Fein on the boil. Elected MP for Brent East, June 1987.

McALISKEY
Bernadette
(formerly DEVLIN)

Republican socialist. Civil rights campaigner and founder member People's Democracy, 1968. Participant in PD march Belfast to Derry, attacked by Loyalists at Burntollet, January 1969. Elected to Westminster as independent MP for Mid-Ulster, March 1969. Active in the 'Battle of the Bogside', August 1969. Sentenced to six months' imprisonment for incitement to riot and disorderly behaviour, December 1969. Punched Tory home secretary Reginald Maudling in parliament for lying over Bloody Sunday, January 1972. Lost Mid-Ulster February 1974 after intervention of SDLP. Founder member of the IRSP, December 1974. Left IRSP over objections to the party's ideas about the importance of the armed struggle against Britain. Campaigned in support of the hunger-strikers, 1980-81. Seriously wounded, together with husband, in Loyalist assassination attempt, January 1981. Recovered to challenge Fianna Fail leader Charles Haughey in his North Dublin constituency in both 1982 general elections.

MacGIOLLA
Tomas

Former president of Official Sinn Fein, now leader of the Workers Party. Presided over the 1969-70 split in the republican movement. Deported from Britain twice in 1972 although cleared of charges of Official IRA membership in Ireland. Has guided Official Sinn Fein through its transformation into the moderate Workers Party. This was completed in 1982 when the party removed Sinn Fein from its title entirely and MacGiolla won a seat in the Dail at the general election.

McGUINNESS
Martin

Leading Sinn Fein member. Elected as Ulster assembly representative for Derry on abstentionist ticket, October 1982. Former leader of Provisional IRA in Derry. Member of IRA delegation in secret talks with William Whitelaw in 1972. Imprisoned in the Republic, 1973. Banned from visiting London by Whitelaw, December 1982. In 1984, he dismissed suggestions that Sinn Fein should split from the IRA and concentrate on political campaigns, declaring 'without the IRA we are slaves.' Declared after the successful May 1985 council elections that 'the results are good but, at the end of the day, it will be the cutting edge of the IRA which will bring freedom.' At the centre of BBC censorship scandal over the banning of the *Real Lives* documentary in which he featured with Loyalist bigot Gregory Campbell, July 1985. Vigorously opposed to Sinn Fein's abstentionist position in the South. Blamed its supporters for the 1975 truce debacle when the position was overturned at the 1986 Ard Fheis. At funeral of two of the IRA volunteers slain by SAS, told mourners 'We will remember Loughgall forever, and we will see to it that the British government does as well,' May 1987.

MacSTIOFAIN
Sean

Former IRA chief of staff, 1969-72. Born London 1938. Sentenced to eight years for stealing rifles from a school in Essex, 1953. Central role in building up the Provisional IRA in Northern Ireland after the 1969-70 split. In 1972 said he was interested in peace but on IRA's terms. Arrested in Dublin and jailed for six months, November 1972. IRA made an

unsuccessful rescue bid. In January 1973 gave up 57-day hunger-strike in prison. On release active in Sinn Fein political work. Resigned from Sinn Fein in 1981 after its Ard Fheis showed a majority opposed to the *Eire Nua* policy for a federal Ireland. Called for an IRA ceasefire, March 1983. Was accused of being a spy for the garda by spies for British intelligence working for the scab *Sunday Times,* anxious to stir up strife between different factions in the republican movement.

MAGEE
Patrick

The Brighton bomber. Born Belfast 1951. Moved to Norwich, 1953, where his father found work as a fitter. Returned to Belfast with his family, October 1969. Joined Provisionals early seventies. Interned in Long Kesh, 1973-75. Badly tortured for three days in Castlereagh RUC barracks, 1977. Was sent on active service to England where his accent was thought to be the most use. First saw action in Christmas bombing campaign in London, 1978. Masterminded the attack on the British cabinet at the Grand Hotel, Brighton, during the Tory Party conference, October 1984. Jailed for life in June 1986.

MALLON
Seamus

Deputy leader of the SDLP, 1979 to date. Born in Markethill, County Armagh, 1936. Former Gaelic footballer and head teacher. Worked in civil rights campaigns from mid-sixties, elected to Armagh council, 1973. Appointed to Republic's senate by Haughey, June 1982. Elected to Ulster assembly representing Armagh, but unseated by Unionist Harold McCusker on the grounds that he was a member of a 'foreign' parliament. Became SDLP MP for Newry and Armagh, 1986. Figurehead for green nationalist wing of SDLP until he became MP, when he adopted his leader's openly sycophantic attitude to all things British. After Lord Justice Gibson was blown up by the IRA, called for cross-Border police patrols so that the RUC could operate with official sanction in the Republic, April 1987.

MASON
Roy

Labour's secretary of state for Northern Ireland, September 1976–May 1979. Former miner, MP for Barnsley. Presided over the full implementation of Ulsterisation and criminalisation, and intensified repression through an enlarged RUC, UDR and SAS. Support for RUC interrogation methods led to 'don't vote for torturers' campaign against him in Britain. Earned the label 'Butcher' among nationalists. In 1977 headed off a repeat of the Ulster Workers' Council strike by promising Loyalist workers increased terror against the nationalist community. After his removal from office in the 1979 general election, the Tory *Daily Telegraph* often wished aloud that his brutal hand was still guiding the British war effort. Regularly predicted the imminent collapse of the republican movement. In 1977 claimed that 'the corner' was 'being turned in the war against the terrorists'. Ten years later, spent his last days as an MP still calling for more repression against the Irish. Now lives in retirement in constant fear of a 'terrorist' around every corner waiting to deliver retribution.

MAUDLING
Reginald

Ran Northern Ireland as Tory home secretary, 1970-72. Tried to leave things to Stormont, but ended up having to impose direct rule after internment fiasco and the Bloody Sunday massacre. Talked complacently about achieving 'an acceptable level of violence', but handed over to new Northern Ireland secretary William Whitelaw with violence erupting on an unprecedented scale.

MOLYNEAUX
James

Leader of Official Unionist Party since 1979. Deputy Grand Master of the Orange Order. Presided over the loosening of the Unionists' traditional links with the Conservative Party. Prominent in pressurising the minority Labour government to give Northern Ireland more seats at Westminster. Has fronted Enoch Powell's policy of total integration into the United Kingdom and warned against the dangers of the 'rolling devolution' assembly in 1982. But adopted a softer line on cooperating with the SDLP in response to fears about increased 'alienation' of the nationalist community in 1984. His first preference vote of almost 20 000 was the largest in the assembly elections. Joined with DUP in fighting Anglo-Irish accord, but preferred constitutional opposition like boycotts and resignations to street violence. With his DUP counterpart, retracted compromise deal made with Thatcher in February 1986 in the face of working class opposition. Has cautiously steered his party away from confrontation with the government in the wake of weakening Loyalist resistance to the Anglo-Irish deal.

MORRISON
Danny

Sinn Fein vice-president. Former internee. Editor of *An Phoblacht/Republican News,* the republican movement's weekly paper, from 1981 until his election to the Ulster assembly as the representative for Mid-Ulster in October 1982. His comment at the 1981 Sinn Fein Ard Fheis, 'Who can object if we take power in Ireland with an Armalite in one hand and a ballot paper in the other?' has become the accepted definition of the republican movement's military and political strategy. Member of Sinn Fein delegation banned from visiting London, December 1982. Came within 78 votes of winning Mid-Ulster from the DUP in the June 1983 general election. Won 93 079 votes in the June 1984 Euro-elections, when defeated by John Hume of the SDLP.

NEAVE
Airey

Assassinated Tory Northern Ireland spokesman. Killed by car bomb in house of commons car park in the Inla's most spectacular operation, March 1979. Former British war hero and close Thatcher acolyte, he had called for even more draconian repression in Ireland.

NEWMAN
Sir Kenneth

RUC chief constable, 1976-79. Learnt the basics of repression in Palestine, 1946-48. Reorganised and rearmed RUC in line with Ulsterisation. Pioneered vicious interrogation techniques aimed at extracting confessions to make the conveyor-belt system of British justice run more smoothly. Metropolitan Police commissioner, 1982-87. Now to work for private counter-terrorist agency Control Risks.

O'BRADAIGH
Ruairi
President of Provisional Sinn Fein, 1970-83. Former teacher from Roscommon. Played leading role in IRA Border campaign, 1956-62. Sentenced in Dublin to six months' imprisonment for IRA membership, 1973. Leading role in developing Sinn Fein political programme, *Eire Nua.* Stepped down and replaced by Gerry Adams at 1983 Ard Fheis as his political ideas were rejected by new Northern leadership of Sinn Fein. Broke with Sinn Fein after 1986 Ard Fheis abandoned abstentionist policy for the South and helped launch the breakaway Republican Sinn Fein.

O'CONNAILL
Daithi
Leader of the breakaway Republican Sinn Fein. A Corkman, he was wounded in 1956 IRA campaign, and interned in the Curragh. Escaped by linking arms with O'Bradaigh and pretending to be a courting couple, 1958. Imprisoned again for three years, 1960. Prominent IRA activist in early seventies. Leader of IRA delegation to Whitelaw, 1972. Vice-president Provisional Sinn Fein, 1974-83. Key negotiator in 1975 ceasefire. Arrested and imprisoned again in 1976 and 1977. Promoter of the concept of a federal Ireland adopted by Sinn Fein in 1971, but later rejected at the 1982 Ard Fheis. After the 1986 Sinn Fein Ard Fheis, founded Republican Sinn Fein with O'Bradaigh.

O'HARE
Rita
Editor of *An Phoblacht/Republican News,* Sinn Fein's weekly in Ireland, 1985 to date. Headed Sinn Fein's women's department. Took over paper on death of Mick 'Burke' Timothy in January 1985.

OLDFIELD
Maurice

Chief security coordinator in Northern Ireland, 1979-80. Former head of MI6 from 1965 to 1977, 'M' was brought out of retirement to help coordinate police and Army terror in the North. Was responsible for preparing the ground for the supergrass system to try to break the republican movement. But it all proved too much for him—he suffered a heart attack and retired for good in 1981. His corpse was dug up by Thatcher as part of her campaign to bash prominent homosexuals in the run-up to the 1987 general election.

O'MALLEY
Desmond

Leader of Progressive Democrats, January 1986 to date. Born Limerick, 1939. TD for Limerick East, 1968 to date. Introduced draconian Offences Against the State legislation, 1970-1973, as Fianna Fail minister of justice. Fought Fianna Fail leader Charles Haughey in bid to secure leadership of the party in 1979. Conducted numerous intrigues in succeeding years but always defeated by Haughey's ability to manipulate nationalist aspirations. The two men have been at loggerheads ever since. Adopted guise of figurehead of 'modern' wing of Fianna Fail, only to lose party whip for opposing abortion amendment. Rebelled against party line of opposition to legalisation of contraceptive sales and was expelled, 1985. The Progressive Democrats were soon called the 'Dessicrats'. The party fought the February 1987 general election under the slogan, 'There's a job to be done—only Dessie can do it', and won 14 seats.

O'NEILL
Terence
(later Lord O'Neill of the Maine)
Stormont prime minister, 1963-69.
Presided over the decline of the old-
style Unionist establishment and
attempts to modernise Northern
Ireland's economy, broke Loyalist
tradition by holding negotiations with
the Dublin government. But his half-
hearted attempts at reform and
conciliation only exacerbated
tensions in Northern Ireland. As
nationalist resistance flared and
Loyalist intransigence became more
strident, he had to give way to a
more coercive Unionist approach.

ORME
Stanley
Labour's junior Northern Ireland
minister, 1974-76. This left winger
had links with Gerry Fitt from 1964,
and was involved with the Campaign
for Democracy in Ulster, which
criticised Stormont's excesses before
the war began. His record and
opposition to internment meant
Unionist leaders objected to his
promotion to the Northern Ireland
office. But once installed as right-
hand man to Merlyn Rees, he
became a consistent defender of the,
British occupation and virulent critic
of the liberation movement.

PAISLEY
Ian
Loyalist leader. Founder of Free
Presbyterian Church, 1951. Born
1926. First came to prominence
when he provoked riot over display of
Irish tricolour above republican
headquarters during 1964 general
election campaign. Denounced visit
by Republic's premier Sean Lemass
to Stormont, 1965. Led rallies,
protests and violent demonstrations

against any concessions to the civil rights movement, 1968. Won Westminster seat for North Antrim, June 1970. Established Democratic Unionist Party, 1971. Disrupted power-sharing assembly and supported Ulster Workers' Council strike, 1974. Formed United Ulster Unionist Council with Harry West and William Craig—later collapsed after disagreements over the 1975 convention. Lost prestige through too conciliatory approach towards power-sharing and the collapse of the attempted 1977 Loyalist strike.

Revived popularity around calls for more repression. Won major victory in 1979 Euro-elections, establishing himself as 'Mr Ulster'. In March 1981, organised a 'Carson Trail' culminating in a 30 000-strong rally at Stormont, to protest at Dublin-London 'conspiracy'. Threatened to unleash his paramilitary 'Third Force' against nationalists in the aftermath of the 1981 hunger-strikes. Swung back towards respectability by becoming the staunchest defender of the Ulster assembly. But still managed to stir the Orangemen in the 1984 Euro-elections, winning 230 000 votes on a 'smash Sinn Fein' platform. Loud in opposition to Anglo-Irish accord, but burnt his fingers when he and Molyneaux of the OUP negotiated a compromise with Thatcher which was howled down by Belfast shipyard workers, February 1986.

Physically dragged from Northern Ireland assembly by RUC when it was closed down by the Tories, June 1986. Backed formation of Ulster Resistance, a front for 'direct action' with paramilitaries, November 1986. Ejected from European parliament for interrupting address by Thatcher, December 1986. Has since become increasingly desperate with failure of Loyalist campaign against Anglo-Irish accord. Threatened to resign DUP leadership when his executive objected to having an election pact with the OUP in 1987 general election, April 1987.

PASCOE
Major-General Robert

General Officer Commanding Northern Ireland, 1985 to date. Served in Borneo in mid-sixties, and Northern Ireland in 1974, as commander 1st battalion Royal Green Jackets.

POWELL
Enoch

Tory, turned Unionist, politician. Following his break with Ted Heath's Conservative government in 1973, Powell was selected as Unionist candidate in South Down, which he won with a reduced majority in 1974. Powell has promoted the total integration of Northern Ireland into the United Kingdom, dismissing 'rolling devolution' and London-Dublin talks as an 'Anglo-American' plot to sell out Ulster. He has gone too far for some of his Official Unionist colleagues who see their future in some sort of devolved administration. Nevertheless, his articulate advocacy of British imperialist interests, his condemnations of the Republic and his success in manoeuvring at Westminster to increase the number of Unionist seats staved off defeat at the hands of nationalists. Held his seat by 548 votes in the 1983 general election, despite boundary changes which favoured the SDLP and a hostile campaign against him by the DUP, which claimed an Englishman could not properly

represent Loyalists. Refused to join Unionist boycott of Westminster and held out until the last minute before resigning his seat to fight by-elections in protest at the Anglo-Irish deal, January 1986. Lost his seat to SDLP in June 1987 election.

PRIOR
James

Tory secretary of state for Northern Ireland, September 1981 to September 1984. Leading Tory 'wet'. Sent to Belfast—the Siberia of British politics—as a way of silencing his opposition to Thatcher's economic policies at home. Presided over the end of the hunger-strike. Tried to restore Britain's international image by introducing a 'rolling devolution' assembly, but rolled straight into a brick wall as the SDLP boycotted it and Sinn Fein won five seats on an abstentionist platform, October 1982. Responded by organising a rolling shoot-to-kill and supergrass campaign. Rolled out of office under a cloud after a storm of protest against the mass RUC attack on a Belfast republican rally in August 1984.

PYM
Francis

Tory secretary of state for Northern Ireland, 1973-74. Caretaker direct ruler for three months between Whitelaw and Rees, took part in Sunningdale conference at which the ill-fated power-sharing scheme was launched. Later organised British military terror on the other side of the world, as foreign secretary during the South Atlantic War, 1982.

REES
Merlyn
Labour's shadow spokesman on Northern Ireland, 1971-74. Secretary of state for Northern Ireland, 1974-76. Took over just as the power-sharing assembly, executive and the proposed Council of Ireland were on the verge of disintegration. Used period of 1975 truce with IRA to phase out internment in December 1975, only to supervise the introduction of its replacement: criminalisation, no-jury Diplock courts and the conveyor-belt system. Now makes dubious claim to be mystified over the existence of British death squads during his period of office in the North. His bumbling and waffling was believed by his colleagues to be his 'major virtue' at a time when cover-ups were central to state policy. Promoted to home secretary after his own political initiative, the constitutional convention, collapsed.

RICHARDSON
General Sir Robert
General Officer Commanding British forces in Northern Ireland, 1982-85. Commanded infantry brigade in the Six Counties, 1974. Keen advocate of low-profile role for the Army on the streets of Northern Ireland.

ROBINSON
Peter
Deputy leader of DUP, MP for East Belfast, 1979 to date. Born in Belfast, 1948. In 1966 attended Paisley rally and then joined Lagan Valley unit of the Ulster Protestant Volunteers, a militant section of the Free Presbyterian church. Founder member of DUP, 1971. DUP general secretary, 1975. Won William Craig's East Belfast constituency from him in 1979 with a slim majority of 64 votes.

Elected to Ulster assembly, 1982.
First came to public notice when
expelled from commons in December
1981, protesting over the IRA
assassination of a fellow Unionist MP.
Appeared in court as character
witness for Loyalist bigot George
Seawright, 1984. Prominent in
backing paramilitary Ulster
Resistance during the 1986 Loyalist
campaign against the Anglo-Irish
agreement. In August 1986, he
boosted his sectarian credentials by
leading a mob attack on the village of
Clontibret, County Monaghan, where
he was arrested. His reputation and
challenge to Paisley took a knock
when he pleaded guilty to the
Clontibret incident and paid a fine to
a Dublin court, January 1987.

SANDS
Bobby

Leader of the IRA hunger-strikers in
H-Blocks, 1981. Born 1954 in Belfast.
Forced out of a job and Rathcoole
home by Loyalists, moved to
Twinbrook area of the city, 1972.
Special category prisoner 1973-76.
Sentenced to 14 years for
possession of weapons, 1977.
Became Officer Commanding
Provisional IRA prisoners in the Maze
during abortive 1980 hunger-strike.
Began own hunger-strike for political
status, 1 March 1981. Elected
Westminster MP for Fermanagh and
South Tyrone with 30 000 votes, April
1981. Refused appeals to give up his
heroic protest from many quarters,
including the Pope. Died after 66
days on strike, 5 May 1981. Funeral
followed by 100 000 nationalists.
Vacated parliamentary seat was then
won by his election agent, Owen
Carron, with an increased majority.

SEAWRIGHT
George
Loyalist extremist. Describes himself as 'an honest bigot'. Born Glasgow, 1951. Moved to Belfast 1974. Former shipyard worker with close links with paramilitary organisations. Elected to Belfast council for Upper Shankill, 1981. DUP representative for North Belfast in Ulster assembly, 1982. In May 1984 won notoriety when he told Belfast education and library board that all Catholics should be incinerated. Expelled from the DUP and imprisoned as a result. In November 1985 assaulted Tom King at Belfast city hall, in campaign against Anglo-Irish agreement, and got another spell in prison. An attempt by the RUC to arrest him in Portadown in July 1986 led to a major riot between Loyalist mobs and the police. In September 1986 attended funeral of his election agent and UVF commander John Bingham, shot dead by the IRA, whom he described as a 'close friend'. Retains popular support in Belfast's Shankill Road and won just under 6000 votes in North Belfast for his newly formed Protestant Unionist Party in 1987 general election.

SOLEY
Clive
Labour deputy Northern Ireland spokesman, 1981-84. Tried to give Labour's Irish policy a distinctive appeal. Argued Irish unity could be achieved 'by consent' of the Loyalists, and opposed PTA. But backed Britain all the way against the republican movement. Loud protagonist of all-Ireland courts and police force to stamp out liberation movement. Met Sinn Fein during trip to Northern

Ireland and asked what minimum terms would be for an IRA ceasefire, 1983. Replaced as part of Labour's drive to appoint even more pro-imperialist spokesmen.

SPRING
Dick

Irish Labour Party leader, November 1982 to date. Deputy premier (Tanaiste), December 1982 to January 1987. Owes his support in republican County Kerry to the memory of his father Dan, a Labour politician who led the county's Gaelic football team to the All-Ireland trophy and was close friends with an executed IRA man. The colourless Spring junior has tried to keep up the family's nationalist credentials, but in coalition government backed every Fine Gael measure against the republican movement. Under his leadership, the popularity of the party has plummeted to less than four per cent, an all-time low. Resigned from Fine Gael coalition, January 1987.

STALKER
John

Former deputy police chief, Greater Manchester. Joined Manchester police, 1958. Worked as top detective on Moors murder case in mid-sixties. Headed city's Special Branch during IRA bombing campaigns in early seventies, and helped in capture of a number of IRA active service members. Assistant chief constable Greater Manchester, 1980-86. Selected for course at Royal College of Defence Studies, 'designed to train those people who would run the country in the event of war', 1983. Headed inquiry into RUC shoot-to-kill policy, 1984-85. Handed over report to DPP, recommending serious charges to be made against up to a dozen top RUC officers, October

1985. Suspended from duty after
corruption allegations, June 1986.
Reinstated in job, but not RUC inquiry,
September 1986. Resigned from
Manchester police, December 1986.
Scapegoat because his over-
enthusiastic investigation threatened
to expose the British controllers of
the RUC's shoot-to-kill policy. Now
writing his own account of the
episode.

TAYLOR
John
Official Unionist member of the
European parliament. Former
Stormont MP, part of hardline Loyalist
opposition to O'Neill. Survived Official
IRA assassination attempt, 1972.
Staunch defender of the Union in
Strasbourg and resister of European
interference in the affairs of the
'United Kingdom', his long service
earned him the title 'father of the
house' when the assembly opened in
1982. Became MP for new
constituency of Strangford, 1983. A
leading figure on integrationist wing
of the OUP, his notable lack of
fervour in opposing the Anglo-Irish
agreement made him a target for
DUP invective.

THATCHER
Margaret
Prime Minister, 1979 to date. Born
Grantham, 1925. Tory MP for
Finchley, 1959. Leader of
Conservative Party, 1975. Dismissed
the demand of the 10 Irish hunger-
strikers for political status by arguing
that they were criminals and that
'Murder is murder is murder',
December 1980. After hunger-strikes,
boasted that the IRA had 'played their
last card'. Presided over the
introduction of the supergrass system
and the shoot-to-kill policy. Visited
Drummadd barracks in South

Armagh, Christmas 1983, on morale-
boosting trip for the troops just after a
dozen UDR members had been
arrested for murdering nationalists.
Narrowly escaped assassination
when IRA bombed her Brighton hotel
during Tory Party conference,
October 1984. Threw out South's
New Ireland Forum options with the
words 'Out, out, out!', November 1984.
Told Unionists 'I am a Loyalist' after
signing Anglo-Irish accord, November
1985. Surrounded herself with SAS
bodyguards during 1987 election,
claiming to be a top IRA target after
the Loughgall killings.

TUZO
General Sir Harry

Army General Officer Commanding in
Northern Ireland, 1971-73. Famous
for blunt declarations of British
strategy, he reckoned that about half
the Catholics in Northern Ireland had
republican aspirations and about a
quarter were prepared to support the
IRA. Set up the undercover dirty
tricks Military Reconnaissance Force
and directed Operation Motorman.

TWOMEY
Seamus

Former Belfast IRA leader. Leading
role in the reorganisation of the
Provisional IRA after the 1969-70
split. Member of the IRA delegation to
negotiate with William Whitelaw,
1972. Arrested and imprisoned within
three months of becoming the
Provisionals' chief of staff, March
1973. Spectacular helicopter escape
from Dublin's Mountjoy prison,
October 1973. Recaptured and
imprisoned in Dublin, 1977-82. Active
in Sinn Fein's election campaigns
after release but split to join
Republican Sinn Fein when it was
formed in November 1986.

TYRIE
Andy
Loyalist paramilitary leader, commander Ulster Defence Association, 1973 to date. Associated with the New Ulster Political Research Group, the UDA's political front, and its ideas of an independent Ulster, 1979. This leader of Northern Ireland's most viciously active Loyalist murder gang, responsible for hundreds of sectarian killings, was sympathetically interviewed in the British Communist Party's *Marxism Today* in December 1981.

WEST
Harry
Leader of Official Unionist Party, 1974-79. Rich Fermanagh farmer and former Stormont minister, succeeded Faulkner as OUP leader. Rejected power-sharing and other reforms and concessions to the nationalist community. Outflanked by Paisley as a result of his involvement in devolution talks with Mason, 1977-79. Lost heavily to Paisley in 1979 Euro-elections, resigned leadership in favour of Molyneaux. Lost narrowly but crucially to Bobby Sands in the Fermanagh and South Tyrone by-election of April 1981.

WHITELAW
William
(later Lord)
Tory Northern Ireland secretary, 1972-73. First direct ruler. In the turmoil that followed the collapse of Stormont, Whitelaw's most celebrated initiative was inviting an IRA delegation for talks in London in July 1972. No terms could be agreed and a fragile truce soon collapsed. As home secretary almost a decade later Whitelaw banned a Sinn Fein delegation including two of the same

people from visiting London for
informal talks. In 1972 he also
conceded political status to
republican prisoners in response to a
hunger-strike. At the same time he
launched Operation Motorman to
reclaim the nationalist 'no-go' areas
and moved ahead with the scheme
for a power-sharing assembly. In
1984 some commentators suggested
he was advertising to get his old job
back when he shot two civilians while
hunting, during the Tories' search for
a new Northern Ireland secretary.

YOUNG
Sir Arthur
Former Metropolitan Police
commissioner, RUC chief constable
1969-70. Sent in by Harold Wilson to
reorganise RUC after the outbreak of
'the troubles'. Gained vital experience
of fighting 'terrorism' in Malaya.

2.

Political organisations and parties

Alliance Party

Launched in 1970 with a 'non-sectarian' appeal, the Alliance has never been more than a marginal Protestant middle class organisation. At the beginning it attracted some support away from the Official Unionist Party and the Northern Ireland Labour Party. It won around 10 per cent of the vote in the mid-seventies' power-sharing assemblies. The polarisation of the communities as the war continues has left little space for the Alliance's moderate approach and its fortunes have stagnated. Although it won 10 seats in the 1982 assembly elections, it has since lost thousands of votes, many of which have gone to the SDLP in an attempt to stop the rise of Sinn Fein. In the 1983 general election it contested 12 seats but won none. In the January 1986 by-elections, its five unsuccessful candidates got just over five per cent of the poll with no competition from the SDLP. Shared the same manifesto as the British SDP/Liberal Alliance in 1987 general election and won less than 10 per cent of the vote. They expressed their fundamental commitment to Unionism when they declined to stand in West Belfast, and asked their supporters there to vote tactically for the SDLP to try to unseat Sinn Fein president Gerry Adams.

Campaign for a Democratic Ulster

British Labour Party pressure group, prominent in supporting demands for civil rights in Northern Ireland in the sixties, and now moribund. Backed by up to 100 left-wing Labour MPs in its heyday, the CDU pressed Westminster to introduce democratic reforms—against the opposition of the Unionist establishment at Stormont. When the Six Counties state proved resistant to reform and conflict burst on to the streets, the same MPs approved Westminster's next move—the despatch of thousands of British troops to Northern Ireland. The Labour Party justified a measure necessary to preserve imperialist law and order as a progressive step to defend the Catholic community from Loyalist pogroms. Many CDU members—Stan Orme, Roy Hattersley, Michael Foot—have become consistent supporters of Britain's determination to keep Ulster undemocratic by continuing the military occupation.

Campaign for Social Justice

Catholic middle class pressure group which began in Dungannon in 1964. It had close links with the British Labour Party.

Communist Party of Ireland

A Stalinist rump, based in Belfast, with a membership heavily dependent on ageing trade union officials. From its beginning in 1920 the CPI has been small and isolated, achieving some influence only transiently in the militant unemployed struggles of the thirties. Hence it has always relied heavily on the Soviet Union. After 15 years of war it is still appealing to the British state to introduce democratic reforms in Northern Ireland as a preliminary stage to reuniting the country. It condemns the liberation struggle as an obstacle to Britain fulfilling its progressive role. The CPI played some part in the early civil rights movement and influenced the degeneration of the Official IRA. As the war has continued the CPI has become more and more irrelevant, but its members are still powerful on the pro-Loyalist Northern Ireland Committee of the Irish Congress of Trade Unions, where they keep a characteristically low profile. The party's Northern and Southern sections were only reunited in 1970, but today separate policies are still pursued on either side of the Border. The party campaigns for a devolved assembly in the North and a 32-county United Ireland in the South. Its opposition to the Anglo-Irish accord was also packaged to find favour with both Loyalists and nationalists. A pro-republican faction, based in the South, had their motion calling for joint work with Sinn Fein routed by the Northern leadership at the 1986 party conference.

Connolly Association

A social circle of ageing Irish Stalinists in London. Publishes the *Irish Democrat,* a curious collection of articles aimed at lobbying Labour MPs to oppose the Prevention of Terrorism Act, features on Irish history and extensive lyrics of Irish ballads.

Conservative Party

The party's formal title is the Conservative and Unionist Party, but the war has broken the traditional ties between British Tories and Ulster Unionists. The abolition of the Stormont parliament by Edward Heath's Conservative government in 1972 was a bitter blow to the Unionist establishment. The division became even more bitter when Heath proposed power-sharing in 1973 and the majority of Unionists came out against it. After the February 1974 general election Unionist MPs no longer accepted the Conservative whip. Enoch Powell's defection to the Unionists—and his recommendation to vote Labour in 1974—further soured relations. When Labour negotiated tacit Unionist support for its government in return for more Unionist seats in the next parliament, links with the Tories deteriorated still further. Under Margaret Thatcher's leadership the Tories initially tried to mend a few fences, guaranteeing the Union more loudly than ever and setting up the Unionist-run assembly at Stormont. In April 1983 the Official Unionists' executive voted narrowly to seek restoration of its links with the Tories.

All reconciliation attempts collapsed, however, when Thatcher sat down with Southern premier Garret FitzGerald at Hillsborough in November 1985 and signed the Anglo-Irish accord. Only one leading Tory, treasury minister Ian Gow, resigned in protest. The OUP severed its historical links with the Conservative Party in protest in April 1986. Two months later the Tories closed down the assembly and OUP members accused Thatcher of treason to the Crown. But come what may, the Tories remain consistent defenders of the Union. Their position as the most forthright supporters of British imperialism was recognised by the republican movement when the IRA bombed their Brighton conference in October 1984.

Democratic Unionist Party

Ian Paisley's political organisation. Founded in 1971 by Paisley on a platform of militant populist Loyalism. In the 1973 assembly elections the DUP won 10 per cent of the first-preference votes, which it increased to almost 13 per cent in the 1975 convention elections; in both contests the DUP stridently repudiated power-sharing. Paisley established his position as the dominant figure in Loyalist politics through his massive votes and victories in the 1979 and 1984 Euro-elections. But while his party has increased its support, particularly at local level, it has not matched its meteoric rise. The DUP share of the vote doubled to 20 per cent between the 1979 and 1983 general elections, but its representation at Westminster held steady at just three MPs. The party lost some support in the eighties because of its association with a homosexuality scandal at the Kincora boys' home in Belfast, and because of the more moderate, statesmanlike demeanour of its fiery leader. Paisley expelled the bigoted George 'burn the Catholics' Seawright in 1984.

The DUP has won the support of working class Loyalists by its intransigent defence of the Union and its intense sectarian hostility towards Catholics. Any compromise on these principles damages its popularity. When Paisley accepted Thatcher's offer of a compromise on the Anglo-Irish deal in February 1986, he was howled down by Belfast shipyard workers. He promised never to negotiate with Thatcher again while the accord still existed.

The DUP was at the forefront of the Loyalist campaign against the Anglo-Irish agreement, and won much support for its rabble-rousing resistance. In the aftermath of the failure of the campaign, however, Loyalist populism has fallen into temporary disrepute and the DUP has been thrown into a leadership crisis. Up to 50 activists staged a walk-out of a strategy meeting in protest at Paisley's plan to have an election pact with OUP, April 1987. Their chief whip quit politics the following month after he was blocked from standing against the OUP in the safe Unionist seat of East Antrim. The pact could not stop the spread of Loyalist demoralisation, however, and the DUP vote dropped heavily in the June 1987 poll.

Fianna Fail

The largest party in the Dail (Irish parliament). Its origins lie in the republican faction in Sinn Fein which opposed the partition treaty and fought a brief Civil War against the pro-treaty forces of the 'Irish Free State' backed by Britain. First came to power under Eamon de Valera in 1932 and has been the ruling party, except for brief periods, ever since. Currently led by Charles Haughey, Fianna Fail has long come to terms with partition and British domination over Ireland. An essentially middle class party, it sustains rural and working class support through republican rhetoric and periodic anti-British gestures. Despite its formal commitment to Irish unity, Fianna Fail has ruthlessly suppressed republicans in the Free State ever since it came to power in the thirties. Likewise, it initially opposed the Anglo-Irish agreement, but swung round to backing it before the February 1987 election. As in previous governments, Fianna Fail in power has cooperated fully in British legal and military cross-Border arrangements for dealing with 'terrorists'. It has fraternal relations with the SDLP in Northern Ireland.

Fine Gael

The second largest party in the Dublin Dail. It originated in the pro-partition treaty faction of Sinn Fein which formed the first Free State government under British patronage in 1921. Based on the big farmers and the pro-British professional and administrative elite, Fine Gael since the twenties has proved incapable of mobilising sufficient popular support to form a majority government. Hence its brief spells in office from 1948-51, 1954-57, 1973-77, 1981-82, have always been in unstable coalitions—usually with the Labour Party. Under Garret FitzGerald, the party came out of the November 1982 election in a strong enough position to team up with Labour in another coalition. The relatively long period in office between 1982 and 1987 was due more to the weakness of the opposition than to any popular support for the two governing parties. Eventually Labour buckled under the strain and broke the partnership, precipitating a general election. However, Fine Gael had sustained major setbacks on its own—over the divorce referendum in 1986, the lack of progress with the Anglo-Irish accord, and the dire state of the economy. The party dropped 19 seats, down to 51, in the February 1987 general election, and its rival Fianna Fail formed the new government. Fine Gael remains the more explicitly pro-British and pro-partition of the two major parties.

Friends of Ireland

Opportunist grouping of Irish-American politicians, including Edward Kennedy, Tip O'Neill, and Daniel Moynihan. They condemn the national liberation struggle and propose a British-imposed political solution.

Irish in Britain Representation Group

Radical Irish community organisation. Formed in 1981 as Britain's Irish community responded angrily to events around the H-Block hunger-strikes. The IBRG is primarily concerned with local community and cultural affairs, but supports the Labour left's campaigns against Irish jokes and chauvinist gutter journalism. The IBRG's views are broadly reflected in the weekly *Irish Post*. It is sympathetic towards the Labour Party in Britain and Fianna Fail in Ireland.

Irish Independence Party

Formed in 1977 to articulate nationalist demands in response to the SDLP's capitulation to British imperialism and the republican movement's neglect of the political sphere, the Irish Independence Party formed a temporary bridge between the SDLP and Sinn Fein. Its support came largely from Catholics in rural areas of Northern Ireland. Won three per cent of the vote in the 1979 general election, but did much better in the 1981 council elections as nationalist alienation intensified during the hunger-strike. Squeezed badly by the republican movement's return to electoral politics in 1982, its call for a boycott of the assembly elections was largely ignored by hardline nationalists who turned out to vote for Sinn Fein's abstentionist platform. The party failed to contest the 1983 general election and lost heavily to Sinn Fein in the 1985 local council elections.

Irish Labour Party

Ever since it abstained from taking a position on independence in 1918 and partition in 1920, the Irish Labour Party has demonstrated the marginal scope that exists for a social-democratic party in a country dominated by imperialism. In 1930 it split from the trade unions and became a rump supported by the rural poor. The party repaired its relations with the unions during industrialisation in the sixties, but it retained its petit-bourgeois political approach. The Irish Labour Party has fully adapted to the partitionist middle class politics of the Free State establishment. Deferential to Britain, the Dublin state and the Catholic Church, it has consistently condemned the national liberation movement. It has pursued its own fortunes in coalitions with the explicitly pro-imperialist and anti-working class Fine Gael. Under Dick Spring, the party was in coalition government with Fine Gael from December 1982 until January 1987. By 1985, it was torn in a struggle between its middle class leaders and its trade union supporters who were pushing for Labour to withdraw support from Fine Gael's austere counter-crisis measures. By the following year, even moderates were beginning to swing behind the campaign to end the coalition as the party's poll ratings slid precipitously. When called by Fine Gael to commit electoral suicide by voting for an austerity budget immediately before a vote of confidence that the coalition was going to lose, Labour lost its nerve and resigned from the government—thus causing the February 1987 general election in the South. Discredited after its four years in coalition, Labour lost two seats in the general election, down from 14 to 12.

Irish National Caucus

Washington-based split from Noraid noted for its hostility to the republican movement and its prolific output of creative begging letters. Prominent members include Father Sean McManus, Fred Burns O'Brien and Rita Mullen. It does not send money overseas but seeks political influence through the congressional committee on Irish affairs, campaigning against US arms sales to the British security forces and American investment in Northern Ireland firms with sectarian employment records. Currently campaigning to implement the MacBride principles. These duplicate the Sullivan principles for South Africa, which ask investors to threaten disinvestment unless discrimination is ended. It is supported by 130 congressmen including Mario Biaggi, and seeks an orderly British withdrawal underwritten by American cash.

Irish National Liberation Army

Military wing of the Irish Republican Socialist Party, formed in 1974. Its most celebrated operation was the assassination of Tory Northern Ireland spokesman Airey Neave in March 1979 at the house of commons. One of its former leaders, Dominic McGlinchey, was the most wanted man in Ireland for a time. He was the first republican to be extradited from the Republic to the North on St Patrick's Day, March 1984. Inla has also conducted a campaign against leading Loyalist politicians and attacked British military installations in Germany. Badly damaged by supergrasses, it was torn apart by a deadly feud in early 1987.

Irish Republican Army

The leading force in the anti-imperialist struggle in Ireland. The IRA, or Provisionals, emerged from the split in the republican movement in December 1969-January 1970. They responded to the immediate need to defend the nationalist community. Under the leadership of Sean MacStiofain, the Provisionals reorganised their military activities from scratch, especially relying on veteran Belfast republicans Joe Cahill, Seamus Twomey and Billy McKee. They soon attracted a new generation of activists to the republican cause. Once the British began to shoot nationalists dead, from July 1970, the Provisionals were in a position to assume the leading role in the war. In the succeeding months their operations took a heavy toll of military and business targets. In July 1972 the British flew a Provisional delegation including MacStiofain, Adams, Twomey, O'Connaill and McGuinness to London for abortive peace talks.

The arrests of MacStiofain and Cahill in 1972 and 1973—and of Twomey in 1977—opened up the leadership of the movement to a younger generation. In the mid-seventies there were a series of attempted ceasefires and republicans operated 'truce incident centres' in the erroneous belief that Britain was about to withdraw from the North. There were even (unsuccessful) attempts at reaching a rapprochement with the Loyalists. Increased sectarian murders and intensified state repression damaged the authority and effectiveness of the Provisionals. However, the reorganisation of the IRA from a brigade into a cell structure improved morale and operational efficiency in 1978 and 1979. The assassination of Lord Mountbatten and 18 British soldiers on the same day in different corners of the country was a spectacular achievement in August 1979.

The hunger-strikes, led by IRA prisoners and supported by Inla prisoners in the H-Blocks in 1980 and 1981, did much to raise the prestige of the Provisionals in the nationalist community. Republican prisoners gave the IRA another boost when 38 got out of the Maze in the Great Escape of September 1983. The success of the Provisional IRA in shooting soldiers and policemen in response to the shoot-to-kill policy between 1982-85 confirmed its essential role as the military resistance to the British occupying forces. In February 1985 the Provisionals silenced crowing establishment commentators when a mortar attack on Newry RUC station killed nine officers—the IRA's biggest success against the force since the war began. In 1986 its attacks on contractors and suppliers to the security forces further restricted their room for manoeuvre.

In October 1986, at their first Army convention for 17 years, IRA delegates voted in favour of continuing the armed struggle and abandoned the policy of abstaining from taking seats in the Dublin Dail. The results of the February 1987 election in the South proved disappointing, however, and the military offensive was prosecuted with renewed vigour from April 1987. Rapid success was secured by blowing up Lord Justice Gibson, who had applauded the RUC for bringing three IRA volunteers to 'the final court of justice', April 1987. The IRA sustained their heaviest casualties since the Tan War in the twenties when eight volunteers were executed by the SAS at Loughgall, North Armagh, in May 1987. But it remains a vital and effective defender of the nationalist community, and the British government's most feared opponent.

Irish Republican Socialist Party

Formed out of split from Official Sinn Fein, December 1974. Its birth was marked by a murderous feud with the Official IRA in which several members, including its leader Seamus Costello, were assassinated. The IRSP has faced intense repression in Northern Ireland, the Republic and in Britain. Its members have been framed by supergrasses, imprisoned, detained under the PTA, deported and shot. Bitterly opposed as they were to the Officials' betrayal of the armed struggle, the IRSP proved incapable of breaking from their reformist politics while at the same time unable to pose a viable alternative to Sinn Fein's traditional brand of republicanism. It therefore experienced difficulty in consolidating a base beyond its pockets of supporters on either side of the Border. In 1984 it tried to broaden its working class appeal by formally adopting 'the teachings of Marxism-Leninism', but its paper, the *Starry Plough,* subsequently folded and its few remaining members became embroiled in the deadly Inla feud in early 1987.

Labour Party

Pro-imperialist organisation of the British labour bureaucracy. The Labour Party, in opposition and in government, has consistently supported Britain's domination of Ireland. It approved partition in 1920 and consolidated it under the Labour government in 1949. All wings of the party have repeatedly condemned the national liberation struggle. The Labour government sent in the troops in 1969 and reinforced them under the 1974-79 Labour administration. Labour built the H-Blocks, brought in the Prevention of Terrorism Act and enforced criminalisation. The Labour Party backed the Tories all the way against the hunger-strikers in 1980 and 1981 and acquiesced to the shoot-to-kill strategy from 1982-85. At the same time, the Labour Party has always had to cope with pressure from socialist and Irish nationalist supporters of the party. Hence it has often deprecated the excesses of British terror in Ireland, especially when the Tories have been in office, from the Black and Tans, through the 'B' Specials to the use of torture under internment or plastic bullets against children. Labour has often expressed its sympathy for Irish unity as a distant goal (like socialism in Britain). Thus since 1981 Labour has officially favoured eventual Irish reunification, while approving the British occupation for the indefinite future. In early 1987, as the general election in Britain drew closer, Kinnock endorsed the negotiations his senior Northern Ireland spokesmen had been conducting with elected Sinn Fein leaders with an eye on Irish votes in Britain. But Labour's election manifesto backed the British occupation and Thatcher's Anglo-Irish agreement. When the Tories accused Labour candidates of fraternising with Sinn Fein in the closing days to the election, Kinnock declared that his party would never talk with 'terrorists', June 1987.

Labour Committee on Ireland

The Labour left's Irish campaign. The LCI is fronted by leading left wingers such as Ken Livingstone and Joan Maynard. It came to prominence around the 1981 conference decision in support of 'eventual Irish reunification'. While the Labour Party has stepped up its support for the British occupation, the LCI has popularised the notion that Labour is becoming more radical in its attitude to the Irish War. It condemns the republican movement, supports a progressive British solution, and uses campaigns against Irish jokes and anti-Irish racism to win Irish votes for the Labour Party.

Labour and Trade Union Group

A small sect originally based in Derry. Closely linked with the Militant entrist groups in the Irish and British Labour parties, it seeks the establishment of an 'independent' Labour Party in Northern Ireland, 'based on the trade unions'. Its attempts to portray the North's virulently Loyalist official labour movement as a genuine workers' organisation reaches the absurd in its call for a 'trade union militia' to combat sectarianism. The group's condemnation of the liberation struggle means it is set to go down the same road as the old Northern Ireland Labour Party, and become a Unionist rump. In the 1983 general election it won 584 votes in largely Protestant East Belfast. Failed to stand in 1987.

Liberal Party

A middle class pro-imperialist party. Originally the party of Gladstone's Home Rule Bills, the Liberals are best remembered as the party of Lloyd George's treaty and partition in 1921. Throughout the war the Liberals have maintained consistent support for Britain's occupation and repression. In 1979 the Young Liberals decided in favour of British withdrawal as part of a long-term solution involving the defeat of the national liberation struggle. They were warmly greeted by the British left, and a few Young Liberals fronted the left's march commemorating 10 years of the war. In 1983 the Young Liberals got the full party conference to adopt their policy. The fact that the party of partition could effectively adopt the Labour Party's policy, supporting 'eventual Irish reunification' while backing British domination in the present, exposed the myth that Labour had 'broken with bipartisanship'. The party leadership soon pigeon-holed the new policy, and agreed instead to share a common programme in the 1987 general election not only with its SDP allies, but also with the pro-Union Alliance Party based in the North.

Noraid (Irish Northern Aid Committee)

Republican fund-raising organisation in North America, led by veteran republican Martin Flannery. Its slogan is 'IRA all the way'. It hit the headlines in August 1984 when its publicity officer, Martin Galvin, was banned from entering Northern Ireland and the RUC's brutal attempt to arrest him at a Belfast rally ended in the murder of Irish man John Downes. Noraid has become the target of a concerted propaganda campaign as the British, Irish and American governments try to discourage US support for the republican movement.

Northern Ireland Civil Rights Association

The respectable face of the civil rights movement, set up in January 1967. Nicra incorporated the Campaign for Social Justice and included representatives of the British National Council for Civil Liberties, the Northern Ireland Labour Party, the Ulster Liberal Party and even the Young Unionist Group from Queen's University, Belfast. It also included some republicans and socialists. However, its demands—one man, one vote in council elections, an end to gerrymandering, public complaints machinery, fair allocation of housing, repeal of the Special Powers Act, the disbandment of the 'B' Specials—were profoundly subversive in the context of Northern Ireland's institutionalised system of sectarian discrimination. Once the campaign provoked the violent reaction of the state and its Loyalist allies, Nicra tried to curb nationalist protests. It was soon swept away as its moderate middle class politicians pulled back from the fray, and the nationalist people took the fight for democratic rights into their own hands.

Official Irish Republican Army

The now defunct consequence of the take-over of the republican movement by Communist Party fellow-travellers in the sixties. This led to the split in December 1969-January 1970 from which the Provisional republican movement emerged. Demoralised and isolated after the defeat of the 1956-62 Border campaign, the republican movement came under the influence of a small group of intellectuals formerly associated with the British Communist Party. As popular support and old activists withered away, this faction won the movement over to the three-stage theory of how to win national liberation, a formula familiar in the degenerated official communist movement since the days of Stalin. The first stage was to unite Catholics and Protestants within a 'democratised' Northern Ireland state; the struggle for national unity and independence was postponed until the second stage; the final stage—socialism—lay in the indefinite future. The first stage meant the rejection of the two central pillars of the republican tradition—abstention from participation in the electoral institutions imposed on Ireland, North and South, by the British, and the commitment to take up arms against the oppressor.

When police and Loyalist gangs attacked the nationalist community in 1969, the consequences of the political degeneration of the republican movement became apparent. It was still pressing for democratic reform within the Six Counties state that was oppressing the Catholics and, worst of all, the republican movement had neither the organisation nor the weapons to defend the nationalist ghettos. Although in a minority, the Provisionals walked out to build up mass support for the military struggle against British imperialism. The Officials, dubbed the Stickies from their use of adhesive labels for their Easter lilies at the 1970 commemoration of the 1916 Rising, stagnated. After a few military operations—the assassination of a Unionist senator and an off-duty British soldier from Derry, and the attempted assassination of Unionist MP John Taylor and the bomb attack on the Parachute Regiment's Aldershot base that killed seven people—the Officials declared a ceasefire in May 1972. Their military activities have subsequently been directed at anti-imperialists in the Provisionals and the IRSP, several of whom they have murdered. The Officials have also been involved in several armed robbery and forgery scandals in the Republic.

The Officials have directed their political activities into the Workers Party, North and South. The party combines bureaucratic community and trade union politics with strident condemnations of the national liberation struggle. Its representatives claim that the Official IRA has long been defunct.

Official Unionist Party

The dominant political party in Northern Ireland from partition until direct rule and still the majority representative of the Loyalist community. The tensions caused by the civil rights protests, culminating in the suspension of Stormont, destroyed the power-base of the Loyalist establishment and fragmented the Unionist Party. Supporters of Terence O'Neill (party leader 1963-69) moved to the Alliance Party in 1970 after he was squeezed out by Chichester-Clark (leader, 1969-71). O'Neill's more extreme opponents followed William Craig into the Vanguard movement in 1972 or even joined Ian Paisley's Democratic Unionist Party. Others followed Brian Faulkner (leader, 1971-73) into the Unionist Party of Northern Ireland in 1973.

Loyalists have dealt harshly with any of their leaders who have shown any sign of making concessions to the nationalist community. Terence O'Neill was ousted for introducing minor reforms to the advantage of the Catholics. Chichester-Clark was dismissed for not pursuing a sufficiently coercive approach towards the emerging republican movement. Faulkner suffered humiliation after his endorsement of the 1974 power-sharing executive. Each Unionist Party leader has been succeeded by a more intransigent Loyalist. Faulkner was succeeded by Harry West who was replaced by James Molyneaux in 1979 after West was trounced by Paisley in the Euro-elections.

In the old days the Unionist Party held four fifths of the seats at Stormont and 10 of the 12 Westminster seats for Northern Ireland. At the 1970 general election OUP representation dropped to eight as Ian Paisley and three nationalists won seats. In the February 1974 general election the OUP linked up with Vanguard and the DUP in an anti-power-sharing bloc—the United Ulster Unionist Council. The UUUC won 11 of the 12 seats, but of these three went to Vanguard and two to the DUP candidates. The UUUC collapsed in 1977 after Vanguard leader William Craig adopted a conciliatory approach to the SDLP. As Craig followed the same fate as O'Neill, Chichester-Clark and Faulkner before him, the struggle for the mandate of the Loyalist community was now between the OUP and Paisley's DUP. At the October 1974 general election the OUP won five seats to the DUP's three. The DUP continued to advance, but fell short of winning a majority over the OUP in the 1982 assembly elections. In the 1983 general election the OUP consolidated its leading position, taking 11 seats and 34 per cent of the vote to the DUP's three seats and 20 per cent—the Official Unionists' best result since the fall of Stormont.

The OUP has survived in the past by adopting more extreme Loyalist postures, but direct rule still weakens and divides the party. It is split between two factions. One led by party leader James Molyneaux and MEP John Taylor favours total integration into the United Kingdom. The other, fronted by Upper Bann MP Harold McCusker, calls for the return of some devolved government to the Loyalist establishment in Northern Ireland. The OUP initially joined Tory right wingers in campaigning against the 'rolling devolution' assembly, and later boycotted its meeting after three Protestant church elders were killed in November 1983. But the party's internal tensions soon reappeared, as four of its assembly representatives broke the boycott and resumed their seats. The split was healed when the rest of the party eventually agreed to follow them.

In opposition to the November 1985 Anglo-Irish agreement, the party joined in the constitutional aspects of the Loyalist campaign against it, such as the boycotts of Westminster and the local councils. They backed the one-day strike in March 1986, but opposed any further industrial action. As the Loyalist campaign against the accord began to falter, the OUP's position in the Loyalist camp was strengthened. The Official Unionists refused to join the DUP's Ulster Resistance initiative and concentrated on organising constitutional protests like petitions. The old integration/devolution split in the party resolved itself into a division between 'realists' who want to negotiate a suspension of the deal with the British, and 'fundamentalists' who hold that the boycott strategy will force the British to abandon it altogether. By mid-1987, as the Loyalist campaign against the accord ground to a halt, the 'integrationist' faction returned to the ascendant in the party. They hope to end the party's boycott of Westminster after the election pact with the

Democratic Unionists resulted in a drastic slump in their vote in the 1987 general election. As long as direct rule continues the OUP leaders are destined to squabble over the favours dished out by Westminster. And always present in the background is their fear of being out-manoeuvred by Paisley or some other extreme populist manifestation of Loyalism.

Orange Order

Loyalist community organisation. The Loyal Orange Lodge institution owes its name to King William the Third of the Netherlands (William of Orange) who, with the support of the Pope, defeated the forces of the Catholic King James the Second at the historic battles of the Boyne (1690) and Aughrim (1691). Originally formed in Loughgall in 1795 to unite Protestant landlords and tenants in North Armagh against Catholics, it now encompasses the whole Protestant community. It fought home rule until partition and has subsequently staunchly defended the Union. Most Unionist politicians are Orangemen and there is a branch at the house of commons. It has between 80 000 and 100 000 members in Northern Ireland and lodges among Loyalist expatriates in places as far from Belfast as South Africa and Canada. Many of the riots which broke out during protests against the Anglo-Irish agreement started out as Orange parades. Although they were routed through Catholic areas they were not banned as republican marches always are. The authorities let them pass because, under the aegis of the Orange Order, they were designated as 'traditional'.

Progressive Democrats

Founded by expelled Fianna Fail minister Des O'Malley, January 1986. Appealing to the Dublin yuppy set, the party has tried to project a modern image, and claims to have broken the mould of Irish politics, in imitation of the SDP in Britain. Fundamentally conservative and anti-nationalist, the 'Dessicrats'—as they came to be known—rejected the Civil War heritage that ostensibly divides the two main establishment parties, Fianna Fail and Fine Gael. It secured 25 per cent vote in the opinion polls at its birth, but as each of its policies was announced it slid further down the polls. It won 14 seats in the February 1987 general election, but didn't make it into a hoped-for coalition with Fine Gael.

Protestant Action Force

Loyalist paramilitary gang responsible for campaign of sectarian assaults, bombings and murders in the eighties. Largely made up of Ulster Defence Regiment members who pick out nationalists for harassment while in uniform and attack them when off-duty. In November and December 1983 a dozen UDR members in County Armagh were arrested in connection with the PAF's murder of a Catholic man. Became active again during the Loyalist protests against the Anglo-Irish accord, and was responsible for a series of sectarian murders in 1986.

Red Hand Commandos

A Loyalist paramilitary group involved in sectarian assassinations in 1972 and 1973. Linked to the Ulster Volunteer Force and the Ulster Defence Association and banned in 1973 at the same time as another UDA front, the Ulster Freedom Fighters.

Republican Sinn Fein

Formed in November 1986 by Daithi O'Connaill and Ruairi O'Bradaigh after the Sinn Fein Ard Fheis voted to end its abstention policy in the South. Has some support among the old guard of 'Provisional' Sinn Fein, who led the organisation until after the 1975 truce. Republican Sinn Fein justified its split from Sinn Fein on the grounds that every republican party that abandons abstentionism to enter a 'partition parliament' like Dublin's Dail sooner or later gives up the armed struggle and goes over to the pro-British camp.

Sinn Fein

The political wing of the IRA on both sides of the Border. 'Provisional' Sinn Fein rejected the consequences of the programme of the Officials, but never produced a systematic critique of its politics. Instead Sinn Fein returned to the 'democratic socialist republic' formula outlined by radical republicans in the period before partition. *Eire Nua,* the programme produced in 1972, calls for extensive nationalisation and the widespread formation of cooperatives. It also proposed a federal system of government devolved to the four historical provinces of Ireland. The programme expresses the dreams of small farmers and small businessmen in the Ireland of 70 years ago. It is no answer to the needs of the working class today. The 1982 Ard Fheis rejected the concession to Loyalism implicit in the federalist proposals—but the rest of the programme stands.

In 1982 Sinn Fein declared its intention of contesting elections in both Northern Ireland and the Republic, alongside the continuing military struggle against British rule. In the Six Counties its candidates—especially those most associated with the IRA's campaign—did well in the 1982 assembly elections, winning five seats on an abstentionist ticket. In the 1983 general election Sinn Fein's vote topped the 100 000 mark and its president, Gerry Adams, was elected to Westminster—again on a platform of abstaining from the imperial parliament. In the South Sinn Fein has not fared so well. Although it has some representatives on local councils in rural areas it has failed to win elections to the Dail or consolidate significant urban support. Its best effort was in the 1984 Euro-elections, when it won around six per cent of the votes in the Free State. Southern support for the liberation movement has been contained by the republican rhetoric of Fianna Fail.

In an effort to overcome its isolation in the nationalist ghettos of the Six Counties, and to appeal to those in the South who view an abstentionist candidate as a 'wasted' vote, Sinn Fein followed the IRA Army convention by voting to end the abstentionism policy at its 1986 Ard Fheis. A number of members who occupied leading positions in the organisation in the past refused to accept the decision and left to form Republican Sinn Fein. Sinn Fein stood 27 candidates in 24 constituencies on a non-abstention ticket in the February 1987 general election in the Twenty-six Counties, but failed to win a seat, polling 1.9 per cent of the vote. Despite a vigorous campaign to unseat him by the Loyalists, Gerry Adams kept his West Belfast seat in the June 1987 British general election returning with an increased share of the poll. But the impact of the Anglo-Irish deal took its toll, cutting Sinn Fein's overall vote by 20 000. Even so, hardcore support for republicanism held up, with Sinn Fein capturing a third of the nationalist vote in the North.

Social Democratic and Labour Party

Middle class Catholic party in Northern Ireland. Formed in August 1970, in response to British requests for a single moderate nationalist body to deal with, it incorporated a number of Catholic nationalist groupings and several Stormont politicians. The party included Gerry Fitt who became its first leader, civil rights campaigners John Hume, Ivan Cooper, Paddy O'Hanlon and Austin Currie; Paddy Devlin, formerly Northern Ireland Labour Party MP, expelled from the SDLP in 1977, now with his own Labour Party of Northern Ireland; and Paddy Wilson, murdered in a sectarian attack in 1973. Set up to promote reforms through Stormont, the SDLP was forced to withdraw from the Loyalist parliament in July 1971 in response to pressure from the nationalist community after the security forces killed two youths in Derry.

The SDLP has participated in every charade performed by the British state to disguise its coercive strategy in Northern Ireland. In late 1971 it set up an assembly—the Dungiven parliament—to court a British solution which would give some recognition to moderate representatives of the nationalist community. After Britain imposed direct rule the SDLP proposed a new assembly under joint London and Dublin control. In 1973 it settled for the power-sharing assembly and executive set up under British control after the Sunningdale conference, with the token Council of Ireland tacked on. When Loyalist intransigence wrecked this sham in 1974, the SDLP moved on to pursue new forms of collaboration—through the convention in 1975, and talks with successive Northern Ireland secretaries.

Until the 1982 assembly elections the SDLP commanded virtually unchallenged support within the nationalist community. In the 1973 assembly elections it won more than 20 per cent of the first-preference votes and party leader John Hume polled almost 25 per cent of the first-preference votes in the European parliament election. But in the 1982 assembly elections, the 1983 general election and the 1984 Euro-election, the SDLP has been challenged with increasing vigour by Sinn Fein. In 1983-84 the SDLP joined the parties of the Dublin establishment in the New Ireland Forum, an attempt to come up with a political proposal which could restore the credibility of constitutional nationalism. Thatcher's 'Out, out, out' response to the Forum's ideas in November 1984 marked the nadir of the SDLP's efforts to resist republicanism. It was torn in two in 1985 when one section advocated a pact with Sinn Fein to ensure nationalist control of certain local councils, while another wing wanted the SDLP to adopt Dublin's approach and refuse to meet with or speak to Sinn Fein representatives.

London stepped in to save the day for the SDLP. A major function of its Anglo-Irish agreement with Dublin was to bolster the SDLP's fortunes by pretending to offer a few crumbs to Northern nationalists. In the January 1986 by-elections, SDLP candidates considerably improved their performance, while support for Sinn Fein dropped. SDLP deputy leader Seamus Mallon beat all his opponents to become the new MP for Newry and Armagh. The deal enabled the SDLP to secure its best performance in a decade in the June 1987 general election, with the party's South Down candidate and chief whip Eddie McGrady defeating Enoch Powell to give them a total of three Westminster MPs. Nevertheless, the repression continues and little or no crumbs have fallen from the British table in the aftermath of the accord. The SDLP's future is by no means secure.

Troops Out Movement

Leading Irish solidarity organisation in Britain in the seventies. Formed in 1973, it modified its demands for 'Troops out' from the beginning in the hope of attracting liberal and reformist support. These hopes were never fulfilled and the movement virtually collapsed in the late seventies as the left-wing groups that sponsored it—the International Marxist Group (now Socialist League) and the Socialist Workers Party—turned away from the Irish War in the face of the pressures of British public opinion. The movement has staggered on, turning from women, to blacks, to the Irish community in the search for some response to its moralistic appeals. It has come to rest within the orbit of the Labour Party, refusing to organise anything that might embarrass Labour's chances of getting back into government. Now moribund, TOM still organises periodic excursions to Northern Ireland and regular social events in London to revive the spirits of its dwindling band of supporters.

Ulster Clubs

Umbrella group set up by Unionist parties to coordinate Loyalist grassroots opposition to the Anglo-Irish accord in November 1985. Based in the localities, the Ulster Clubs allowed activists from the political parties, the OUP and the DUP, to work alongside members of paramilitary organisations like the UDA and UVF in mobilising for mass rallies and protests. In the aftermath of the failure of the Loyalist campaign against the accord, the Ulster Clubs began increasingly to follow the UDA's political line. During the 1987 general election they came out in favour of 'Ulster independence'.

Ulster Defence Association

Loyalist paramilitary organisation. Populist-style movement which linked up Loyalist vigilante groups in 1971, and excluded MPs and clergymen from its ranks. Organised thousands of Loyalist workers in military parades in Belfast in 1972 and patrolled 'no-go' areas. The major force behind the 1974 Ulster Workers' Council strike that brought down the power-sharing assembly. The membership of the UDA overlaps with that of the RUC and the British Army's Ulster Defence Regiment. Its involvement in the campaign of sectarian murders in Northern Ireland is beyond dispute, but the UDA remains a legal organisation. Its political wing is the Ulster Political Research Group, founded in 1978.

Many of its members have been imprisoned on charges of murder and other firearms offences. In 1979 11 members of the UDA in Scotland were given heavy prison sentences on gun-running and intimidation charges. However, the British readily accept the organisation's denial of responsibility for these actions, and have turned down frequent requests from the SDLP to ban it on the grounds that the UDA has never claimed responsibility for any acts of 'terrorism'. To pursue its terror campaign against nationalists the UDA set up a front called the Ulster Freedom Fighters.

The upsurge in Loyalist violence around the Anglo-Irish accord boosted the fortunes of the UDA. It was invited by the main Unionist parties to participate in the Ulster Clubs initiative, and did most of the legwork to make the one-day strike in March 1986 effective. But once the tide of Loyalist anger against the British government began to abate at the end of 1986 they once again distanced themselves from the paramilitaries. The UDA tried to promote itself politically again in the new year with their policy document 'Common Sense', but to little avail. The UDA's support is based only on its willingness to assassinate Catholics, and nobody cares much about its half-baked political programmes.

Ulster Freedom Fighters

A UDA front, banned by the British authorities in 1973 but responsible for the UDA's more gruesome sectarian attacks. In March 1984 it failed in an attempt to assassinate Sinn Fein president Gerry Adams in Belfast. Claimed responsibility for a number of sectarian murders during the Loyalist campaign against the Anglo-Irish accord. Planted bombs in Dublin on the first anniversary of the Anglo-Irish deal in November 1986. Hit the South again in February 1987 when incendiaries burnt out Dublin stores as well as shops in Letterkenny and Ballybofey, County Donegal, causing £2m damage.

Ulster Political Research Group

The UDA's political front. Set up in January 1978 by Andy Tyrie and Glen Barr, on the platform of an 'independent Ulster'. The group has fared badly in elections, even in staunchly Loyalist areas, where people support the UDA for its military activities, and are little concerned about its politics. In early 1987, it enjoyed a reprise as the UDA strove to organise the dwindling bands of Loyalists opposed to the Anglo-Irish agreement. It reissued its old 'independent Ulster' policy, souped-up with a new emphasis on its power-sharing aspect. This is a dangerous path for Loyalists to tread, as can be seen in the experience of Craig's Vanguard Party. The initiative was met with open hostility from the establishment Unionist parties after it had been openly endorsed by SDLP leader John Hume.

Ulster Popular Unionist Party

The private party of maverick Unionist MP James Kilfedder. Kilfedder has pursued his career under several different party labels, and formed the UPUP in 1980. He was elected as the party's sole representative in the assembly in 1982 and selected as a compromise candidate to chair its meetings. In the 1983 general election he held North Down, but has since come under fire from the other Unionist parties for his lack of fervour in campaigning against the Anglo-Irish deal. In the 1987 election Kilfedder narrowly saw off a challenge from arch-integrationist independent Unionist Robert McCartney by joining in the election pact with the mainstream Unionist parties.

Ulster Resistance

A DUP initiative launched at a mass rally in Belfast in November 1986 to add some paramilitary muscle to the flagging campaign against the Anglo-Irish deal. It drew in DUP, UDA and Ulster Club members. The massed ranks of Ulster Resistance pledged themselves to take 'direct action as and when required' to defeat the accord. A number of leading DUP politicians wore red berets to match their militant rhetoric. But Loyalist workers were just as unimpressed by these theatrics as they were by the DUP's failed Third Force initiative in 1981. It is now defunct.

Ulster Volunteer Force

Loyalist paramilitary organisation, deriving its name from Carson's anti-home rule militia in the pre-partition period. Began campaign of sectarian terror with two murders in 1966, for which it was banned and its leader Gusty Spence imprisoned. Spence became a reformed character inside and, after being released in 1984, claimed to be a 'Northern Ireland socialist'. Now this rehabilitated murderer gives his allegiance to Labour: 'I would align my socialism with the British Labour Party. I would take my political philosophy from Neil Kinnock.'

Meanwhile the UVF carried its sectarian assassinations into the seventies. In 1977 26 UVF members were given a total of 700 years in jail on 55 charges including murder. In 1979 nine UVF members were imprisoned in Scotland on firearms and explosives charges. It has suffered bloody leadership feuds. Lenny Murphy, notorious leader of the Shankill Butchers, shot his way to the top in the early eighties only to be topped by the IRA in 1982.

In the early eighties the UVF was hit by Britain's attempt to make its supergrass strategy appear even-handed. By 1986, however, they were all back on the streets—just in time to launch their biggest murder campaign since the early seventies. The signing of the Anglo-Irish deal at the end of 1985 led the security forces to downplay their shoot-to-kill policy temporarily. The UVF carried on where the covert army squads and the RUC left off, and 16 nationalists were brutally murdered. Their offensive received a blow when the IRA shot dead Belfast UVF commander John Bingham in September 1986. Leading OUP and DUP politicians attended his funeral as a mark of respect. Another UVF commander was shot dead by the IRA in April 1987.

Ulster Workers' Council

Organising committee of the 1974 Loyalist strike which brought down the power-sharing assembly. A model of efficient and coordinated industrial action which paralysed the Northern Ireland economy within days with the object of blocking even a token gesture away from British domination. The council included Unionist politicians, Loyalist paramilitaries and Loyalist trade unionists. West, Paisley and Craig represented the different factions of Unionism; Tyrie (UDA), Hannigan (UVF) and several others provided military muscle; Jim Smyth, Harry Murray and Billy Kelly mobilised engineers, shipyard workers and power workers to bring the economy to a standstill.

The British security service, MI5, has been accused of planning the strike and directing the activities of the UWC. Together with Army fraternisation with pickets and BBC broadcasts against the government, secret service involvement in the 1974 strike indicates that the bulk of British establishment opinion moved decisively against the limited concession to the nationalists that power-sharing represented.

The UWC mobilised again in 1977 to press for more vigorous repression of the nationalist community. When the British authorities acquiesced immediately to its key demands, support for strike action dwindled away.

Vanguard

Unionist political movement led by William Craig, 1972-77. Began as extreme Loyalist opposition to the conciliatory approach of the Official Unionist Party before direct rule. It had strong paramilitary support and staged massive Nazi-style rallies. In 1973 the Ulster Vanguard became the Vanguard Unionist Progressive

Party and won 10 per cent of the first-preference votes in the assembly elections. In the 1974 general election it won three seats under the United Ulster Unionist Council (with the DUP and OUP). When Craig came out in favour of negotiations and even cooperation with the SDLP after the 1975 Convention the Vanguard split, to collapse in 1977.

Workers Party

Moderate reformist organisation in both the Twenty-six Counties and the Six Counties (where it was previously called the Republican Clubs). The degenerated political product of the Official IRA, via Official Sinn Fein and Sinn Fein the Workers Party. It finally dropped Sinn Fein from its title in 1982.

The Workers Party pursued the logic of the Official IRA's stages theory of political development in Ireland in its programmatic document, *The Irish Industrial Revolution,* published in 1977. The Officials had already reduced their sights from socialism (on the most distant horizon), and even from national independence (still a remote object), to campaigning for reforms within the structures established by British domination on both sides of the Border. The Workers Party has identified imperialism as a progressive force in Ireland. It came out in favour of government measures to promote European, American and British investment. The only obstacles to progress in Ireland were its 'incompetent, inefficient and greedy' small employers—and the struggle against imperialism being carried out by the republican movement.

In the South, the Workers Party promotion of state intervention and its dogged bureaucratic style of operation have won it some support among trade union officials in Ireland's large public sector. Its advocacy of tax reform and other trade union concerns has drawn a degree of electoral support in urban areas. In 1981 its first TD (MP) Joe Sherlock was elected in Cork, to be followed in February 1982 by Proinsias de Rossa in Dublin and Paddy Gallagher in Waterford.

In the November 1982 general election Gallagher and Sherlock lost their seats, but party leader Tomas MacGiolla was returned along with de Rossa in Dublin. The party had already proved willing to cooperate in imposing anti-working class budgets. Its reliance on Ireland's fragile trade union bureaucracy is pulling it even further to the right as the country plunges deeper into recession. In the February 1987 general election the party gained another two seats—Pat McCartan in Dublin North East and Joe Sherlock in Cork East. In the North the Workers Party retains minimal support among diehards loyal to the Officials, but its condemnations of the liberation struggle and concentration on community work has won few new sympathisers in the nationalist community. In the 1983 general election it won two per cent of the vote. It was the only party apart from Sinn Fein to contest the Euro-elections on an all-Ireland basis, and was soundly beaten by the republicans. During the January 1986 by-elections, five Workers Party candidates standing in Unionist constituencies with no other nationalist competitor won just over 15 500 votes between them, while their four candidates standing in nationalist areas could only muster 2600 votes. Did slightly better in the 1987 general election, when its vote went up by 5000 on 1983. The party's involvement in protection rackets in the North, especially in the construction industry, has earned it the title of the 'Building Workers Party'.

3.

What happened when

The build-up to war

1921 Partition finalised, Stormont and the Irish Free State established.
1949 Free State declared Republic of Ireland.
Integration of Northern Ireland into the United Kingdom reinforced by Labour government.
1956-62 Border campaign by IRA; internment introduced in North and South.
1966 UVF opens campaign of sectarian murders, killing two Catholics.
1967 Northern Ireland Civil Rights Association formed.
1968 **October:** Civil rights march in Derry attacked by RUC.
1969 **January:** Civil rights march attacked by Loyalists at Burntollet bridge en route from Belfast to Derry.
March: Power station blown up by UVF—IRA blamed.
April: Terence O'Neill succeeded by James Chichester-Clark as Stormont prime minister.
July: Rioting. First Catholic killed by RUC in Derry.
August: Rioting in Belfast and Derry. Battle of the Bogside leads to intervention of British Army, first in Derry and then in Belfast.

Repression and resistance

1969   **August:** Northern Ireland invaded by British Army; by end of year almost 8000-strong.

October: 'B' Specials to be disbanded—and replaced by the Ulster Defence Regiment, under direct British Army control. RUC reorganised. First RUC man killed—by Loyalists in Belfast.

December: Split in IRA—into Provisionals and Officials.

1970   **January:** Sinn Fein follows IRA and splits into Provisionals and Officials.

April: UDR inaugurated. Army uses batons and CS gas against nationalist rioters in Belfast. Army General Officer Commanding Freeland threatens to shoot rioters on sight.

June: Provisionals defend Short Strand from Loyalist attack.

July: British Army imposes Falls Road curfew—five Catholics killed, 60 injured and hundreds of homes devastated.

1971   **February:** Provisionals shoot dead first British soldier.

March: Chichester-Clark replaced by Brian Faulkner at Stormont.

April: Provisionals' bombing campaign begins—37 explosions in one month.

July: Army shoots two boys dead in Derry—three days of rioting, SDLP forced to withdraw from Stormont. Bombing campaign intensifies: 91 explosions.

August: Internment—340 Catholics and two Protestants detained. Rioting and street-fighting all over Northern Ireland. 'No-go' areas established; sectarian pogrom in Belfast. In four days, 22 killed—mainly Catholic civilians. Nationalist rent and rate strike begins.

September: All marches declared illegal—15 000 attend anti-internment protest in Belfast.

December: McGurk's bar blown up by UVF in Belfast: 15 Catholics killed. Thirty simultaneous bombings across Six Counties. On Christmas day, anti-internment march from Belfast to Long Kesh blocked by British Army.

1972   **January:** Bloody Sunday in Derry: 13 unarmed civil rights demonstrators shot dead by British Army, another died later from injuries.

February: British embassy burned down during mass Dublin protests over Bloody Sunday. Campaign of sectarian intimidation in Six Counties intensifies—many Catholics lose their jobs, some their lives.

March: Stormont minister John Taylor survives Official IRA assassination attempt. Belfast's Abercorn restaurant bombed—two women killed and 130 injured. Stormont suspended and direct rule imposed—William Whitelaw becomes first secretary of state for Northern Ireland.

May: Official IRA kill Ranger William Best, a Derry Catholic in the British Army—prompts angry response from some nationalist women. Official IRA calls unconditional ceasefire. Kelly's pub bombing—five Catholics killed. UDA begins open drilling.

June: Provisionals declare truce. Whitelaw concedes special-category status after hunger-strike by republican prisoners.

July: Whitelaw meets Provisional delegation in London. Ceasefire breaks down after clashes between nationalist residents and British troops in Lenadoon, Belfast. 'Bloody Friday': 26 bombs in Belfast kill two soldiers and nine civilians. Operation Motorman: 'no-go' areas smashed in Belfast and Derry by more than 20 000 troops.

November: IRA leader Sean MacStiofain arrested in Republic; starts and gives up hunger-strike. Provisionals launch RPG7 rocket attacks on British Army posts.

December: Bombs in Dublin kill two people and injure 80 while the Dail is debating new repressive legislation. In Northern Ireland total death toll for year reaches 467.

1973   **March:** IRA arms shipment intercepted on the *Claudia* off Waterford, and Joe Cahill arrested.

June: Elections to power-sharing assembly.

July: Diplock no-jury courts established.

October: Helicopter escape from Mountjoy prison by Seamus Twomey and two other IRA leaders.

November: Belfast-Derry railway link blown up, three police and Army posts attacked in Derry, bomb attack on Army post in Belfast.

December: In 12 months, 250 dead.

1974   **January:** Republican air force drops two milk-churn bombs on Strabane police station from hijacked helicopter.

March: Labour returns to power in London and Merlyn Rees takes over in Belfast. Two massive car bombs devastate central Belfast.

April: RUC to be reorganised and reinforced to take on 'responsibility for law and order'.

May: Power-sharing executive formally approved by assembly; Loyalist Ulster Workers' Council strike declared immediately, assembly collapses in a fortnight. During strike 27 killed by Loyalist bombs in Dublin and Monaghan.

August: Mass escape of 19 republican prisoners from Portlaoise in the Republic. Police chief assassinated in Omagh.

September: Two judges shot in Belfast.

October: Long Kesh burnt down in prison riot; prisoners brutally assaulted by Army and prison guards. Disturbances at Magilligan and Armagh prisons.

November: Mass escape from Long Kesh through tunnel—but prisoners later recaptured; one prisoner shot dead. Prevention of Terrorism Act rushed through in response to Birmingham bombings in Britain, extended to Northern Ireland.

December: Dublin government introduced new law to allow courts to try republicans for their military activities in Britain or the Six Counties. Negotiations between IRA and British authorities through Protestant clergymen at Feakle, Co Clare, lead to temporary Christmas ceasefire. Irish Republican Socialist Party formed in split from Official IRA. Riot of republican prisoners at Portlaoise prison. In 1974, 216 people died in Irish War.

1975 **January:** IRA ceasefire extended to 16 January, then called off.
February: IRA call new ceasefire and set up incident centres to monitor it in liaison with government officials.
March: Price sisters, convicted for London car bombings, transferred from Durham prison to Armagh after hunger-strike.
April: Two pub bombings in Belfast leave seven dead and 75 injured.
July: Rees promises to release all internees before Christmas. Miami Showband attacked by UVF—three Catholics killed and one seriously injured (two UVF blew themselves up in the attack).
October: A spate of UVF attacks leaves 12 people (including four UVF men) dead and 26 injured.
November: Rees closes down incident centres. Renegade republican group led by Eddie Gallagher and Marian Coyle kidnap Dutch industrialist but are captured after siege in Free State. Provisionals and Officials clash in Belfast shoot-out.
December: Two British soldiers shot in Derry after visit by prime minister Harold Wilson. End of year death toll: 247.

1976 **January:** In two separate incidents five Catholics killed in sectarian assassinations in South Armagh. The following day 10 Protestants killed by 'Republican Action Force' in retaliation at Kingsmills, South Armagh. SAS unit despatched to South Armagh 'bandit country'.
February: Truce ended.
March: Labour government withdraws special-category status. Great train robbery at Sallins, Co Kildare, for which IRSP members framed— although IRA admit responsibility.
April: First prison official killed by IRA in Tyrone. Relatives' action committees formed by nationalist women to demand reinstatement of political status for republican prisoners.
May: Nine IRSP members escape from Long Kesh through tunnel.
July: Three RUC men killed in bomb explosion in Co Fermanagh. RUC reorganised to improve intelligence gathering and operational efficiency. New British ambassador to Dublin, Christopher Ewart-Biggs, blown up by remote control mine.
August: Death of three children hit by a car whose IRA driver had been shot dead by British troops leads to formation of women's peace campaign, later anti-republican Peace People.
September: Kieran Nugent begins blanket protest in H-Blocks refusing to wear prison uniform and demanding political status. Roy Mason succeeds Merlyn Rees as Northern Ireland secretary.
October: Sinn Fein vice-president Maire Drumm shot dead in Mater Hospital, Belfast.
December: IRA fire bombs cause £1m damage to Derry shops. IRA declare Christmas ceasefire. In another 12 months of war, 297 people died.

1977 **March:** Eight SAS men fined £100 each by a Dublin court for carrying guns without a licence after being apprehended South of the Border.
May: Loyalist strike demanding tougher repression. Mason announces the deployment of more SAS units and reinforcements for the RUC and UDR, and strike is called off.
July: Feud between Officials and Provisionals leads to four deaths.

August: Queen's Jubilee visit marked by IRA bomb attacks and intensified repression in nationalist areas.

October: IRSP leader Seamus Costello shot dead in Dublin.

December: IRA leader Seamus Twomey recaptured in Dublin with IRA reorganisation plans found in his pocket. Five hotels blown up by IRA. No Christmas ceasefire. End of year death toll down dramatically to 112.

1978   **January:** European Court of Human Rights rules that internees suffered 'inhuman and degrading' treatment, but not torture. Abortive Coalisland conference meets to coordinate campaign to restore political status for prisoners.

February: La Mon restaurant bombing in Co Down kills 12 and injures 23—IRA responsible.

March: After systematic harassment H-Block prisoners begin 'dirty protest', coating the walls of their cells with their own excrement—continues until 1981 hunger-strike.

October: Riots in Derry as Sinn Fein commemorates the tenth anniversary of the first major civil rights march and the DUP stages counter-demonstration.

November: IRA launch simultaneous bomb attacks on commercial targets in Belfast, Dungannon, Enniskillen, Cookstown, Armagh and Castlederg. Deputy governor of Belfast prison shot by IRA. Another wave of fire bomb attacks in 14 towns and villages.

December: Bomb attacks across the Six Counties, three soldiers shot dead in main street through Crossmaglen, South Armagh. Total deaths for year—81.

1979   **March:** Bennett report confirms torture in Castlereagh. Tory spokesman Airey Neave assassinated by Inla car bomb on house of commons. British ambassador to Netherlands shot dead by IRA.

April: Four RUC men killed by IRA landmine in South Armagh.

May: Tories replace Labour in government and Humphrey Atkins replaces Mason in Northern Ireland.

August: Armed IRA volunteers join Sinn Fein demonstration in West Belfast, to the outrage of Loyalists. Eighteen British soldiers killed in twin IRA bomb blasts at Warrenpoint. Lord Mountbatten and three others killed on same day, as IRA blow their boat off Sligo. Thatcher is helicoptered into Warrenpoint and pledges to smash the IRA—increases RUC strength by 1000.

September: Pope John Paul appeals for peace at Drogheda, Co Louth—IRA call for British withdrawal.

October: London and Dublin governments agree to intensify repression and to impose joint security arrangements. National H-Block/Armagh Committee set up after conference in Andersonstown's Green Briar Hotel to step up the prison campaign.

November: A cache of rifles and machine guns en route from USA to IRA seized in Dublin. IRA carry on campaign against prison staff, killing fifth in three months.

December: Down bus depot devastated in IRA attack. Bomb attacks on shops in Lisburn. Five soldiers killed in two IRA attacks. RUC to be boosted by 1000 in 1980. In 1979 the Irish War claimed 113 lives.

1980   **January:** Two undercover soldiers shot by mistake by fellow paratroopers in South Armagh. Three UDR men killed by landmine in Co Down.
February: IRA incendiary attack on Belfast bus depot destroys 20 buses.
April: Hotels bombed in Lisburn, Strabane and Armagh. IRA attack Newry police barracks with mortars.
May: IRA bombs cross-Border electricity link.
June: Massive IRA bombs in Markethill, Co Armagh, and Fintona, Co Fermanagh, destroy commercial premises. Republican activists John Turnly and Miriam Daly assassinated by Loyalist paramilitaries.
October: Seven republican prisoners go on hunger-strike in the H-Blocks for 'five demands' concerning prison conditions which amount to political status.
December: Hunger-strike called off after 53 days in response to vague promises—which are not fulfilled by the British authorities. Total deaths for the year fall to new low of 76.

1981   **January:** Bernadette and Michael McAliskey seriously wounded in Loyalist assassination attempt.
March: Second hunger-strike for political status begins under leadership of Bobby Sands.
April: MP for Fermanagh-South Tyrone Frank Maguire dies suddenly and Sands is elected to his Westminster seat while still on hunger-strike in the H-Blocks.
May: Sands dies—100 000 attend his funeral.
June: Two other hunger-strikers elected to Dublin Dail in the Republic's general election.
July: Paisley launches Third Force initiative—a Loyalist militia to supplement the RUC and UDR.
August: Republican Owen Carron elected to succeed Bobby Sands as MP for Fermanagh-South Tyrone.
September: Atkins succeeded by James Prior, a more heavyweight figure in the Tory hierarchy, as Northern Ireland secretary.
October: British Labour Party conference adopts policy of Irish reunification, but confirms support for criminalisation and direct rule in foreseeable future. Hunger-strike ends after death of 10 republicans.
November: IRA assassinate Loyalist MP Robert Bradford in Belfast. Series of IRA attacks on security forces. Loyalists embark on renewed spate of sectarian assassinations.
December: Annual death toll of 101—including seven shot by plastic bullets during protests in support of hunger-strikers.

1982   **January:** Inla assassinates John McKeague, leading Loyalist paramilitary reputed to be founder of Red Hand Commandos.
February: Wave of arrests and charges against republicans on basis of information supplied by supergrasses. IRA scuttles British tramp steamer in Lough Foyle.
March: Five IRA bombs detonated simultaneously in Banbridge, Armagh, Newtownstewart and Belfast.
October: Sinn Fein wins five seats in new Ulster assembly. Three RUC men killed in landmine explosion near Lurgan.

November: In response to Sinn Fein's success, security forces launch shoot-to-kill policy. Three IRA members and a 17-year old youth gunned down by RUC in Co Armagh. IRA executes Shankill 'Butcher' Lennie Murphy.

December: Two Inla volunteers ambushed and shot dead by RUC. Inla blows up Army disco in Ballykelly killing 11 soldiers and six civilians. Sinn Fein delegation banned from visiting London under Prevention of Terrorism Act. Death toll for the year reaches 97.

1983 **January:** IRA shoot dead Belfast judge William Doyle. Inla declared illegal in the Republic.

February: GLC leader Ken Livingstone visits Belfast and condemns liberation struggle. Undercover soldiers visit the Derry home of an Inla volunteer and shoot him dead in cold blood.

March: Dublin government announces New Ireland Forum.

May: 1000lb IRA bomb wrecks Andersonstown RUC barracks, causing £1m of damage.

June: Tories win general election, Sinn Fein's Gerry Adams wins West Belfast on abstentionist ticket.

July: Former pro-British Catholic MP Gerry Fitt, beaten by Adams, is made life peer—people of West Belfast show their opinion by burning down his house. Gerry Adams visits London. Tyrone IRA landmine kills four UDR men—the regiment's biggest loss in any attack. Two nationalist civilians shot dead by shoot-to-kill squads.

August: First major supergrass trial, the Christopher Black case, ends with 22 nationalists jailed for more than 4000 years. Two Inla men killed in Dungannon shoot-out with RUC.

September: 'Great Escape' from H-Blocks—38 republican prisoners escape via food lorry, only 19 re-arrested.

November: Jackie Grimley Inla supergrass trial thrown out of court—several other informers retracting evidence. RUC gun down 80-year old nationalist woman in Co Tyrone. IRA blow up Ulster Polytechnic class full of RUC men, killing two and injuring 13. IRA's mortar attack on new Carrickmore RUC station kills another policeman. Three Protestant church elders killed at Darkley, Co Armagh, by 'Catholic Reaction Force'—in retaliation for two-year campaign of sectarian terror by Protestant Action Force.

December: UDR members arrested in Drummond, Co Armagh, in connection with Protestant Action Force murders. Gun battle at Ballinamore in the Republic between thousands of Free State troops and police and a handful of IRA men ends in death of a Free State soldier and policeman.

1984 **January:** Catholic joy-rider shot dead by troops in Belfast.

February: SAS execute two IRA men wounded in Co Antrim gun battle.

March: IRA shoot dead deputy governor of Long Kesh prison. Ulster Freedom Fighters wound Sinn Fein president Gerry Adams in failed Belfast assassination attempt. RUC cleared of shoot-to-kill charges in court case which reveals the force's operations in the Republic. Inla chief Dominic McGlinchey extradited from South to stand trial in Belfast.

April: IRA shoots Catholic magistrate and kills his daughter in Belfast. British soldier shot by IRA in Derry after Army convoy attacked with new sweetjar petrol bombs.

May: New Ireland Forum report published in Dublin. On third anniversary of death of hunger-striker Ray McCreesh, IRA kills two RUC men with 1000lb bomb near his home town of Camlough, Co Armagh. On same day, IRA blow up two off-duty British soldiers at Enniskillen angling contest.

June: Sinn Fein wins 93 000 votes in Euro-elections. British Labour Party leadership orders left-wing Euro-candidates to get republicans off their platforms.

July: Loyalist riot through nationalist areas of Co Down. SAS execute IRA volunteer in Co Tyrone. While RUC attack his funeral, IRA blows up two local UDR members.

August: Tory government bans American republican fund-raiser Martin Galvin from Northern Ireland—mass RUC attack on Belfast rally addressed by Galvin ends in murder of nationalist John Downes. Seamus Shannon extradited from Dublin to Belfast to stand trial for killing former Stormont speaker Sir Norman Stronge.

September: Joint operation by British/Irish/US security services hijacks trawler *Marita Anne* carrying eight tonnes of IRA guns off Kerry.

November: Thatcher dismisses Dublin's proposals for diplomatic deal after Anglo-Irish summit.

December: New wave of SAS/RUC shoot-to-kill attacks leaves five IRA men dead in two weeks—one SAS assassin killed. Private Ian Thain becomes first soldier sentenced for murder of a nationalist while on duty. Raymond Gilmour Inla supergrass trial thrown out of court—14 Loyalist supergrass accused also released on appeal soon after. Dominic McGlinchey sentenced to life imprisonment on Christmas Eve.

1985

February: RUC shoot joy-rider dead, West Belfast. SAS stake-out squad blasts three IRA volunteers dead in Strabane. IRA shoot dead senior Maze prison officer and RUC community relations officer. SDLP leader John Hume meets IRA leadership for talks but refuses to be filmed and leaves. IRA mortar attack on Newry RUC barracks kills nine officers, 30 injured. Death toll is largest inflicted on RUC in any one incident. Seventeen Loyalists released after trial of UVF informer James Crochard collapses.

May: Paisley leads Loyalist mob through Catholic estate in Cookstown after forcing his way through RUC cordon. Riots break out at end of month. Sinn Fein wins 59 seats in local council elections. IRA kill four RUC men by car bomb at Kilkeel, Co Down.

July: Riots in Portadown between nationalists and RUC, and then Loyalists and RUC, as Orangemen try to march through Catholic 'tunnel' area. Loyalists petrol-bomb homes of RUC officers. BBC bans *Real Lives* documentary on Derry featuring leading Sinn Fein member Martin McGuinness and psychotic Loyalist councillor Gregory Campbell.

August: IRA commences campaign against security forces' contractors, shooting two dead—but also a Sinn Fein election worker in error.

September: Hurd promoted to home secretary and replaced as Northern Ireland secretary by Tom King.

October: Appeal court in Belfast quashes Dominic McGlinchey's murder charge. Immediately whisked to Border to be handed back to Dublin for further charges. Stalker hands report against RUC's shoot-to-kill policy to DPP, recommending serious charges against senior RUC officers.

November: OUP, DUP and UDA launch Ulster Clubs to organise grassroots resistance to Anglo-Irish deal. Accord signed at Hillsborough by Thatcher and FitzGerald. Treasury minister Ian Gow resigns in protest. Tom King assaulted by Loyalists at Belfast city hall.

December: IRA blow up Ballygawley RUC barracks with car bomb. Other barracks attacked at Castledawson, Tynan and Castlederg. Seamus Shannon freed by Belfast court after being extradited from South. Twenty seven convicted in Kirkpatrick supergrass trial. RUC dawn swoop after Christmas lifts 18 Sinn Fein members.

1986   **January:** Sectarian murders of Catholics in aftermath of Anglo-Irish agreement start—two die. It also boosts SDLP, who increase their vote at Sinn Fein's expense in four of the by-elections caused by Unionist resignations from Westminster.

February: SAS murder Catholic, Toomebridge, Co Derry. IRA volunteer shot dead by Army patrol, Derry. Paisley and Molyneaux agree compromise with Thatcher over Anglo-Irish deal, but forced to retract by Loyalist shipyard workers.

March: Loyalist one-day strike against accord. British deploy another battalion of troops in North to calm Loyalist fears. Loyalists riot in Portadown, Craigavon and Lisburn over right to march through Catholic areas. One nationalist beaten to death by Loyalists in North Belfast. Republican Evelyn Glenholmes chased through Dublin high street after being released by courts. Garda fires gun in crowded street, but no one injured. She goes into hiding.

April: 79 nationalist families and 50 RUC members burnt out of homes across Six Counties by Loyalists on rampage. First Protestant is killed by RUC plastic bullet. IRA volunteer shot dead in SAS stake-out, Rosslea, Co Fermanagh.

June: Stalker suspended from RUC shoot-to-kill inquiry. Tom King dissolves Ulster assembly. Unionist politicians dragged out by RUC.

July: Loyalist riots throughout North. At Rasharkin, Co Antrim, isolated Catholic enclave attacked by 50 axe-wielding Loyalists. Three Catholics murdered by sectarian gangs. Belfast appeal court throws out Christopher Black supergrass convictions—18 freed. IRA wearing 'butcher's aprons' kill three RUC men in Newry market at midday.

August: DUP deputy leader Peter Robinson arrested while leading Loyalist invasion of Monaghan village of Clontibret. Loyalist riots peak during height of 'marching season'. Loyalists accompanying Robinson to Dundalk hearing get garda protection after they are petrol-bombed and chased out by enraged nationalists. Clocking-in cards of Catholics burnt at Short's factory, Belfast. Stalker reinstated to police post, but kept out of RUC inquiry.

September: IRA shot dead UVF commander, North Belfast, on same day that Army shot IRA volunteer in back in West Belfast. Later, RUC attacks IRA funeral but provides guard for UVF man's. Courts free RUC officer Nigel Hegarty after finding him not guilty of manslaughter of John Downes in August 1984.

October: Irish Congress of Trade Unions launches campaign against sectarianism in the workplace. Charges dropped against two people held on word of supergrass Angela Whoriskey. RUC man killed in IRA mortar attack on New Barnsley barracks, West Belfast. IRA organises first Army convention in 17 years, and delegates agree to drop abstentionism policy.

November: Sinn Fein Ard Fheis drops abstentionism, and former leaders quit to form Republican Sinn Fein. Eight Derrymen freed on appeal against supergrass Robert Quigley. UFF plant four bombs in Dublin, but two defused in time. No injuries. Low-key protests by Loyalists on first anniversary of Anglo-Irish deal. DUP sets up Ulster Resistance.

December: Two IRA volunteers, including organiser of 1983 'Great Escape' from H-Blocks, extradited from Netherlands and taken to Northern Ireland. DUP leader Ian Paisley expelled from European parliament in Strasbourg for interrupting speech by Thatcher. IRA bomb reduced RUC's Lisburn Road barracks to rubble, Belfast. Two nationalists murdered by Loyalists—amounting to 14 in total for the year. Total death toll for 1986 is 62.

1987 **January:** Three leading Inla members killed in faction fight, including Mary McGlinchey, wife of jailed former leader Dominic. DUP deputy leader Peter Robinson let off with fine by Dublin court after invading South with Loyalist mob previous August.

February: Fianna Fail wins majority of seats in Southern election. Two more Inla members killed in bitter feud.

March: Charles Haughey agrees to maintain Anglo-Irish accord after being elected as Southern premier. Further six Inla members killed, including faction leader Gerard Steenson, before truce is finally agreed. Their funerals are the subject of intense RUC intimidation. IRA attack policeman's funeral to warn the RUC to 'keep their distance' from republican funerals. IRA kill one prison lecturer and two RUC in Derry. Soldier dies in IRA attack in Divis flats, Belfast.

April: UVF kill IRA volunteer in Belfast. Funeral has to be postponed twice due to RUC harassment of mourners. IRA shot UVF second-in-command in response. Unionist 'Day of Defiance' and general strike against Anglo-Irish agreement flops. Loyalist march in Portadown at Easter passes of peacefully. IRA offensive continues with attacks on RUC in seaside resorts of Portrush and Newcastle, letter bombs posted to leading British civil servants and blowing up of Lord Justice Gibson and wife on South Armagh Border.

May: UVF murder Catholic civilian, the thirteenth member of his family to be killed by Loyalists. Tom King promises more SAS death squads for Ireland in revenge for death of Gibson. Eight IRA volunteers on active service and one passing motorist assassinated in SAS trap in Loughgall, the birthplace of the Orange Order in North Armagh. Assassination attempt on Belfast Sinn Fein councillor Alex Maskey leaves him seriously wounded.

June: Tories returned for a third term in general election. Sinn Fein president Gerry Adams retains West Belfast seat, but Official Unionist Enoch Powell loses South Down to SDLP.

4.

'Vote early, vote often'

'Vote early—vote often' runs the old slogan about elections in Northern Ireland. It refers to the well-established tradition of 'personation', the practice followed by all parties of voting in elections in the name of people who have emigrated or died. Like everything else in Irish politics, corrupt electoral practices are a consequence of the system that has been imposed by British rule.

Voting changes nothing in Northern Ireland. It merely registers the balance of forces for and against British rule, and the balance of forces within each camp in favour of harder or softer approaches to the basic conflict that dominates life in Ireland. Yet because the whole character of people's lives hangs in these balances, every election in Northern Ireland is hard fought. Every party goes to great lengths—not ruling out personation—to pull out the voters.

Voters in Northern Ireland have a reputation for being among the most sophisticated electorates in Europe. This is partly because they get so much practice. Up to the imposition of direct rule in 1972 they voted representatives to their own parliament at Stormont as well as to Westminster. Since then they have voted in a series of polls for devolved local assemblies. They also have elections to local government and to the European parliament. The distinctive feature of different elections in Northern Ireland is that they are all about the same issue—the war.

We include here tables covering the major elections that have taken place in the Six Counties over the past 18 years of war.

● 1970 Westminster general election

The 1970 Westminster general election revealed the fragmentation of the old Unionist establishment under the impact of the upsurge of violence and the British military invasion nine months earlier. The Official Unionists' share of the seats fell from 10 out of 12 to eight. Ian Paisley (under the Protestant Unionist label) won North Antrim, Gerry Fitt (Republican Labour) held West Belfast and Bernadette Devlin held the seat in Mid-Ulster she had won at a by-election the previous year as an independent. Nationalist Frank McManus won Fermanagh-South Tyrone as a 'Unity' candidate.

1970 Westminster general election		% of total	
Party	Votes	poll	Seats
Official Unionists	422 036	54.1	8
Northern Ireland Labour Party	98 464	12.6	0
Unity (McManus)	76 204	9.7	1
Independent (Devlin)	37 739	4.8	1
Protestant Unionist (Paisley)	35 303	4.5	1
Republican Labour (Fitt)	30 649	3.9	1
Others	78 358	9.9	0
Total	**778 753**	**99.5**	**12**

● 1973 assembly election

In 1973 the British government attempted to set up a power-sharing assembly and executive to give politicians in Northern Ireland something to do and give the world the impression that Britain was seriously trying to resolve the conflict in Ireland. Elections took place in June. The polls revealed the emergence of the Social Democratic and Labour Party, founded in 1970, as the leading constitutional voice of the nationalist community. The election also revealed the growing hostility among Loyalists to what they perceived as concessions to the nationalists. Paisley's Democratic Unionists, Craig's Vanguard, the West Belfast Loyalists and a significant section of the Official Unionists were opposed to the very existence of the assembly to which they campaigned to be elected.

1973 assembly election

Party	Votes	% of total poll	Seats
Official Unionists	211 362	29.3	24
Unionists	61 183	8.5	8
Democratic Unionists	78 228	10.8	8
Vanguard	75 759	10.5	7
West Belfast Loyalists	16 869	2.3	3
Other Loyalists	3 734	0.5	0
SDLP	159 773	22.1	19
Alliance	66 541	9.2	8
Others	48,792	16.0	1
Total	**722 241**	**100.00**	**78**

● February 1974 Westminster general election

The first election in 1974 was held in Britain under the shadow of the miners' strike and Edward Heath's question—'who rules, the government or the unions?' The electorate answered by returning a Labour administration. In Northern Ireland the issues were quite different.

The British authorities had just established the power-sharing executive in addition to the assembly, a move which bitterly divided the Loyalist ranks. The executive was defended by Brian Faulkner's Unionists (as well as the SDLP and the Alliance) but opposed by the bulk of the Official Unionist Party, Paisley's Democratic Unionists and William Craig's Vanguard. The election brought the Unionist hardliners together in the 'triple-U C' bloc. The United Ulster Unionist Council won 11 of the 12 seats, with Gerry Fitt retaining his West Belfast seat, now under the flag of the SDLP. Three months later the Loyalist Ulster Workers' Council strike finally buried power-sharing.

February 1974 Westminster general election

Party	Votes	% of total poll	Seats
UUUC	366 703	50.8	11
Pro-Assembly Unionists	94 301	13.1	0
SDLP	160 437	22.2	1
Alliance	22 660	3.1	0
Others	73 525	10.2	0
Total	**717 626**	**99.4**	**12**

● October 1974 Westminster general election

The second election in 1974 returned Wilson in London and ratified the Loyalists' rejection of power-sharing in Northern Ireland. The UUUC remained the dominant force among the Unionists and Faulkner's moderate breakaway, the Unionist Party of Northern Ireland, suffered the fate of many earlier departures from the Loyalist hard line against the nationalists—it was crushed. Nationalist Frank Maguire won Fermanagh-South Tyrone as an independent and Enoch Powell, a renegade from the Tory ranks at Westminster, won South Down.

October 1974 Westminster general election

Party	Votes	% of total poll	Seats
UUUC	407 778	57.4	10
UPNI	20 454	2.9	0
SDLP	154 193	21.7	1
Alliance	44 644	6.3	0
Others	75 025	10.6	1
Total	**702 094**	**98.9**	**12**

● 1975 convention election

The seventh poll in Northern Ireland in two years was for elections to the constitutional convention, another ill-fated attempt to bridge the divide created by war. The issue was solely the constitution of Northern Ireland. The UUUC (Official Unionists, Democratic Unionists, and the Vanguard Unionist Progressive Party) stood for no surrender and no concessions to the nationalist people. The parties which had backed the earlier power-sharing initiative—Faulkner's UPNI, the SDLP and the Alliance—favoured a measure of cooperation under British rule. The poll simply ratified the results of the earlier elections on a similar theme.

1975 convention election Party	Votes	% of total poll	Seats
UUUC			
Official Unionists	169 797	25.8 ⎫	19
Democratic Unionists	97 073	14.8 ⎪ 54.8	12
Vanguard	83 507	12.7 ⎬	14
Other Loyalists	10 140	1.5 ⎭	2
SDLP	156 049	23.7	17
Alliance	64 657	9.8	8
UPNI	50 891	7.7	5
Others	26 047	4.0	1
Total	**658 161**	**100.00**	**78**

●1979 Westminster general election

The 1979 general election registered a considerable advance by Paisley's Democratic Unionists and he was joined at Westminster by Peter Robinson and John McQuade. The Official Unionists also lost North Down to James Kilfedder, the sitting MP, who set himself up as an independent Unionist.

1979 Westminster general election

Party	Votes	% of total poll	Seats
Official Unionists	254 578	36.2	7
SDLP	126 325	18.0	1
Alliance	82 892	11.8	0
Democratic Unionists	70 975	10.1	3
Independent Unionist (Kilfedder)	39 856	5.6	1
Others	121 261	17.2	0
Total	**695 887**	**98.9**	**12**

● 1979 elections to the European parliament

The first European elections were a triumph for Paisley who easily topped the poll and defeated his Unionist rivals. He was elected on the first count under the proportional representation system. The poll was also a considerable personal success for the SDLP leader John Hume who gained a voice for his party in Strasbourg.

1979 elections to the European parliament

	1st pref votes	% of total poll
I Paisley (Democratic Unionist)	170 688	29.8
J Hume (SDLP)	140 622	24.6
J Taylor (Official Unionist)	68 185	11.9
H West (Official Unionist)	56 984	9.9
O Napier (Alliance)	39 198	6.7
B Devlin-McAliskey (Independent)	33 969	5.9

After serial recounts under the proportional representation system, Paisley, Hume and Taylor were elected.

● *1981 Westminster by-elections*

Two by-elections took place during the H-Block hunger-strike, in the full glare of worldwide publicity. The results were a severe blow to the British establishment and a dramatic demonstration of the extent of popular support for the republican movement in the nationalist areas of Northern Ireland.

The first by-election in Fermanagh-South Tyrone resulted from the death of independent nationalist MP Frank Maguire in April. Both the SDLP and the DUP declined to contest the seat leaving it a straight fight between hunger-strike leader Bobby Sands and the local Official Unionist Harry West. The result was a narrow win for Sands.

April: Fermanagh-South Tyrone

	Votes
Bobby Sands (Anti-H-Block/Armagh Political Prisoners)	30 492
Harry West (Official Unionist)	29 046
	Anti-H-Block majority 1 446
% poll 86.8	

The British authorities refused to recognise Sands' mandate and concede the prisoners' demands for political status. He died in May, but the Labour Party colluded with the Tories to put off another by-election until August in the hope that they could avoid further embarrassment. In the event local Sinn Fein activist Owen Carron won the seat by an increased majority as a 'proxy political prisoner'.

August: Fermanagh-South Tyrone

	Votes
Owen Carron (Anti-H-Block/Proxy Political Prisoners)	31 278
Ken Maginnis (Official Unionist)	29 048
Seamus Close (Alliance)	1 930
Others	1 471
	Anti-H-Block majority 2 230
Poll 88.2%	

● 1982 assembly election

In the aftermath of the hunger-strikes the British government again attempted to set up a local assembly to cover up the increasingly coercive drift of British strategy. The most significant feature of the election was that Sinn Fein decided for the first time to contest elections in Northern Ireland, though making it clear that its successful candidates would not take up their seats in the assembly. The result confirmed the popular support for the republican movement that had been widely demonstrated during the hunger-strikes. The poll also showed the revival of the Official Unionists at the expense of Paisley's Democratic Unionists.

1982 assembly election		% of total poll	Seats
Party	1st pref votes		
Official Unionists	188 277	29.7	26
Democratic Unionists	145 528	23.0	21
SDLP	118 891	18.8	14
Sinn Fein	64 191	10.1	5
Alliance	58 851	9.3	10
Others	57 382	9.1	2
Total	**633 120**	**100.0**	**78**

● 1983 Westminster general election

Reorganised constituency boundaries brought five new seats to Northern Ireland in the 1983 election, making a total of 17. The most significant breakthrough of the election was Gerry Adams' success in winning Sinn Fein's first Westminster seat, though Adams made clear he had no intention of going to London to occupy it. Sinn Fein passed its target of 100 000 votes and Danny Morrison came within 100 votes of winning in Mid-Ulster. John Hume won a seat for the SDLP at Foyle. The Official Unionists confirmed their advance over the Democratic Unionists, winning 11 seats to the DUP's three.

1983 Westminster general election

Party	Votes	% of total poll	Seats
Official Unionists	259 952	34.0	11
Democratic Unionists	152 749	20.0	3
SDLP	137 012	17.9	1
Sinn Fein	102 601	13.4	1
Alliance	61 275	8.0	0
Independent Unionist (Kilfedder)	22 861	3.1	1
Others	28 375	3.6	0
Total	**764 825**	**100.00**	**17**

● 1984 elections to the European parliament

The 1984 European election confirmed Paisley's claim to speak as 'Mr Ulster', as he increased his share of the poll to win more than a third of the first-preference votes. While the Democratic Unionist Party slipped behind the Official Unionists, Paisley remained the dominant personality in Loyalist politics. John Hume and John Taylor were returned for the other two seats.

1984 election to the European parliament	1st pref votes	% of total poll
I Paisley (Democratic Unionist)	230 251	33.6
J Hume (SDLP)	151 399	22.1
J Taylor (Official Unionist)	147 169	21.5
D Morrison (Sinn Fein)	91 476	13.3
D Cook (Alliance)	34 046	5.0
J Kilfedder (Independent Unionist)	20 092	2.9

After several serial recounts, Paisley, Hume and Taylor were elected.

● 1985 elections to local councils

In 1985 Sinn Fein decided to contest council seats across the Six Counties, declaring that its candidates would take their seats if elected. Given the fact that local government powers in Northern Ireland are restricted to refuse collection, and maintaining graveyards and parks, representation on the council is of little importance. The elections once again allowed the people of Northern Ireland to express their views on the British occupation. On the nationalist side the polls allowed voters to express their choice between the SDLP's pleading for a stake in running the system under British rule and the republican movement's armed resistance to the British state.

The results demonstrated the consolidation of republican support. Sinn Fein won 59 seats at its first attempt and 12 per cent of the poll. The SDLP remained fairly steady and the Official Unionists advanced at the expense of the Democratic Unionists.

1985 elections to local councils Party	Seats	% of total poll
Official Unionists	190	29.8
Democratic Unionists	142	24.3
SDLP	101	17.8
Sinn Fein	59	11.8
Alliance	34	7.1
Irish Independence Party	4	1.2
Workers Party	4	1.6
Others	32	6.4

Number of councillors elected per party compared with 1981

Party	1985	1981	Gain/Loss
Official Unionists	190	151	+39
Democratic Unionists	142	142	-1
SDLP	101	104	-2
Sinn Fein	59	-	+59
Alliance	34	38	-4
Irish Independence Party	4	21	-17
Workers Party	4	3	+1
Others	32	67	-35

● *1986 Anglo-Irish accord by-elections*

As part of their campaign against the Anglo-Irish deal, signed by Thatcher and FitzGerald in November 1985, all 15 Unionist MPs at Westminster resigned their seats to precipitate by-elections to indicate the strength of Loyalist feeling on the issue. The elections were held in January 1986, and 72 per cent of poll—418 230—voted for candidates opposed to the agreement. Although the anti-accord parties did not stand candidates against each other, the Official Unionists did lose one seat—Newry and Armagh. It went to SDLP deputy leader Seamus Mallon, who became his party's second representative at Westminster. His election marked an upturn in the fortunes of the SDLP. The SDLP's vote went up at Sinn Fein's expense, as floating nationalist voters put the Anglo-Irish agreement to the test.

1986 Anglo-Irish accord by-elections		% of total	
Party	Votes	poll	Seats
Official Unionists	302 192	52.0	10
Democratic Unionists	85 239	15.0	3
SDLP	70 917	12.0	1
Sinn Fein	38 821	7.0	0
Alliance	32 095	5.0	0
Independent Unionist (Kiifedder)	30 793	5.0	1
Workers Party	18 148	3.0	0
'Peter Barry'	6 783	1.0	0
Total	**584 982**	**100.00**	**15**

Loyalist anti-agreement total share of votes: 72%

Nationalist anti-agreement total share of votes: 11%

● 1987 Westminster general election

Sinn Fein scored an important success in the general election when its president Gerry Adams polled 16 862 to hold on to his West Belfast seat. Adams' win was especially important, as the SDLP made advances at Sinn Fein's expense elsewhere. The total republican vote was down from 102 000 in the 1983 election to just over 83 000. The SDLP is clearly still enjoying some benefits from the illusory promises of reform under the Anglo-Irish agreement. But the results also showed that the core of republican support cannot be swayed by phoney schemes such as Thatcher's accord with Dublin. The SDLP's biggest success came in South Down, where it unseated the former Tory turned Official Unionist MP Enoch Powell. Powell's defeat was part of a pattern of falling Unionist support and increased divisions, as Loyalists displayed their disenchantment with the ineffective campaign against the Anglo-Irish agreement. The Unionists' poor electoral showing suggests they will now have no choice about dropping their Westminster boycott.

1987 Westminster general election

Party	Votes	% of total poll	Seats
Official Unionists	276 230	37.8	9
Democratic Unionists	62 638	11.7	3
SDLP	158 087	21.1	3
Sinn Fein	83 389	11.4	1
Alliance	72 671	9.9	0
Independent Unionist (Kilfedder)	18 420	2.6	1
Workers Party	19 294	2.6	0

The emerging patterns of the past seven years can be seen by comparing the first preference votes in the key elections since 1980. This demonstrates a fairly even split in the Loyalist community between Paisley's Democratic Unionists and Molyneaux's Official Unionists. When personality is to the fore—as in the Euro-elections—Paisley comes off best. When it is a party to party contest the Official Unionists are stronger.

In electoral terms the SDLP remains the dominant party of the nationalist community. John Hume has a strong personal following in Derry and the party has solid support among middle class Catholics. Sinn Fein has picked up support in the working class nationalist ghettos in Belfast and Derry and the poorer country areas. It has marginalised the smaller nationalist parties, while leaving much of the SDLP's base intact. Northern Ireland politics is hard on attempts to cultivate the middle ground. In a situation of war the polls reflect the fact that people are forced to take sides and that those who try to stand in the middle are pushed aside. The middle class Protestant Alliance Party and the pro-British Workers Party have been consistently marginalised at the polls.

● *Election summary 1981-87*

	General 1987	Anglo-Irish accord 1986	Local 1985	Europe 1984	General 1983	Assembly 1982	Local 1981
Official Unionists	37.8	52.2	29.8	21.4	34.0	29.7	26.5
Democratic Unionists	11.7	15.0	24.3	33.6	20.0	23.0	26.6
SDLP	21.1	12.0	17.8	22.0	17.9	18.0	17.5
Sinn Fein	11.4	7.0	11.8	13.4	13.4	10.1	—
Alliance	9.9	5.0	7.1	4.9	8.0	9.3	8.9
Independent Unionists (Kilfedder)	2.6	5.0	—	—	—	—	—
Irish Independence Party	—	—	1.2	—	—	—	3.9
Workers Party	2.6	3.0	1.6	1.2	2.0	2.7	1.8
Others	2.9	1.0	6.4	3.2	4.7	6.3	16.1

5.

The bombing campaign in Britain

1972   **February:** Aldershot: Official IRA bomb Parachute Regiment barracks, in reprisal for Bloody Sunday killings in Derry. Bomb leaves seven dead—including chaplain and women cleaners.

1973   **March:** London: Two IRA car bombings outside Old Bailey and Scotland Yard—one man killed, 180 injured.
August: Midlands: Nine blasts in three weeks—police bomb disposal expert killed. London: Series of small incendiary and booby-trap bombs in big stores, stations, the stock exchange—20 injured.
September: London: Chelsea bomb—five injured.

1974   **January:** London: Explosions at Madame Tussaud's wax museum and the boat show at Earl's Court.
February: M62: Coach carrying British military personnel blown up by parcel bomb—12 people killed, nine of them soldiers.
June: London: Bomb explodes at Westminster.
July: London: Bomb explodes at Tower of London—one woman killed, 40 children injured.
October: Guildford: Two pubs frequented by soldiers bombed—four military personnel and one other killed, about 50 more injured.
November: Woolwich: Soldiers' pub bombed—two killed, 35 injured. Coventry: Birmingham-based republican blows himself up while planting a bomb outside telephone exchange. Birmingham: Two pubs blown up—21 killed, more than 150 injured.
December: London: Bomb attack on Edward Heath's private flat in Belgravia—he is out. Several bombs in central London, as well as in Bath, Bristol and Aldershot.

1975   **January:** London and Manchester: Six bombs—26 injured.
Autumn: London bombing and shooting campaign culminates in Balcombe Street siege in which four IRA volunteers are captured. Car bombs and attacks on West End hotels and restaurants leave five dead, including a bomb disposal expert and a professor killed accidentally by a bomb attached to the car of leading Tory MP Hugh Fraser. After he offered a reward for information leading to the arrest of republicans, notorious reactionary and *Guinness Book of Records* compiler Ross McWhirter was himself assassinated.

1976   **April:** London: Bomb explodes on underground train. Explosion at Ideal Home Exhibition—80 injured.

1977   **January:** London: Eight bomb explosions.

1978   **December:** London: Three car bombs—and seven explosions in five other British cities.

1979   **January:** London: Two car bombs and a failed attempt to blow up a gas storage tank at Greenwich and an oil refinery plant at Canvey Island.
March: London: Airey Neave assassinated by Inla car bomb at house of commons.

1980   **March:** Salisbury Plain: Inla bomb attack on Army base—several injured.

1981   **October:** London: Coach full of soldiers hit by massive nail bomb outside Chelsea barracks—two civilians killed, many soldiers injured. Retired marines' commander Sir Steuart Pringle severely injured by car bomb at his Dulwich home. Bomb disposal expert killed by explosion at Wimpy bar, Oxford Street.
November: London: Home of attorney general Sir Michael Havers blasted by IRA bomb. Booby-trap bomb triggered by dog at Woolwich Arsenal, injuring two soldiers' wives.
December: London: Attempted bombing of gas storage tank, East London.

1982   **July:** London: Eleven soldiers and some horses killed by bombs in Regent's Park and Park Lane. One injured horse, Sefton, is singled out for media concern.

1983   **December:** London: IRA unit plants several bombs in West End, including Harrods in Knightsbridge, two policemen and three others killed, 91 injured.

1984   **October:** Brighton: IRA bomb Grand Hotel during Conservative Party conference—five Tories killed, Thatcher and the rest of her cabinet narrowly escape.

1985   **November:** London: Inla fails in attempt to blow up Chelsea barracks.

6.

Irish prisoners in English jails

The following prisoners are recognised by the republican movement. Readers are encouraged to send birthday cards for the dates indicated and to attend the regular pickets of the prisons.

Name	Prison	Sentence	Number	Birthday
Martina Anderson	Durham	Life	D25134	16 April
William Armstrong	Frankland	Life	119085	26 December
Liam Baker	Long Lartin	24 years	464984	6 September
James Bennett	Long Lartin	20 years	464989	4 December
Martin Brady	Albany	Life	119087	22 September
Eddie Butler	Long Lartin	Life	338637	17 April
Donal Craig	Maidstone	4 years	—	—
Gerry Cunningham	Long Lartin	20 years	132016	24 March
Robert Cunningham	Long Lartin	20 years	131877	12 July
Hugh Doherty	Wakefield	Life	338636	7 December
Vincent Donnelly	Wormwood Scrubs	Life	274064	25 September
Brendan Dowd	Frankland	Life	758662	17 November
Harry Duggan	Albany	Life	338638	31 October
Noel Gibson	Long Lartin	Life	879225	11 December
Patrick Hackett	Parkhurst	20 years	342603	20 April
Sean Hayes	Albany	24 years	341418	8 July
Paul Holmes	Frankland	Life	119034	22 June
Paul Kavanagh	Leicester	Life	L31888	12 August
Brian Keenan	Leicester	21 years	B26380	17 July
Sean Kinsella	Albany	Life	758661	5 November
Bernard McCafferty	—	16 years	—	—
Ronnie McCartney	Gartree	Life	463799	3 September
John McComb	Long Lartin	17 years	851715	25 February
Gerald McDonnell	Parkhurst	Life	B75882	19 December
Con McFadden	Wakefield	20 years	130662	19 June
Sean McShane	Parkhurst	8 years	B75879	—
Patrick Magee	Leicester	Life	B75881	29 May

Andy Mulryan	Long Lartin	20 years	461576	18 November
Patrick Mulryan	Long Lartin	20 years	461575	23 March
Stephen Nordone	Gartree	Life	758663	2 August
Paul Norney	Parkhurst	Life	863532	11 November
Joe O'Connell	Gartree	Life	338635	15 May
Ella O'Dwyer	Durham	Life	D25135	3 March
Eddie O'Neill	Frankland	20 years	135722	15 January
Thomas Quigley	Parkhurst	Life	B69204	23 July
Peter Sherry	Parkhurst	Life	B75880	30 June
Natalino Vella	Wakefield	15 years	B71644	24 December
Roy Walsh	Gartree	Life	119083	1 November

Prison Addresses

HM Prison Albany, Newport, Isle of Wight PO30 5RS
HM Prison Durham, Old Elvet, Durham DH1 3HU
HM Prison Frankland, Finchale Avenue, Brasside, Durham
HM Prison Gartree, Leicester Road, Market Harborough, Leics LE16 7RP
HM Prison Leicester, Welford Road, Leicester LE2 7AJ
HM Prison Long Lartin, South Littleton, Evesham, Worcs WR11 5TZ
HM Prison Maidstone, East Sutton Park, YCC Sutton Valence, Maidstone, Kent
HM Prison Parkhurst, Newport, Isle of Wight PO30 5NX
HM Prison Wakefield, Love Lane, Wakefield, West Yorkshire WF2 9AG
HM Prison Wandsworth, PO Box 757, Heathfield Road, London SW18 3HS
HM Prison Wormwood Scrubs, PO Box 757, Du Cane Road, London W12 0AE

The following Irish political prisoners have consistently proclaimed
that they are not guilty of the charges on which they have been
convicted. They have been framed on the basis of forced confessions
and bogus forensic tests and despite strong contradictory evidence.

In connection with the M62 coach bombing, February 1974:
Judith Ward   Life   Durham

**In connection with the Guildford and Woolwich pub bombings, October and
November 1974:**

Patrick Armstrong	Life	Gartree
Gerry Conlon	Life	Long Lartin
Paul Hill	Natural life	Wormwood Scrubs
Carole Richardson	Indefinite	Styal

Anne Maguire and her family have served their sentences in relation to the above,
but are now actively campaigning to clear their name.

In connection with the Birmingham pub bombing, November 1974:

Hugh Callaghan	Life	Long Lartin
Patrick Hill	Life	Long Lartin
Gerry Hunter	Life	Long Lartin
Richard McIlkenny	Life	Wormwood Scrubs
Billy Power	Life	Wormwood Scrubs
John Walker	Life	Long Lartin

7.

Britain's machine of terror

In 1969 the Six Counties state was sustained by a body of around 10 000 armed men. This was bad enough for the nationalist population, but since the war began the repressive apparatus has mushroomed. At first British soldiers were in the front line of the war. In 1972—the worst year yet for deaths and casualties—their numbers passed 20 000. Subsequently the Army forces have been steadily reduced, and the indigenous Loyalist forces built up. The Royal Ulster Constabulary is a paramilitary police force; the Ulster Defence Regiment is the former 'B' Specials incorporated into the British Army. Their combined numbers now far exceed those of the British Army. The total strength of the security forces is now almost three times the level of 1969—and those are just the official statistics.

	RUC	RUC Reserve	'B' Specials	UDR	Combined Ulster forces	British Army	Total
1969	3044	—	8100	—	11144	—	11144
1970	3809	625	—	3869	8303	8100	16403
1972	4256	1909	—	9102	15267	20300	35567
1974	4563	3860	—	7900	16323	16000	32323
1976	5255	4697	—	7800	17752	14900	32652
1978	5789	4689	—	8010	18488	13400	32978
1980	6935	4752	—	7500	19187	12100	31287
1982	7500	4900	—	7150	19550	12500	32050
1984	8555	4500	—	7111	20071	9516	29587
1986	8250	4500	—	6600	19350	10200	29550

8.

Death toll

The following list was drawn up by Father Raymond Murray of Armagh in response to the inadequate and prejudiced statistics produced by the British government. His breakdown of fatalities of the Irish War provides a more accurate picture than the statements of the British authorities. The list covers more than 17 years from August 1969 to 31 December 1986. It excludes those killed in the Republic and in Britain.

	Catholic	Protestant	Total
Civilian deaths due to republican activity			
Explosions	64	84	148
Cross-fire, accidents	45	14	59
Assassinations	115	277	392
Riots	—	12	12
Totals	**224**	**387**	**611**
Civilian deaths due to British/Loyalist activity			
Explosions	94	17	111
Cross-fire, accidents	6	7	13
British Army/RUC/UDR killings	107	19	126
Loyalist assassinations	417	138	555
Riots	30	4	34
Totals	**654**	**185**	**839**
Deaths due to military activity			
Security forces killed by republicans	101	655	756
Republicans killed by security forces	106	—	106
Republican 'own goals'	109	1	110
Security forces killed by Loyalists	2	12	14
Loyalists killed by security forces	—	14	14
Loyalist 'own goals'	—	27	27
Totals	**318**	**709**	**1027**
Deaths of uncertain cause	**27**	**22**	**49**
TOTALS	**1223**	**1303**	**2526**

9.

Information on Ireland

People in Britain have long been ill-informed about events in Ireland. To some extent this is due to deep-rooted ignorance and indifference. But it is also because much of the information available on Ireland is superficial, prejudiced and outdated. The British authorities have also fed the public a large amount of misinformation, especially about the events in the Irish War. We provide here a brief guide to the useful sources of news and information and a survey of background reading.

It is not easy to keep abreast of developments in Northern Ireland. Even though the authorities insist that the Six Counties are part of the United Kingdom, government reports and statistics from this part of the Empire are often difficult to obtain. Some reports, like those of the Fair Employment Agency, are often suppressed. Television documentaries are frequently banned. Detentions under the Prevention of Terrorism Act usually go unreported. The TUC never publishes the cases of trade union members who have been detained. Much research remains to be done on particular aspects of British rule in Ireland, for example, on the role of particular companies and the collaboration of the trade unions.

Making allowances for bias, establishment publications remain a useful source of information. The government's official *Ulster Year Book* provides an annual digest of facts and figures and periodic reports of committees of inquiry often include some reliable information.

Reading the papers

The British press generally limits itself to publishing Army and government press releases. However, the *Independent* sometimes covers the war and repression in more detail. The *Financial Times* and the *Economist* keep their readers attuned to changing British strategy. The *Sunday Times* seems to have the closest links with the intelligence services in Northern Ireland and hence gets the best 'scoops'. The *Irish Times,* published in Dublin but available in most British cities, provides the most consistent coverage of the war in Northern Ireland.

An Phoblacht/Republican News, the republican movement's well-produced weekly, carries regular 'war news' and commentary on Irish politics. It is indispensable for understanding the republican point of view. More extensive analyses can be found in *Iris,* their occasional Dublin-produced journal. *Magill,* another Dublin-based magazine, sometimes contains useful investigative articles, particularly on politics in the South. *Fortnight* is a Belfast journal broadly sympathetic to the SDLP, and it publishes a wide variety of Northern opinion. *Phoenix* is the Irish equivalent of *Private Eye.* A flavour of Loyalist reaction can be obtained from the Democratic Unionist Party's *Belfast Telegraph.*

Many British left-wing publications deal with the Irish War. The best combination of reporting from Ireland and analysis of British strategy can be found in *the next step,* the weekly paper of the Revolutionary Communist Party. The views of the Labour Party-dominated left can be found in *Labour and Ireland.*

Making a start

To get a broad background to the current troubles it is useful to read at least one of the general histories of modern Ireland. Unfortunately they tend to be rather heavy going. Their treatment of the period since partition is particularly unsatisfactory as the pro-British and anti-republican prejudices of our own day take over.

FSL Lyons' *Ireland since the Famine* (1971) is probably the best all-round introduction. Robert Kee's *The Green Flag* (1979) was popularised by his television series. It provides a superficial assessment from a liberal point of view. Desmond Greaves' *The Irish Crisis* (1972) and TA Jackson's *Ireland Her Own* (1946) are the two standard left-wing accounts, but offer less information than Lyons without providing a superior analysis.

From civil rights to war

The early stages of the conflict produced some fine journalism. The *Sunday Times* Insight team's *Ulster* (1972) remains one of the best accounts of the drift from the civil rights marches into open warfare. Eamonn McCann played a prominent role in the civil rights movement in Derry and his *War and an Irish Town* (1974) is a stirring personal testimony. Michael Farrell's *Northern Ireland: The Orange State* (1976) is another book by a civil rights activist which covers the sectarian state and the resistance against it. Andrew Boyd's *Holy War in Belfast* (1969) provides further background on how the war erupted. Bernadette Devlin's *The Price of My Soul* (1969) tells the story of how she became involved in the civil rights movement, became MP for Mid-Ulster and was imprisoned for her role in the battle of the Bogside.

The republican movement

Most studies of the nationalist movement tend to be anti-republican. Some claim a sympathy with the objectives of the republican movement while criticising the armed struggle. J Bowyer-Bell's *The Secret Army: A History of the IRA 1916-1979* (1979) is the most thorough survey of the origins of the modern republican movement. Sean Cronin's *Irish Nationalism: A History of Its Roots and Ideology* (1980) covers much of the same ground. Mike Milotte's *Communism in Modern Ireland* (1984) covers the important subject of the relationship between the left and republicanism in Ireland since the twenties.

Tim Pat Coogan's *The IRA* (1980) has better coverage on the emergence and early years of the 'Provisional' IRA, but Kevin Kelley's *The Longest War: Northern Ireland and the IRA* (1982) is more comprehensive and more up to date. Both draw the line at support for the armed struggle. Sean MacStiofain's *Memoirs of a Revolutionary* (1973) tells his own story as the first Provisional IRA chief of staff. Gerry Adams' *The Politics of Irish Freedom* (1986) is a combination of personal recollections, plus a political motivation of the programme of Sinn Fein by its current president.

The prisoners and the women's struggle

John McGuffin's *Internment* (1973) details the harrowing events surrounding the August 1971 mass arrests and detention of republican suspects. His *The Guineapigs* (1974) contains graphic accounts of how the internees were tortured. Tim Pat Coogan's *On the Blanket: The H-Block Story* (1980) provides the background to the hunger-strikes. Neil McCafferty's *The Armagh Women* (1981) is a parallel account of the struggle for political status of republican women. *Only the Rivers Run Free: Northern Ireland, the Women's War* (1984) by Eileen Fairweather, Roisín McDonagh and Melanie McFadyean is a fuller survey of the role of women in the Irish War.

Loyalist reaction

Most accounts of the Loyalist paramilitaries tend to emphasise the sensational aspects. Robert Fisk's *The Point of No Return* (1974) is an excellent account of the 1974 Ulster Workers' Council strike, by a much-acclaimed British war correspondent. Jack Holland's *Too Long a Sacrifice* (1981) includes a chilling account of the Loyalist paramilitaries as part of a wider journalistic survey of life in the war zone of Belfast. D Boulton's *The UVF 1966-73* (1973) concentrates on the early history of the paramilitaries and suggests that they were about to move in a progressive direction—at the very moment that they launched the biggest sectarian murder campaign so far. Dillon and Lehane's *Political Murder in Northern Ireland* (1973) details the murders of 1972 and 1973 and the power struggles inside the UDA. *Silent Too Long* (1982) is a pamphlet produced by relatives of the victims of Loyalist terror, including detailed case histories.

A number of historical studies of Loyalism are now available. Michael Farrell's *Arming the Protestants* (1983) focuses on the role of the Ulster special constabulary in the twenties. Henry Patterson's *Class Conflict and Sectarianism* (1981) is a detailed study of Loyalist workers in the period before partition. Patterson puts forward the view that Loyalist populism can become a progressive force. This view is updated in Sarah Nelson's *Ulster's Uncertain Defenders: Loyalists and the Northern Ireland Conflict* (1984). Irish journalists Ed Moloney and Andy Pollak's *Paisley* (1986) is a biography of your man himself.

Legalised terror

Two trios of authors have provided detailed surveys of the processes of legal repression during the course of the war. As academics they have studiously avoided taking sides. These are—Boyle, Hadden and Hillyard, *Ten Years On in Northern Ireland* (1980) and O'Dowd,

Rolston and Tomlinson, *Northern Ireland: Between Civil Rights and Civil War* (1980). Boyle and Hadden's *Ireland: A Positive Proposal* (1985) was more political, while retaining an academic guise. It ruled out the South's Forum report as 'colonialist' and advocated the acceptance of the Anglo-Irish deal. Boyle has since declared that the accord concedes too much to the nationalist side.

Peter Taylor's *Beating the Terrorists?* (1980) is an account of the late seventies' conveyor-belt system, concentrating on the RUC torture centres, such as Castlereagh. Its impact is spoilt by Taylor's underlying preoccupation with showing that repression breeds more recruits for IRA 'terrorists'. SC Greer and A White's *Abolishing the Diplock Courts* (1986) argues that the jury trial should be restored in Northern Ireland, but unfortunately does not include a comprehensive assessment of the supergrass strategy, which is still awaited. Fathers Denis Faul and Raymond Murray have produced a stream of pamphlets including detailed case histories of British repression. Kader Asmal's *Shoot to Kill?* (1985) is the report of an international lawyers' inquiry into the RUC's shoot-to-kill policy and provides a graphic indictment of British 'justice' for the Irish. Factual accounts of the frame-ups of the Birmingham Six and the Guildford Four can be found in Chris Mullin's *Error of Judgement: The Truth about the Birmingham Bombings* (1986) and Robert Kee's *Trial and Error: The Maguires, the Guildford Pub Bombings and British Justice* (1986).

British strategy

The classic account of British military strategy in Northern Ireland is Frank Kitson's *Low Intensity Operations* (1971), supplemented by his explicit *Bunch of Five* (1977). In recent years the soldiers' role has begun to be celebrated. AFN Clarke's *Contact* (1983) reveals the full barbarity of the occupying forces—it has since been made into a play and an award-winning television film. Tony Geraghty's *Who Dares Wins: The Story of the SAS 1950-1980* (1980) glorifies the murderous activities of the SAS in South Armagh. Desmond Hamill's *Pig in the Middle: The British Army in Northern Ireland 1969-1984* (1985) provides a more sober account from a television journalist who has interviewed all the top brass. From the left, French journalist Roger Faligot's *The Kitson Experiment: Britain's Military Strategy* (1983) provides interesting information, but underestimates the forces preventing a British withdrawal from Northern Ireland.

There are very few books that provide a fuller analysis of British policy in Ireland, though there are a number of valuable historical surveys. These include DG Boyce's *Englishmen and Irish Troubles* (1972) and George Dangerfield's *The Damnable Question* (1979) which cover the 'Irish question' in British politics around the time of partition. Emile Strauss' *Irish Nationalism and British Democracy* (1957) provides an excellent background for understanding anti-Irish chauvinism in Britain. In the modern period the writings of right-wing Tories and Unionists such as Enoch Powell, John Biggs-Davison and TE Utley provide the most forceful justification for British terror in Ireland, though they frequently allow their bigotry to distort their judgement.

Official reports

Ireland has never lacked government inquiries and special reports. While Ireland starved during the famine years of the 1840s the British government commissioned a stream of detailed investigations. Government reports remain a useful source of information and a guide to establishment thinking.

Cameron report, Disturbances in Northern Ireland: Report of the commission appointed by the governor of Northern Ireland, September 1969.

Hunt report, Report of the advisory committee on police in Northern Ireland, October 1969.

MacRory report, Report of the review body on local government in Northern Ireland, 1970.

Compton report, Report of the inquiry into allegations against the security forces of physical brutality arising out of the events on 9 August 1971, November 1971.

Parker report, Report of the committee of privy councillors appointed to consider authorised procedures for the interrogation of persons suspected of terrorism, March 1972.

Scarman report, Violence and civil disturbances in Northern Ireland in 1969: Report of a tribunal of inquiry (2 vols), April 1972.

Widgery report, Report of the tribunal appointed to inquire into the events on Sunday 30 January 1972 which led to loss of life in connection with the procession in Londonderry on that day, April 1972.

Diplock report, Report of the commission to consider legal procedures to deal with terrorist activities in Northern Ireland, December 1972.

The 1973 white paper, Northern Ireland constitutional proposals, March 1973.

Gardiner report, Report of a committee to consider, in the context of civil liberties and human rights, measures to deal with terrorism in Northern Ireland, January 1975.

Quigley report, Economic and industrial strategy for Northern Ireland: Report of a review team, 1976.

Shackleton report, Review of the operation of the Prevention of Terrorism (Temporary Provisions) Act, August 1978.

Bennett report, Report of the committee of inquiry into police interrogation procedures in Northern Ireland, March 1979.

Rolling devolution, Northern Ireland: a framework for devolution, April 1982.

Jellicoe report, Review of the operation of the Prevention of Terrorism (Temporary Provisions) Act, February 1983.

Baker report, Review of the operation of the Northern Ireland (Emergency Provisions) Act 1978, April 1984.

The Irish working class

There are few substantial works on the Irish working class. Published books tend to be either long out of date or turgid academic works. The development of the working class in the Twenty-six Counties since the sixties is particularly poorly documented. JD Clarkson's book *Labour and Nationalism in Ireland* (1925) is the classic historical account. Peter Beresford Ellis' *A History of the Irish Working Class* was republished in 1984 in an updated edition. Though its analysis is superficial and it is weak on the modern period it is the most easily available historical introduction. Charles McCarthy's *Trade Unionism in Ireland 1894-1960* provides a thorough industrial relations approach to the subject. Bew and Patterson's *Sean Lemass and the Making of Modern Ireland 1945-1966* (1982) contains useful material on the formative period of today's Irish working class.

The South

A beginner's guide to the complexities of the political scene in the South can be found in M Gallagher's *Political Parties in the Republic of Ireland* (1985). The notorious relationship between the Catholic Church and the Free State is thoroughly examined in JH Whyte's *Church and State in Modern Ireland 1923-1979* (1980). The myth of Irish neutrality is effectively disposed of in Robert Fisk's *In Time of*

War: Ireland, Ulster and the Price of Neutrality 1939-45 (1985), which details the Republic's wartime collaboration with Britain behind a facade of impartiality. The seamier side of one of the Republic's political machines can be found in journalists Joe Joyce and Peter Murtagh's lively account of dirty tricks by the 1982 Fianna Fail administration and its charismatic leader, *The Boss* (1983). Ursula Barry's *Lifting the Lid: Handbook of Facts and Information on Ireland* (1986) contains much useful material, especially on the Republic's economy, its repressive apparatus and the position of women.

Radical academic analysis

In recent years a number of left-wing academics have published books on Ireland. While many of these authors claim to be Marxists, the academic school is influenced by the traditions of British Labourism rather than Marxism. British socialists have long looked to the British state as the agency that they hope will transform capitalist society into socialism through a programme of sweeping nationalisation and welfare reforms. Hence they are hostile to the Irish national liberation struggle which is a direct attack on the British state. They interpret the class struggle in Ireland in trade union terms, failing to appreciate that the anti-capitalist struggle in Ireland takes the form of the struggle against British imperialist domination.

Academic Marxists argue that the concept of imperialism is obsolete and deny that Britain can be characterised as the oppressor in modern Ireland. They prefer to use the language of the media and explain the conflict in Northern Ireland in terms of 'sectarianism' and atavistic religious loyalties. They constantly proclaim the elusive goal of uniting Protestant and Catholic workers, while rejecting the struggle against the force that divides the working class—British rule. The academics' hostility towards the anti-imperialist movement often leads to a greater interest in the Loyalist working class which some identify as a more progressive force than the nationalist community.

Tom Nairn's *The Break Up of Britain* (1976), although not strictly about Ireland, provides the framework for radical analysis. He argues that 'imperialism *in the sense required* by the theory does not operate in any part of the Irish island.' Bew, Gibbon and Patterson individually and in collaboration have produced the most sophisticated versions of the anti-republican radical theory. Their book *The State in Northern Ireland 1921-1972* (1979) summarises the argument. Workers Party supporters Bew and Patterson updated their prejudices in *The British State and the Ulster Crisis: From Wilson to Thatcher* (1985), which nevertheless contains some useful material on the war during the seventies.

The political consequences—an appeal to limit the struggle to the reform of the Stormont state—are drawn out in 'Some Aspects of Nationalism and Socialism in Ireland, 1968-78' in the collection edited by Morgan and Purdie, *Ireland: Divided Nation, Divided Class* (1980). Belinda Probert draws the argument to its logical conclusion in *Beyond Orange and Green* (1978), in which she claims that Ian Paisley's bitterly sectarian Democratic Unionist Party 'is fundamentally a working class movement'. While most British left wingers baulk at these explicitly pro-imperialist conclusions, the thrust of academic analysis—Marxist and Labourist—is widely endorsed on the British left. It is adopted in the reporting and commentary of organisations such as the Communist Party, Militant, Socialist Organiser and the Socialist Workers Party. For a taster, see the SWP's *Ireland's Permanent Revolution* (1986) by Chris Bambery.

Mainstream Labourism

While academic Marxists have worked single-mindedly to make the most basic points about the Irish War complex and obscure, more practical British socialists have tried to rally liberal sympathy for the victims of British terror in Ireland. Their demon is the media; their vehicle for changing British strategy, the Labour Party. Liz Curtis is one of the leading advocates of this school of thought. Her books *Ireland: The Propaganda War* (1984) and *Nothing but the Same Old Story: The Roots of Anti-Irish Racism* (1984) blame the failures of the British solidarity movement on the influence of press propaganda and anti-Irish stereotypes.

Geoff Bell's *Troublesome Business* (1982) surveys Labour Party policy on Ireland. There he tries to justify a futile hope expressed in his *The British in Ireland: A Suitable Case for Withdrawal* (1984): that the party which has sent the troops in can be swung round to pulling them out. David Reed's *Ireland: The Key to the British Revolution* (1984) shares the left's repudiation of the anti-imperialist potential of the British working class and its illusions in Labour.

The memoirs of top Labour politicians provide a more accurate guide to the likely direction of the Irish policy of any future Labour government. Harold Wilson's *The Labour Government 1964-70* (1971), Richard Crossman's *The Diaries of a Cabinet Minister* (1971),

James Callaghan's *A House Divided* (1973) and Merlyn Rees' *Northern Ireland: A Personal Perspective* (1985) all include some characteristically cynical insights.

Marxist studies on Ireland

Marx and Engels wrote little about Ireland, but what they wrote remains valuable reading. It is included in the collection *Marx and Engels on Ireland*. At the time that he wrote about it, Lenin appreciated Ireland's significance for British workers better than most of their leaders. His views can be found in the collection *British Labour and British Imperialism*. The writings of James Connolly are a comprehensive attempt to understand class relations in Ireland from the point of view of a newly emerging working class. Many of his key writings are included in *The Selected Works of James Connolly*, edited by Peter Beresford Ellis. Desmond Greaves' *Life and Times of James Connolly* is a good introduction.

Further research

The following texts are useful as a guide to further research. MD Shannon's *Modern Ireland* (1981) is a general bibliography available in large reference libraries. Deutsch and Magowan's *Northern Ireland: A Chronology of Events* (1974) covers the early stages of the war. WD Flackes' *Northern Ireland: A Political Directory 1968-83* (1984) provides a useful 'who's who' and detailed election statistics.

If you want to fight for Irish freedom...
...join the Irish Freedom Movement

The Irish Freedom Movement fights around the demands:

- Self-determination for the Irish people
- Troops out now
- Smash the PTA

The Irish Freedom Movement has branches in England, Scotland and Wales organising solidarity action

- against the PTA
- in support of Irish political prisoners
- for the immediate withdrawal of British troops

To join the Irish Freedom Movement and find out more about its activities, send £5 to BM IFM, London WC1N 3XX.

Weekly paper of the Revolutionary Communist Party

The expanded and redesigned 16-page *tns* will be continuing its high-level coverage of Irish events, with interviews, news and analysis from North and South. Don't be without it!

40p weekly

SUBSCRIPTION RATES

Britain/Ireland £19
Europe/Irish Republic £24
Middle East/North Africa £26
Americas/Asia/Southern Africa £27
Australasia £32
Libraries/institutions £30

SPECIAL OFFER!

Five issues of *tns* for £1
Send cheques or postal orders to Junius Publications, BCM JPLtd, London WC1N 3XX

Junius Publications
Books and pamphlets in print

THE SOVIET UNION
DEMYSTIFIED
Frank Füredi

The Soviet Union Demystified

A Materialist Analysis
Frank Füredi

A Marxist assessment of Soviet society, its development and its prospects.

£5.95 paperback plus 85p p&p
£12.50 hardback plus £1.20 p&p

Confrontation 1

The Revolutionary Communist Party's theoretical journal

Includes **Frank Richards** on 'Marxism in Our Time', a critique of academic Marxism, and **Mike Freeman** on 'The Road to Power', an outline of the RCP's approach to building a revolutionary working class party in Britain.
£2.95 plus 50p p&p

Confrontation 2

The Revolutionary Communist Party's theoretical journal

The second issue contains articles by **Linda Ryan** on 'Labour or The Red Front?' **John Gibson** on 'The Working Class under Thatcher', and **Frank Richards** on 'The Myth of State Capitalism'.
£2.95 plus 50p p&p

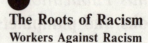